PORT JEWS

Parkes-Wiener Series on Jewish Studies
Series Editors: David Cesarani and Tony Kushner
ISSN 1368-5449

The field of Jewish Studies is one of the youngest, but fastest growing and most exciting areas of scholarship in the academic world today. Named after James Parkes and Alfred Wiener, this series aims to publish new research in the field and student materials for use in the seminar room, to disseminate the latest work of established scholars and to re-issue classic studies which are currently out of print.

Other Books in the Series

Cultures of Ambivalence and Contempt: Studies in Jewish-Non-Jewish Relations
[ISBN 0 85303 324 2]
Edited by Siân Jones, Tony Kushner and Sarah Pearce

The Berlin Haskalah and German Religious Thought: Orphans of Knowledge
[ISBN 0 85303 365 X]
David Sorkin

The Jewish Immigrant in England 1870-1914, Third Edition
[ISBN 0 85303 410 9]
Lloyd P. Gartner

State and Society in Roman Galilee, A.D. 132-212, Second Edition
[ISBN 0 85303 380 3]
Martin Goodman

Sir Sidney Hamburger and Manchester Jewry: Religion, City and Community
[ISBN 0 85303 363 3]
Bill Williams

Remembering Cable Street: Fascism and Anti-Fascism in British Society
[ISBN 0 85303 361 7]
Edited by Tony Kushner and Nadia Valman

Anglo-Jewry in Changing Times: Studies in Diversity 1840-1914
[ISBN 0 85303 354 4]
Israel Finestein

Disraeli's Jewishness
[ISBN 0 85303 366 8]
Edited by Todd M. Endelman and Tony Kushner

Claude Montefiore: His Life and Thought
[ISBN 0 85303 369 2]
Daniel R. Langton

PORT JEWS

Jewish Communities
in Cosmopolitan Maritime
Trading Centres, 1550–1950

Editor

David Cesarani
University of Southampton

FRANK CASS
LONDON • PORTLAND, OR

First published in 2002 in Great Britain by
FRANK CASS PUBLISHERS
Crown House, 47 Chase Side, London N14 5BP

and in the United States of America by
FRANK CASS PUBLISHERS
c/o ISBS
5824 N.E. Hassalo Street
Portland, Oregon 971213-3644

Website: http://www.frankcass.com

British Library Cataloguing in Publication Data
Port Jews: Jewish communities in cosmopolitan maritime
trading centres, 1550–1950. – (Parkes-Wiener series on
Jewish studies)
1. Jews – History 2. Jews – Europe – History 3. Maritime
anthropology
I. Cesarani, David
305.8'924'0903

ISBN 0 7146 5349 7 (cloth)
ISBN 0 7146 8286 1 (paper)
ISSN 1368-5449

Library of Congress Cataloging-in-Publication Data:
Port Jews: Jewish communities in cosmopolitan
maritime trading centres, 1550–1950 / edited by
David Cesarani
    p. cm. – (Parkes-Wiener series on Jewish studies)
Includes bibliographical references and index.
    1. Jews–Civilization. 2. Jews–History–16th century.
3. Jews–History–1789–1945. 4. Jews–Commerce–
History. 5. Jewish merchants–Europe–History. 6.
Sociology, Urban. 7. City and town life–Europe–
History. I. Cesarani, David. II. Series.
    DS112.P74 2002
909'.04924–dc21   2002006819

This group of studies first appeared in a special issue of
Jewish Culture and History [ISSN 1462-169X],
published by Frank Cass and Co. Ltd.

Printed in Great Britain by
Antony Rowe Ltd., Chippenham, Wiltshire

Contents

Acknowledgements

This volume is based on the papers presented at a symposium about 'Port Jews' held at the University of Southampton on 28–29 June 2001, as part of a five-year research project on Port Jews being run in conjunction with the Kaplan Centre for Jewish Studies, University of Cape Town. The Port Jews project forms one strand of a major research programme under the auspices of the AHRB Parkes Centre for the Study of Jewish/non-Jewish Relations. The AHRB Parkes Centre, which is devoted to research and post-graduate training, was established in October 2000 thanks to an initiative of the Arts and Humanities Research Board (AHRB). Funding from the AHRB thus made possible the launch of the Port Jews research project, and the organisers of the symposium, as well as all those associated with this publication, would like to express their gratitude to the AHRB for its support. Dr Jo Reilly made the arrangements for the symposium and ensured that it ran smoothly. In addition to those whose essays are included in this volume, several other members of the Department of History at the University of Southampton contributed to the discussions, including Dr John Oldfield, Dr Alistair Duke, Dr Nils Roemer, Dr Nadia Valman, Dr Donald Bloxham, and Dr Gemma Romain, who subsequently took up a two-year fellowship in connection with the project and since then has taken a leading role in organising the follow-up to the first symposium. Dr Nadia Valman, the editor of *Jewish Culture and History*, has taken a lively interest in port Jews and offered useful advice regarding the publication. Professor Milton Shain, director of the Kaplan Centre, was sadly prevented from attending the symposium, but has been a constant source of counsel by email. Cathy Jennings at Frank Cass Publishers has been an efficient editor and Frank Cass has taken the kind of personal interest in the project that is all too rare amongst publishers today.

Port Jews: Concepts, Cases and Questions

DAVID CESARANI

I

Jews are commonly thought of as a pre-eminently earthbound and urban people, a stereotype that is not wholly charitable nor entirely unfounded. Yet the sea has played a curious, often un-remarked, role in Jewish history – particularly in the modern era. Thanks to new research and new approaches, the sea and the port cities that circumscribe it may assume a pivotal position in the great debate among Jewish historians about the dawning and the course of modern Jewish history.

In the first great history of the Jews, published by Heinrich Graetz in the 1850s, a special role in their transition from the mediaeval to the modern era was assigned to the court Jews of Central Europe and the Haskalah, the Jewish Enlightenment, which they helped to sponsor. Court Jews, like Joseph Oppenheimer of Wurtemburg or Moses Wulff of Dessau, served kings and princes as bankers, tax collectors, and army suppliers. Some were patronised in order to develop trade or industry. In return for privileges, such as the right to settle in cities formerly closed to Jews, and to set up small communities, they serviced the emerging modern, centralised state. Thanks to their proximity to high society, court Jews absorbed the ideas and customs of the day and began to act in imitation of non-Jews. Court Jews have consequently been described as the first 'modern Jews', whose identity was divided between the secular and the religious, European culture and Jewish tradition. They, in turn, used their wealth and influence to promote the modernisation of Jewish life: the Haskalah agenda.[1]

However, in the 1930s the great Jewish scholar Salo Baron noted that a similar phenomenon was visible in the ports on the Atlantic seaboard which were settled by Jews fleeing Spain and Portugal. As conversos or New Christians they too had experienced life outside the boundaries of Jewish tradition, until they were rooted out by the Inquisition as secret Jews or fled simply in fear of such accusations. The New Christians migrated to mainly Protestant lands where mercantile capitalism was flourishing and trade was oriented towards the New World. This environment favoured the incoming Jews who were perceived less according to traditional anti-Jewish animosity and more in the light of new social and economic doctrines that privileged a person's utility to the state and the economy over their faith. In Bordeaux, Amsterdam, London, and Hamburg the refugees from the Inquisition were allowed to settle as Portuguese and Spanish merchants and permitted over time to emerge openly as Jews because they were regarded pragmatically as an asset to trade and commerce. Their diasporic connections and accumulated expertise lay in exactly the areas of overseas expansion that were then of interest to mercantilist governments. Consequently, they were afforded extensive privileges and liberties. They responded by acculturating quickly and effectively, something that was not difficult given their bifurcated backgrounds. In this sense, they too could claim to be the earliest modern Jews.[2]

Yet, despite Baron's corrective, the Ashkenazim of central Europe, especially the court Jews and their intellectual protegés, such as the philosopher Moses Mendelssohn, continued to hold centre stage and Berlin was seen as the pace-setter in the saga of Jewish modernisation. This may have been because in the troubled decades that followed it was considered unwise to associate Jews with the flowering of capitalism. For whatever reason, Baron's insight did not lead to many further studies along these lines.[3] It was not until the 1980s and 1990s that Jewish historians revisited his discovery that the Jews who settled on the Atlantic seaboard rivalled the better-known court Jews of Central Europe as the avatars of modernisation in a Jewish accent.

Lois Dubin, in the course of her work on the Jews of Trieste, identified the singularity of this port city in fostering many of the patterns of behaviour and habits of thought that were associated with the Haskalah, the Jewish Enlightenment of Berlin – yet without any apparent ideological input from that direction. On the contrary, many Central European Jews striving to modernise Jewish life looked to the Triestine Jews as exemplars.[4] David Sorkin pointed out that the stress on court Jews and maskilim had marginalised the Sephardim even though in certain ways they preempted the modernisation of the Central European Jews. Their experience was different from that of the 'typical' Berlin Jews, but was no less important. Sorkin identified five features of the Sephardi port Jew in the eighteenth century that defined them as a 'social type' with a leading role in the transformation of the Jews. Port Jews were associated with migration and commerce; they lived and operated in milieux that valued commerce; they eschewed the traditional autonomous Jewish community and enjoyed improved legal status which

permitted voluntary affiliation to the Jewish collectivity; they were
enthusiastic about Jewish education, or re-education, and engaged in
vigorous intellectual debate among themselves and with Christians; they
questioned Jewish religious tradition, having been estranged from it for
so long, and displayed a form of ethnic Jewish identity.[5]

The work of Dubin and Sorkin, as well as other scholars, helped to
inspire a new wave of research. In only the last few years, the study of
'port Jews',[6] the involvement of Jews in seafaring and maritime trade,[7]
and the place of Jews in the expansion of Europe, has burgeoned.[8] It is an
exciting new area of scholarly endeavour in which ideas are constantly
being thrown up, tested, and pushed further. This volume, which grew
out of a symposium about port Jews held at the University of
Southampton in June 2001, testifies to the freshness and vitality of the
subject matter. It presents summations of work based on the current
understanding of the 'port Jew' as a 'social type' and essays or work-in-
progress intended to extend the concept both in terms of definition and
application. This involves not only a critical use of the concept for new
periods and location, but also a sharpening of the heuristic tools so that
more is gained by their use. Readers will note that the authors refer
frequently to each other's work, sometimes quizzically and sometimes
deferentially, but always in a collegiate spirit. There is a signal lack of
uniformity in the essays presented here: they represent an early stage of
research, inquiry, dialogue, and work in a new field and it is hoped that
they will inspire other scholars to join this exciting, collective endeavour
to understand how seaways, ports, and cities fostered change in Jewish
society.

II

Although research into port Jews is by necessity interdisciplinary, much
of the historical work has been informed by only a shallow appreciation
of geography. Yet geographers – social, economic, human, and historical
– have done more than any other group to elaborate the characteristics of
the port city, and without their insight historians would be labouring in
a darkened room.[9] Consequently, this volume begins with an essay by
Brian Hoyle, a geographer who pioneered the study of port cities.[10] He
begins by showing that the city and the port have been closely associated
since the beginning of human civilisation. The port, which at its most
essential is 'a place where the mode of transportation changes from land
systems to water-borne systems', is also a nodal point of economic life.
Because it is a hub for worldwide maritime communications it is the
interface between the local and the global. It faces landward, too, and

therefore interacts with its hinterland and region. For these reasons the
port city (although not all ports become cities and not all coastal cities
had commercial ports) from its inception featured cultural diversity and
functioned as a 'window on the world'. The functions of a port city
enabled the growth of 'diverse specialised communities' among which
were the Jews. Brian Hoyle demonstrates that although the port city has
been a constant of civilisations it has perpetually mutated in form and
function, with significant consequences for social relations within its
boundaries and in its environs. His definitional exactitude and caution
against generalisation should alert historians to the specificity of the port
city at any one time and place.

David Sorkin, who did so much to focus attention on the port Jew, is
less concerned with the particularity of the port city location than with
the specificity of the 'social type' which he identified as original to it.[11] In
his contribution he argues for reserving the definition of the 'port Jew' to
predominantly Sephardi or Italian Jews, residing in ports of the
Mediterranean, the Atlantic seaboard, or around the West Indies. While
it may be valid and useful to explore 'Jews in ports' or 'port Jewries'
across chronologies and continents, he maintains that it confuses the issue
to so stretch the original typology. Sorkin underlines the importance of
its specificity by weaving it into a uniform theory of the emancipation
process. Traditionally emancipation has been studied in terms of its
origins or its consequences rather than as a process, and models of
emancipation have tended to polarise eastern and western Europe. The
distinctive role of Sephardim as precursors, who experienced
emancipation as a gradual development, has been ignored. However,
Sorkin observes that countries with new port Jew communities solved
the 'Jewish problem' sooner and more smoothly than in Central and
Eastern Europe. He suggests that they managed this because they were
untrammelled by medieval Jewry laws and infused with a different ethos,
valuing Jews for their commercial acumen rather than just despising them
for their beliefs. Jews in Bordeaux, London, Amsterdam, and Trieste thus
enjoyed 'equality minus certain specific disabilities'. They benefited from
what Lois Dubin calls 'civil inclusion', a status which easily evolved into
full emancipation without revolutionary upheavals or interminably
successive legal decrees offering Jews varying degrees of partial
emancipation.

Sorkin acknowledges that he adopted the notion of 'civil inclusion'
from Lois Dubin with whom he had earlier held dialogues that led to the
first appearance in print of the 'port Jew' concept. In 'Researching Port
Jews and Port Jewries: Trieste and Beyond', Lois Dubin continues this
fascinating and stimulating exchange by making a plea for elevating the

'social type' to a communal level and applying the concept of a 'port Jewry' beyond the temporal and geographical confines which Sorkin prefers. She argues that, for example, it could apply equally well to Ashkenazi port dwellers or port cities of the Ottoman Empire. 'Study of port Jewries in different locales and periods would allow us to engage broadly in comparative history, and in so doing, to raise general questions about the relations between economy, society, and culture in Jewish history.' Having broached an ambitious research agenda, to which we will return later in this volume, Dubin recurs to the special qualities of Trieste and, in particular, the way in which the regnant idea of 'utility' led to the acceptance of Jews in the city and among its mercantile elite.[12] Jews were given privileges because they were considered 'useful to the state', but they internalised this doctrine and utility became a virtue in itself and one that they shared with other Triestinos. This was the basis for progressive degrees of civil inclusion which, in turn, offered a model for maskilim who looked admiringly at Trieste's Jews. They had no need for the Haskalah or ideologically-driven change because they had already undergone extensive adaptation. The interaction between Jews and non-Jews on the Trieste bourse and in the market place, and the emergence of a 'nondenominational morality' based on utility, had contributed to the intensification of social relations and ultimately to the acculturation of the Jews.

Jonathan Schorsch, like Dubin, is interested in how ideology and discourse beyond the confines of Jewish society reshaped Jewish identity once Jews were exposed to it by virtue of their participation in the economy and ecology of transatlantic trade. Jewish law and tradition was quite explicit about the practice of slave holding, stipulating the conversion and eventual manumission of slaves. Yet, as people and ideas crossed and re-crossed the Atlantic, forging new, hybrid entities and identities, the 'discourse of race' infiltrated into the beliefs and behaviour of Jews in Amsterdam, Surinam, and the Dutch possessions in Brazil. The Sephardim absorbed the racial perception of Blacks that was common among Christians during the early era of transatlantic slavery. Discussion about Blacks and mulattos in seventeenth-century Amsterdam displayed anxieties about the status of Jews as white and their desire to identify with the attitudes of the majority community, even though this involved contradicting traditional Jewish doctrine. Black Jews were gradually excluded from the community in life and in death. The Mahamad, the communal authority in Amsterdam, limited conversion since it obliged Jews to free their slaves. In Surinam, where Jews were major slaveholders, imported notions of the 'pigmentocracy' overrode Jewish tradition. This was a form of acculturation that has been neglected in historical accounts,

for obvious reasons given its potential for causing embarrassment.
Schorsch thus offers a salutary reminder that the milieu of the port and
the mercantilist ethos were not inherently 'progressive'. Just because port
cities were dynamic and cosmopolitan, and 'good for the Jews', does not
mean that they were a haven of human rights.

A similar caveat is made by Rainer Liedtke who reviews the Jewish
presence in Hamburg.[13] Liedtke points out that the dominance of
Lutheranism and the prominence of the local clergy meant that, despite
its mercantile character, for much of its history Hamburg was not a
tolerant location for Jews. Jews were admitted to the city on the grounds
of utility but had to be defended by the city Senate against the burgers
and clergy. Emancipation was protracted and came about as a by-product
of other developments. The domination of merchants and mercantile
values did not lead to the acceptance of others, or to their inclusion in
city governance or guilds. Jews did not gain full freedom of trade until
1860. Although by the standards of other German cities the public sphere
was more open to Jews, Hamburg remained socially, politically, and
culturally segregated. It was symptomatic of the attitude towards Jews,
and the fragile self-confidence of the Jewish community, that both Jews
and non-Jews avoided contact with the vast numbers of Jewish
transmigrants who flowed through the port from eastern Europe en
route to England and America between 1880 and 1914. Few were able to
settle in a city that, despite its global connectedness and cosmopolitan
façade, offered Jews 'partial and selective integration'.

There are significant parallels in this respect between Hamburg and
Southampton, a port city that, as Tony Kushner shows, managed to
combine diversity with a defensive attitude towards difference. Kushner
compares Southampton with Portsmouth, but his comparative approach
ranges more widely. At the outset, he warns against too narrow a
definition of 'port Jews' that would inhibit its wider deployment. He
pleads for an approach that is not simply 'top–down', preoccupied with
economic and intellectual elites, but one that accommodates class as well
as ethnicity. Otherwise it is not even certain that Southampton and
Portsmouth Jews would qualify for inclusion at all! Yet his richly
textured account of these Jews and their communities not only reveals
the value of the port Jew/Jewry as an analytical tool but adds a new
dimension to it. By situating these ports in their regional as well as their
global context – a step which Brian Hoyle deemed essential to
understanding both their external and internal social and economic
relations – Kushner is able to illuminate the attitudes towards the Jews
that helped to shape their behaviour.

Portsmouth had an older, settled Jewish population that benefited from the major Royal Navy base. Southampton had a smaller, newer community that was dwarfed by the volume of transmigrants. In both places Jews were held to be a more or less alien presence. Whereas Portsmouth Jews periodically indulged in apologetics and local 'boosterism', Southampton Jews opted for almost total invisibility and preferred transmigrants to move on as quickly as possible. In both centres Jews tried to efface their difference by adapting their surroundings or adapting to them.

Tony Kushner urges the wider application of the port Jew concept to non-elite Ashkenazim beyond the eighteenth century, and calls for greater attention to the phenomena of transmigration which brought together local and global trends in a conjunction that can be seen in almost every British city with a Jewish population and which must have had a distinctive impact on relations between Jews and non-Jews. This theme is echoed by David Cesarani in a re-examination of London's Jews as port Jews. However, Cesarani also quizzes the static definition of the 'social type' by drawing on the work of geographers who stress the dynamic of port cities. Each phase in the development of the port city has been accompanied by particular economic, social and power relations that have had an impact on their Jewish populations. This suggests that the context and the character of the port Jew must have shifted over time, at least in those cases in which Jewish populations were present for a sufficient duration to experience such alterations.

London as a port city was not consistently or uniformly hospitable to Jews. Jews faced exclusion and opposition from London merchants who feared competition. This well-documented resentment calls into question the assumption that a positive attitude towards commerce automatically fostered a benign attitude towards the Jews. However, the crown protected London's Jews from London's merchants: London is unique because its Jews were both court Jews and port Jews. Changing perceptions of the port also had implications for perceptions of the Jews. From the late nineteenth century, exchange ceased to be the port's primary function and London became a place of trans-shipment and manufacture. Jews moved from being merchants who engaged in exchange to being commodities that were trans-shipped. The positive image of the merchant gave way to that of the negative, imaginary horde of immigrating aliens.

The cautionary approach to the port city as an engine of beneficence is maintained by Mark Levene in his study of Salonika Jewry. While the theory of the port Jew might appeal today because it appears founded on the goodness of the market and the benefits of globalisation, the reality in Salonika was that incorporation into the world economy was a mixed

blessing for the city and its Jews. The Jewish population languished in an
economic backwater of the Ottoman Empire until the 1870s, when it was
revivified by aid from west European Jews and was able to take part in
the boom that resulted from inward investment that was often mobilised
by the same Jews but wearing different hats. Local Jews acted as cultural
and economic mediators, taking on the role of compradors, or agents of
foreign powers and overseas capital. They were thus valued for their
economic function and were protected from the waves of nationalistic
violence that swept the Balkans. Ultimately, however, their role as
intermediaries doomed them. Once Greece acquired Salonika and
incorporated the city into a state that aspired to ethnic and cultural
homogeneity, and that was not dependent on one maritime trading
outlet, they became dispensable. For a time they were shielded by the
ascription to them of mythic associations and access to power. But their
prosperity, prominence as middlemen, and their relationship to outside
powers may have contributed to their isolation in 1943 when Salonika
was under German occupation, and rendered them vulnerable to the
Nazi onslaught which destroyed the community.

In 'Greeks and Jews in Salonika and Odessa', Maria Vassilikou
challenges the traditional way of looking at Greek–Jewish relations solely
through the lens of ethnic conflict and communal violence, as typified in
much of the historiography on these cities. She portrays a more complex
dynamic animating inter-ethnic relationships. Contact ranged from
mutual indifference, cooperation and tolerance, to animosity. Neither
ethnic-faith group was monolithic and the pattern of relations was
refracted through social status and class, with wealthy Greek and Jewish
merchants tending to share salubrious residential districts. They worked
together in municipal administration and the regulation of commerce.
Until the 1910s, the community leadership in neither city supported
nationalist movements. Exclusivism and chauvinism were characteristic
of the lower-middle classes, in both places social and political conflict was
more common along lines of class. Vassilikou thus introduces class into
the consideration of ethnicity and relates both to the functions and
fortunes of major port cities.

John Klier complements Vassilikou's comparative study with an
outline of the development of Odessa and the unusual circumstances of a
Jewish population developing *ad novum* from a variety of regions within
the Russian Empire and Austria-Hungary. Odessa's Jews were often
condemned as being 'unjewish' or 'apathetic' by the Jewish intelligentsia,
but the city's Jewish elite was hugely successful in commerce and there
was a large Jewish middle class active in the city's cultural life. However,
this diverse and newly thrown-together community found it hard to act

in concert politically. Klier reminds us of the importance of Jewish economic activity throughout Odessa's large hinterland and the diversification of occupations in the port. Almost uniquely in Russia, Odessa's Jews had a 'normal' economic profile including rich industrialists and railway entrepreneurs, a professional and mercantile middle class, artisans and plebeian Jews – including dockworkers. Jews were not residentially segregated by ethnicity but were grouped socially.

Finally, Jonathan Goldstein takes up the challenge of extending the concept of the 'port Jew' to India, China and Japan. He applies Sorkin's criteria for distinguishing the port Jew as a 'social type' to the Jews of Baghdad, Bombay and Yokahama; Cochin; the Bnei Israel of India; the American Jews of Canton and Macao; and refugee Jews in 1930s and 1940s Shanghai. Goldstein concludes that the 'social type' was to be found with substantial variations in all these locations, but barely in Shanghai where Jews did not have enough time to establish a settled community. In an interesting and original departure, Goldstein also examines the inland Jewish community of Harbin in Siberia as a counterfactual to the port Jew theory. He finds that the composition and character of the Jewish community in Harbin in the late nineteenth and early twentieth centuries seems closest to the model of the 'port Jew'. This begs the question of whether the maritime location is a critical factor in the emergence of the 'social type'.

III

As in the best traditions of an academic symposium the essays in this volume do not offer a uniform approach or interpretation, despite extensive agreement on certain fundamentals. The extent of the consensus should not be overlooked. Almost every contributor agrees that the 'port Jew' as a 'social type' is an invaluable concept and is wholly appropriate to the Sephardim in Atlantic-oriented port cities from the mid-seventeenth to the mid-nineteenth centuries. There is also unanimity that certain ports with an Ashkenazi population in the Mediterranean exemplified its characteristics. Whether or not the type can be identified in other regions at other times is more of a moot point, but the typology itself and the significance of the port city milieu is undisputed. This is a solid base for future research.

However, throughout the essays in this volume there is a tension between, on the one hand, the specificity of the 'social type' identified with the early modern period, with alternatives to haskalah and with paths to modernity, and on the other, the attempt to locate that type more widely or to apply the term 'port Jew' to very different social subjects such as Jews in Muslim lands, poor Jews, or communities of transmigrants. The term was intended to recover the history of the Sephardim, but arguably it failed to encompass those Sephardim who emigrated to port cities that did not enjoy the same trajectory at the Atlantic ports, such as those in the Ottoman Empire. Certain of the criteria defining the 'port Jew' may also be applicable to Jews in pre-modern cities, such as fifteenth-century Lisbon, as well as in late-nineteenth century and twentieth century contexts.

Several essays point to the limits of mercantilist doctrine and the notion of utility as the source of positive attitudes towards Jews. Progressive thinking was not necessarily in thrall to the market: during the eighteenth century certain thinkers, notably the French physiocrats, distinguished 'useless' trade from useful production. Even in port cities that evinced the undiluted and unchallenged spirit of commerce, the pre-eminence of profit often fostered inter-ethnic rivalry. While class and commercial interests in a port city sometimes cut across ethnicity, it was more frequently the case that ethnic and religious differences sharpened the competitive edge. Commercialism was not always accompanied by cosmopolitanism, nor was trade invariably the handmaiden of tolerance. Religious prejudice and racialism could co-exist with business. Sometimes business itself fostered conservative or intolerant views, most obviously in the case of the transatlantic slave trade. Where Jews were permitted to develop a fully-faceted social structure, class bisected ethnic allegiances and the port city became simply an arena in which 'progressive' Jewish ideologies and movements were pitted against their enemies within and beyond the Jewish community.

Finally, several essays refer to the importance of empire and region in the function of city ports and the fate of their Jewish populations. Port cities might occupy central or peripheral locations, and these situations might alter due to the redrawing of political boundaries. In certain cases heterogeneous port cities were absorbed into nation states, whereupon cosmopolitanism ceased to be an asset and became a liability. Cosmopolitanism and association with foreign interests, economically or politically, is not always a good thing. Jews in certain situations were perceived negatively as 'compradors', having previously been vaunted as the avatars of economic development. These points of agreement and dissent form the basis for a research agenda which will be addressed at the end of this volume.

NOTES

1 For a useful summary of the history and historiography, see Lloyd P. Gartner, *History of the Jews in Modern Times* (Oxford: Oxford University Press, 2001), pp.23–4, 39–46, 55–60, and David Sorkin, 'Into the Modern World' in Nicholas de Lange (ed.), *The Illustrated History of the Jewish People* (London: Auram., 1997), pp.201–9.

2 See Salo W. Baron, *A Social and Religious History of the Jews*, Vol.2 (New York: Columbia University Press, 1937), pp.164–90.

3 One of the most significant early studies of Jews in a port city, and a notable exception, was explicitly devoted to proving that they did *not* play a special role in the emergence of capitalism, so rebutting the thesis advanced by Werner Sombart, and amplified for different reasons by other anti-semites: Herbert Bloom, *The Economic Activities of the Jews of Amsterdam in the Seventeenth and Eighteenth Centuries* (Williamsport, Pa.: Bayard Press, 1937).

4 Lois Dubin, *The Port Jews of Habsburg Trieste* (Stanford, Cal.: Stanford University Press, 1999) and 'Trieste and Berlin: The Italian Role in the Cultural Politics of the Haskalah' in J. Katz (ed.) *Toward Modernity: The European Jewish Model* (New Brunswick, NJ: Rutgers University Press, 1987).

5 David Sorkin, 'The Port Jew: Notes Towards a Social Type', *Journal of Jewish Studies*, 50:1 (1999), 87–97.

6 Yosef Kaplan, *An Alternative Path to Modernity: The Sephardi Diaspora in Western Europe* (Leiden: Brill, 2000).

7 Nadav Kashtan (ed.), *Seafaring and the Jews* (London: Frank Cass, 2001).

8 Paolo Bernadini and Norman Fiering, *The Jews and the Expansion of Europe to the West 1450–1800* (Oxford: Bery, 2001).

9 Brian Graham and Catherine Nash (eds), *Modern Historical Geographies* (London: Longman, 2000) offers an excellent survey of the interconnections and cross-fertilisation between the disciplines.

10 See B.S. Hoyle and D.A. Pinder, *European Port Cities in Transition*, (London: Belhaven Press, 1992).

11 Sorkin, 'The Port Jew: Notes Towards a Social Type' (see note 5) and 'Into the Modern World' (note 1).

12 Lois Dubin (see note 4).

13 Rainer Liedtke, *Jewish Welfare in Hamburg and Manchester, c. 1850–1914* (Oxford: Oxford University Press, 1998).

Fields of Tension:
Development Dynamics
at the Port-City Interface

BRIAN HOYLE

A close association between cities and ports, and their coastal zones and hinterlands, is a recurrent theme throughout the history of civilisation. The port city, or cityport, is a critical element in the global maritime transport and trading system, a major facilitator in the economic life of most countries, and a focus of local/regional and often national/international activity. It symbolises in one dimension the interdependence of environment and society, and in another dimension it often involves a fusion of cultural diversity and historical experience. Jewish communities, among many others, have long played a significant role in the life of port cities, symbolised for many people by Shakespeare's Venice, 'there where merchants most do congregate'.[1] Nearby on the Adriatic coast of Croatia, the urban form and fabric of Dubrovnik still typify intimate medieval port/city interdependence. In the later nineteenth century, Paul Cézanne portrayed the impact of the expanding, industrialising Marseille port-city complex on the adjacent coastal zone between the Vieux Port and L'Estaque, as urban and port functions began to move apart.[2] Today, Rotterdam and Hong Kong represent in different contexts the idea of a modern port city as a fundamental element in the spatial structure, organisation and re-organisation of economies and societies, in the relationships between those societies and their environments, and in terms of the degree of spatial separation between urban areas and port zones now regarded as normal in large cityports worldwide. 'While urban planners tried to use the orientation towards the port as a solid, sustainable basis for the city plan, the port slithered like a slippery eel, constantly changing its position and continuing to grow.'[3]

Diversity is nevertheless a keynote of the modern world cityport system. Ports are located not only on the coasts of the world's oceans and seas, and on estuaries, but also on the shores of lakes and rivers sometimes far inland. The primary function of a port may be commercial or naval. In advanced and less-developed countries today, port cities, and their associated coastal zones, have become foci of increasing planning attention. At Southampton (UK), urban authorities have attempted in recent years, with some success, to bring the city back to the sea, to reunite the urban core with the waterfront from which it became separated during and after the Second World War. In contrast, the cityport of Dar es Salaam (Tanzania) is involved in the United Nations Development Programme's sustainable cities initiative.[4] Changes, in these cityports as in all others, are derived in part from local circumstances, at the interface between land and sea, between terrestrial and maritime transport systems; in part from the national space economy; and in part from the international, global cityport system within which each individual port city is one small but significant element. The management of change, which ultimately is what urban and port administration are all about, requires both an understanding of spatial scales and contexts, within modern cultural frameworks, and an understanding of the varying pace, impact and legacy of temporal evolution. In this way, every port city, however individually distinctive, illustrates principles of global relevance.

This essay explores the cityport concept from a geographical perspective, with historical overtones, and is intended to provide a spatial frame of reference for general or specific research on Jewish port-city communities, migrant or settled, characterised *inter alia* by their association with a particular type of location. The aim is to contribute some ideas and to indicate some relevant material derived largely from research in geography, a discipline essentially complementary with history and within which in recent decades port-city issues have generated a substantial literature. The essay deals with the cityport concept; the distinction between situation and site; port-city linkages, past and present; the port-city interface; coastal zone management; and dimensions, perceptions and interpretations of change. The conclusions question the continuing role of the cityport in the brave new world of intermodal transport, globalisation and economic restructuring.

The Cityport Concept

The idea of the cityport is derived from the frequently close relationships between the port function and coastal urban development. Defined as *a place where the mode of transportation changes from land systems to water-borne systems*, a port normally provides the central and original function of a coastal urban nucleus, and coastal city location is often associated with a harbour within which port development occurs. In one way, the concept of the cityport simply expresses the frequently close association between a port and the city of which it is a major component. Not all ports are associated with cities, of course, nor is the association always close. Association between port and city may be quite new, a result of modern technological innovation or regional planning; or it may be something that goes back to ancient times. On the ground, in a modern urban planning context, a lot of attention is given to the port-city interface, which is often problematical. In a structural sense, the word *cityport* is quite widely used not only to refer to the specifics of the port-city interface in spatial terms but also to express multifaceted socio-economic interdependence and integration in a wider context.

The social, economic and political complexities of port cities are distinguished from those of other cities by the fact that a port city provides, through maritime trade, a window on a wider world. Multidirectional transport and trade through that window provides, in turn, widespread opportunities for the growth of diverse specialised communities – a spatial, socio-economic and political matrix within which Jews have, of course, figured prominently and controversially. Yet any coastal city, large or small, is likely to have something to do with maritime activities, taking advantage of the available water resources. Those water-related activities may involve port development, and over time the port and the city may have remained closely integrated or may have grown apart. So today the modern port–city association may be substantial, varied and complex or it might be almost negligible. How far is the modern urban economy dependent upon port-related employment? How significant is the port function as an influence upon urban planning? Are spatial proximity and functional interdependence supported by cooperative planning and management systems?

Some examples from around the world illustrate the diversity of these relationships. At Sydney and Marseille the main focus of modern port activity has moved a long way away from the original harbour-focused urban core, thus changing and weakening port-city connections as the spatial scale of port activity and urban development has increased. At Southampton and many other European port cities, the city similarly displays today a less intimate relationship with its port than throughout most of its history. In contrast, many smaller port cities – in the Mediterranean, for example, and in the developing countries of Africa, Asia and Latin America – maintain a substantial association between their dual functions. Although it is sometimes tempting to do so, it would however be inappropriate to associate port-city size too closely with the separation of port and city functions, or to suggest that the gradual process of port-city separation is necessarily driven by rising overall levels of socio-economic development.

There is, clearly, no single simple model of the port city. The American historian Josef Konvitz has underlined the variability of relationships between the quality of harbours, the growth of cities, the development of ports, and the decision-making processes involved in these relationships, and reminds us that explanations often involve unknown elements: 'Every coastal town did not become a city, nor did communities exist wherever there was a good harbour, nor did every port city have a good harbour. There are mysteries about why men have chosen to live in cities, to occupy certain sites, and to link their destinies with the movement of ships that cannot be entirely explained by economic, social and political events'.[5]

We can interpret the cityport concept in many dimensions – geographical and historical, social and economic, technological and political. In most modern port cities (except, perhaps, those of very recent origin or artificial design), it is impossible to be unaware of the immense influence of heritage from the past. For centuries, the pursuit of maritime affairs has played a major role in the development of urban systems and, perhaps especially in Europe, port cities are again undergoing rapid and often beneficial transition.[6] Maritime technologies acted as instruments of progress in port growth, and technologies of ship design and cargo handling paralleled eras and scales of cityport development.

Within a globalising economy, technological factors often transcend other considerations, and modern planning and management systems must recognise the opportunities, constraints and problems that modern technology provides. For practical purposes at the local level, the planning and political contexts are very important, because the degree to which port and city affect one another today influences – for example – land-use, urban transport and employment opportunities, all of which may yield critical and controversial politico-economic and social issues. Progress demands a cooperative approach in such contexts and, wherever possible, a unified policy derived from the legitimate concerns of all the 'actors' involved.

Situation and Site

Urban geographers have traditionally distinguished between the *situation* of a city – the broader regional context within which a settlement develops – as opposed to the specific *site* that it occupies. When considering port cities, we must examine the landward side and the maritime side, so we have not two but four sets of factors, the balance between which obviously varies from place to place and over time. For merchants and sailors, as Shylock pointed out, 'there be land-rats, and water-rats, water-thieves, and land-thieves'[7] and for geographers analysing port cities there is the land situation and the water situation, the water site and the land site. It should be borne in mind, however, that in port-city development it is the *port function* that always lies at the root of the physical form of the cityport settlement in terms of location and layout, and, at least for a time, in terms of socio-economic development, including the activities of specific communities such as port Jews identified by locality or role.

The level of port development, and to some extent of urban growth, reflects the *land situation*, the nature and extent of economic development in the tributary areas, including transport infrastructures and services. In part, at least, a port-city develops in response to demand generated within these broad *hinterlands*. The *land site*, however, is a major controlling factor over the pattern of urban growth, and in turn this affects the operation of the port functions on the landward side. There may be some conflict of interest between port and city as to how the land site should be developed. The *water site*, the physical conditions of the harbour, frequently – indeed one might say normally – provides the initial stimulus to port-city development. The *water situation* is critically important in other ways, because this involves a port's relations with other ports – in other words its competitive position – and its location in relation to the major shipping lanes and routes that connect the port with its *forelands* overseas.

The overall general level of cityport development is thus largely a reflection of the broader situation, both on the landward and seaward sides, while the precise and detailed ways in which that development is geographically expressed is a matter of more specific water site and land site conditions. But however attractive a site may be, or however favourable a situation, these attributes do not in any way determine cityport development, although they may of course influence it in positive or negative ways. What matters, far more than the sites and situations themselves, is the way in which such sites and situations were assessed in the past, and continue to be re-assessed today, by those who are in a position to take decisions about the character, scale and pace of cityport development.

Port-city Linkages, Past and Present

A broad view of the evolution of port-city inter-relationships over time is illustrated in Figure 1, which identifies a series of stages from ancient

STAGE	SYMBOL ○ City ● Port	PERIOD	CHARACTERISTICS
I Primitive port/city		Ancient/medieval to 19th century	Close spatial and functional association between city and port
II Expanding port/city		19th–early 20th century	Rapid commercial/industrial growth forces port to develop beyond city confines, with linear quays and break-bulk industries
III Modern industrial port/city		mid-20th century	Industrial growth (especially oil refining) and introduction of containers/ro-ro require separation/space
IV Retreat from the waterfront		1960s–1980s	Changes in maritime technology induce growth of separate maritime industrial development areas.
V Redeevolopment of waterfront		1970s–1990s	Large-scale modern port consumes large areas of land/water space: urban renewal of original core.
VI Renewal of port/city links		1980s–2000 +	Globalisation and intermodalism transform port roles; port-city associations renewed; urban redevelopment enhances port-city integration.

times to the present day. If the idea of the 'port Jew' is interpreted widely, in space and time, it can be claimed that each stage was marked by particular socio-economic and political characteristics that affected, perhaps substantially, the respective roles of port Jews, other urban Jewish groups, and non-Jewish communities in port cities. 'Primitive' port cities showed very close spatial associations and maximal functional interdependence. The urban centre was dominated by merchants' houses, and the waterfront often formed one side of the market square, the focal point of the settlement. Perhaps the original exemplar for this model lies within the ancient Greek city state or *polis*. In Genoa, one of the great Italian medieval cityports, urban growth was closely crowded around a good natural harbour, and the historic core of modern Genoa still displays this intimate association between the city and the sea. By the sixteenth century, numerous port cities originally developed in this way had also become windows on a far wider world as Europe explored and colonised the Americas, India and Africa – a process in which (from a European perspective) Lisbon occupied a seat in the front stalls.

In the expanding port cities of the nineteenth century, rapid commercial and industrial development induced major changes in traditional port-city inter-relationships. Old harbours were overcrowded, new quays and basins were constructed, ports broke out of their traditional urban confines, and port growth was paralleled by industrial and urban expansion. Most of the great European river-based seaports, such as Rotterdam, developed new basins and gradually moved downstream – a process exemplified, at a later date, by sugarports on the Australian littoral, including Brisbane, Townsville and Mackay.[8] In the Mediterranean, Marseille burst out of its original small harbour and in the 1840s began to develop a series of coastal basins paralleled by urban industrial growth.[9] This period also saw, of course, a global spread of port-city development in all the other inhabited continents. Sometimes located on islands (as at Mombasa, Montreal, and Singapore), sometimes on the shores of natural harbours (as at Sydney and Melbourne), and sometimes near the mouths of major rivers (as at Lagos and Philadelphia), these port cities served primarily, for a time, as instruments of European colonisation and development.

Throughout the twentieth century, the modern industrial port city became associated with increasing ship size and increasingly specialised industrial growth. Large modern ports primarily handle vast quantities of containerised cargoes and bulk goods including oil and ores, require enormous land and water areas in which to carry out their activities, and are reliant upon extensive and sophisticated maritime and land transport systems. Security considerations, as well as space requirements, encourage port-city separation rather than integration. The technology and logistics of modern maritime transport, as expressed in the geography and functioning of modern ports, have thus produced and encouraged an increased separation of ports and cities. The character of modern ports is no longer closely related to the cities with which they are associated but is largely dictated by ship designers and operators who invest vast sums of money in economies of scale. 'Unlike the great ports of the era of European expansion, ports today do not generate urban development around them. Just as port cities depend less on the port for their own needs, ports depend less on adjacent cities for markets and services. Hence the paradox, that as maritime trade has become more important to the economy of nations in the post-war era, ports have become less important in the overall spatial order of a nation's port cities. Ports have become peripheral, literally and figuratively, to the cities whose names they carry.'[10]

The urban consequences of these trends in maritime transport and port activity have involved a retreat from old, traditional urban waterfronts. London is a classic case of a cityport where the urban consequences of port evolution have been particularly serious, but virtually all port cities worldwide have experienced to some degree an abandonment by the port function and an urban-based transformation process of those historic 'doorstep' sites where port-cities originated and flourished in the past, sometimes for centuries. An outcome of this significant change in port-city relations is the widespread process of waterfront redevelopment now associated with urban renewal programmes in innumerable port cities around the world.[11]

This process started in North America in the 1960s, spread to Europe, Japan and Australasia in the 1970s and 1980s, and in the 1990s became important in newly-industrialising and developing countries. Today, various organisations are attempting to bring port and city closer together again in a context of cooperation. Globalisation of trade and the growth of intermodal transport have encouraged a redefinition of port functions and a rethinking of port-city relations involving a renewal of links, some convergence of policy and some new forms of cooperation.

The Port-City Interface

Whereas the evolution of the inter-relationships between ports and cities (Figure 1) places the cityport in an historical perspective, the port-city interface today (see Figure 2) illustrates problems and processes that arise from inherited conditions but are expressed in spatial terms. In this analysis, urban land uses are divided from maritime activities by an

FIGURE 2
THE PORT-CITY INTERFACE: CHARACTERISTICS AND TRENDS
(after Hoyle, 2000)

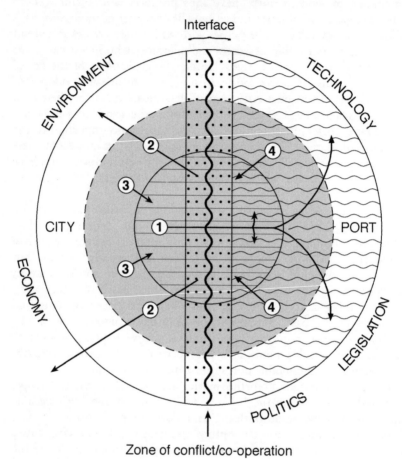

Zone of conflict/co-operation

① Port migration
② Industrial migration
③ Land-use competition
④ Water-use competition

Environmental 'filter'
Traditional port/city core zone

interface zone which may be an area of cooperation or conflict, and may present a scene of degeneration and decay, or alternatively may be characterised by regeneration and lively growth. First published in 1988, this model has generated widespread discussion and has frequently been reproduced.[12]

The dynamics of change include the migration of port activity away from the traditional port-city core zone towards deeper water and more land and water space, sometimes known as 'bluecoast' sites. Port-based industries, no longer dependent upon the break-bulk function or on labour concentration, migrate to other urban zones and to 'greenfield' sites beyond the city. As waterfront sites become available, there is competition for mixed-use land-side redevelopment – for housing, offices, recreational and commercial use. An impulse for redevelopment comes also from the maritime side as demand increases for marinas, berth space and water-related activities of many kinds. Environmental controls act as a kind of filter, reducing pollution and harmonising developments; and the entire system is affected and in part controlled by over-riding factors including technological change, legal requirements, and economic and political conditions.[13]

At the local level, the main reason for these changes is the inability of cityport sites simultaneously to absorb rapidly changing and expanding port development and successive phases of urban growth. Cities and ports once intimately connected have grown apart, and have had to find ways of adjusting to their new relationships. In that process, communities as well as economies have been restructured, relocated, and transformed. But the transformation of the port-city interface is conditioned by and derived from wider, interdependent global trends: the onward march of maritime technology, the spatial scale of modern ports and port-related industries, and a restructuring of the urban economic base involving changes in port-related employment.[14] The dramatic downturn since the 1960s in direct port employment has had a dramatic effect on port-dependent urban communities. What was done by men in the 1950s has rapidly been taken over by machines, in a late-twentieth-century echo of the industrial revolution 150 years earlier. The restructured urban economies of port-cities, however, are sometimes said to employ more people in port-related jobs, thus compensating to some extent for the loss of direct port employment, although it is often difficult to determine precisely in this context what is port-related and what is not.

In a much wider spatial dimension, one of the principal reasons for increasing port/city separation in the nineteenth and twentieth centuries was the changing nature of the relationships, on the one hand, between the services provided by a port and the geographical disposition of its hinterlands, and, on the other hand, the services provided by a city and the geographical character and structure of its urban and regional space economies. Although throughout history ports have always functioned as nodal transfer points in transport systems connecting a wide diversity of *hinterland* places and areas with an extensive range of other *foreland* ports, areas and places across the seas, a modern port often serves not only a large part if not the entirety of the country within which it is located but also a range of other areas beyond national boundaries. The city with which such a port is associated, however, and with which its activities were once closely intertwined, now has a different agenda. It may perform a national role in some respects, but it may be linked with maritime trade only to a limited degree and its essential purpose is to serve the local and regional communities.

If this argument is taken to what may seem a logical conclusion, the inevitable divergence of port and city interests, driven by technology, produces a city that has no real connection with maritime trade, a port that has no substantive links with its city, and a cityport that exists only as an artificial construct preserved by historical accident. Such a view is of necessity an oversimplification, however, partly because it is only in extreme cases where port-city separation reaches extreme lengths, and partly because the separation process is ultimately constrained by the realities of location, community and history. Recognising the need for compromise between separatist trends and sometimes over-idealistic reconvergence plans, many cityports are now looking for fruitful and positive cooperation involving a wide range of participants, in the interests of capitalising on traditional port-city association, modern cityport interdependence, specialisation within urban economies, and competitive port functioning. It is not always entirely beyond the wit of modern authorities, planners and politicians to achieve all of these objectives simultaneously.

Coastal Zone Management

Port cities are involved in a complex web of inter-relationships that far transcend those that simply concern the impact of the port upon the city and vice-versa. In fact there is a need to guard against a tendency to examine, analyse and renovate port cities in relative isolation. There is another particular relationship that is, in some ways, even more important, and that is the interdependence between a cityport, on the one hand, and the region within which it is set, on the other. In developing countries, as well as in advanced countries, this is an important debate.[15] Coastal zone management, especially, must examine littoral regions as dynamic interactive systems within which port cities perform a critical but by no means overwhelmingly dominant role.[16] In this context the balance between cityport and region must be carefully assessed, for each is in part dependent upon the other.

The role of the cityport in regional development planning is also beginning to receive increased attention, in terms of the impacts of rapid urban growth and port activity on neighbouring coastal environments, in terms of the search for a more balanced, integrated approach to the management of port-city regions, and in the wider context of interdependence between cityports and hinterlands. These issues and relationships, for too long disregarded, have been complicated in recent years, again in both advanced and in developing countries, by the introduction of *inland intermodal transport centres*. In Italy, the Quadrante Europa at Verona[17] and the Interporto at Padua are interesting examples. In East Africa, a developing region, there is a growing network of intermodal centres in Kenya, Tanzania and Uganda.[18] The flexibility of new international transport systems based on inter-modalism and multi-modalism is rapidly reducing the relative significance of traditional ports. The modern port is no longer simply a terminal or break-of-bulk point, no longer simply a place where the *mode of* transportation changes. In the world of inter- and multi-modal through transport, there are many such nodes, places, terminals and points, and traditional ports and their associated cities must necessarily adjust to this changing network in terms of competitive positions and planning objectives.[19]

Dimensions, Perceptions and Interpretations of Change

The inter-relationships between ports and cities, in both spatial and temporal dimensions, and the contextual frameworks including coastal zone management within which these inter-relationships are set, have been interpreted in a variety of ways. The broader dimensions of change in this context have been identified by the Israeli scholar Yehuda Hayuth who proposed a threefold categorisation of systems – spatial, economic and ecological – linking port and city, reflecting technological and logistical change on the one hand and attitudinal change on the other, producing new urban waterfront landscapes and growing port/city separation.[20] Philosophical perspectives developed particularly in France have explored the role of ports as creators of cities over time and the diversity of port-city lifestyles today.[21]

From a spatial perspective it can be argued that behavioural geography, rather than physical or social geography, today largely explains the continuing process of differential cityport growth. It is the interaction of decision makers, their economic objectives, political ideas, technological capabilities and environmental attitudes, that ultimately influence what happens at the interface between land and sea, where port cities are located and where they prosper or perish. To a large extent this has always been the case, and although the balance between economics, politics, technology and the environment has clearly varied from one era to another, it can be claimed with little fear of contradiction that at no time have environmental considerations played so large a part in port-city development than at present.

More specifically, the sequence of temporal stages in port-city development has been interpreted, for example in the case of Southampton, as a series of transformations in the politico-economic and socio-cultural life of the port-city.[22] Some of these transformations have been driven by perceived economic opportunity, or by a desire to fight against economic decline, or as a response to the coming of new transport modes and systems (railways, transatlantic passenger liners) that offered opportunities for economic resurgence on an altogether larger scale. The impact of maritime technology has loomed large in many general and specific discussions on port expansion and associated urban change,[23] and there is a growing realisation that what happens in modern ports – and therefore, to some extent, in port-cities – is largely a function of the technology of maritime transport. Ship-owners and ship-operators call the tune, through their emphasis on economies of scale and inter-port competition, so that general levels of port activity are chiefly determined by external forces. At a more local level, however, the precise impact of port activity on the spatial structure of cities – the geographical pattern of the urban mosaic in functional and community terms – has been carefully researched. For example, Wolkowitsch has shown how congestion in the Vieux Port at Marseille, which had handled all port activity there since antiquity, gave rise in the mid-nineteenth century to a need to develop more extensive facilities.[24] The growth of the port towards the north (rather than, as at first proposed, towards the south) started in the 1840s, industrial location patterns changed in response to port developments, and land transport demands necessitated the growth of road and rail networks which in turn have affected patterns of urban and industrial growth. More recently, and in a different context, Gleave has demonstrated the role of port activities in shaping the growing urban area of Freetown (Sierra Leone), arguing that while port activities have been important historically, other influences have become more significant as the basis of the economy has broadened, the structure of society has become more complex and the city has assumed additional functions.[25]

While these two cases are, in many respects, not untypical of the advanced and less-developed countries respectively, the much-debated case of Venice is in a class of its own. The city is preoccupied, in one sense, with the problem of how to deal with the increasing incidence of flooding in the historic core zones, and the inability of the political parties involved to reconcile their differences. In a wider sense, however, the political geography of Venice involves the polarising effects induced by the growth and development of new port areas. First, the Marittima port area was opened in 1880 in the western part of the city, superseding the traditional intimacy between port and city associated with the historic waterfront leading via the piazzetta to St Mark's Square. Second, from the early twentieth century, the Porto Marghera port-industrial zone grew on the nearby mainland. Radical changes in port-city relations throughout the Venice region have been produced by this evolutionary sequence. Soriani has argued for the development of new positive inter-relationships between the component elements of the Venetian cityport and its wider region, invoking a reformulation of the regional role of the port complex as well as a transformation of port-city relations.[26] But in the course of such a reformulation, such a restructuring of relationships, what issues predominate? Where should Venice look for ideas and inspiration? To other cities on water perhaps – Hong Kong, Bruges and Zeebrugge, Sydney; to other port cities based on islands – Mombasa, New York, Singapore; or to other World Heritage Sites where port activity may conflict with the conservation of waterfront palaces – Zanzibar is a recent addition to UNESCO'S list. Lessons from such locations may, however, be of little practical use, for the real problem is how to adapt not only to the *specific* conditions of the case but to the *global* conditions of economic development including new transport systems and new urban lifestyles.

These cases illustrate how, in port-city development, the interdependent processes involved in port activity, industrial change, and urban response create in contrasted locations and time-periods varied patterns that characterise the individuality of place as well as underlining the universality of the inter-relationships concerned. The patterns that result from these processes, however, provide the essential context for the communities that live and work in port cities, contributing to their overall levels of activity and well-being and to those of specific micro-components of the urban mosaic including port Jews. With special reference to Cardiff, the impact of modern port development on maritime communities has been discussed by Hilling who shows how 'the former distinctive, thriving sailortown of Tiger Bay is no more and, as in comparable areas of San Francisco, New Orleans, Hamburg or

Shanghai, is now marked only by residual landscape elements'.[27] Social
and cultural aspects of several other major port cities (Barcelona,
Rotterdam, New York and London) have recently been examined by
Meyer from an urban planning perspective.[28] He poses the question
whether it is still possible to design public urban areas that are
simultaneously meaningful on more than one level, that of large-scale
port-related infrastructure and that of local-scale urban fabric.

Recapturing in a new urban context the key position once held by
traditional port-city centres is the goal of many new waterfront projects,
and the widespread redevelopment of urban waterfronts in port-cities and
elsewhere has generated a substantial literature concerned *inter alia* with
the broader trends involved,[29] with the complex interlinkages between
heritage and tourism[30] and with the political and financial perspectives
involved in managing change.[31] These diverse interpretations of port-city
change conjure up images not only of older communities in decline,
sometimes displaced and neglected, but also of vibrant, younger
communities working and living in revitalised port-city core zones, and
of financial and real-estate entrepreneurs rapidly promoting new
development for an expanding market.

Port-city Associations

Several interdisciplinary organisations have attempted over many years
to address and in part resolve some of the problems associated with port
cities. In France, the Association Internationale Villes et Ports
[International Cities and Ports Association], from its base in Le Havre,
has been trying for many years to resolve some of these disagreements,
and particularly to bring urban and port authorities towards closer
understanding. The association has produced a wealth of documentation
and has organised a series of international conferences (in Europe, North
and South America and Africa) of which the most recent took place in
November 2000 in Marseille. Complementary organisations with related
objectives involving port/city re-integration, each with its own specific
focus, include the Centro Internazionale Città d'Acqua [International
Cities on Water Association] based in Venice, the Waterfront Vitalisation
and Environment Research Center (WAVE) in Japan, and, in the USA,
the Waterfront Center in Washington, D.C.

None of these organisations has found it straightforward to bring
together the diverse opinions, perspectives and attitudes of the various
'actors' involved in port-city inter-relationships; but, with laudable
perseverance, each has succeeded in its own way in getting individuals
and authorities to understand, at least partially, the opinions of others

and the reasons why they are held. There is, unfortunately, no comparable port-city or waterfront revitalisation organisation in the United Kingdom where the structure of local government, and the traditionally commercial attitude of national governments towards ports, renders close cooperation in a continental European mode somewhat difficult. Attempts to persuade Associated British Ports (ABP), for example, to play a positive role in the further development of the International Cities and Ports Association (AIVP) have proved unfruitful. Although the city of Southampton is twinned with Le Havre, where the AIVP headquarters are located, ABP has hitherto declined to participate significantly in AIVP activities.

The debates and interpretations emanating from these various organisations often stress the spatial dimensions of port–city relations although their first pre-occupations may be with economic, political and technological issues. In the 1990s the port-city relationship entered a new era in which concerted action in three contexts – functional, spatial and management – are essential if the fabric of port cities as a whole is to be conserved and developed in rational terms. The functions of ports and cities, although they may seem to remain essentially what they have always been, have in fact changed substantially and become infinitely more complex than heretofore. Changes in the spatial characteristics of port-city development in recent decades have been enormous, as has been explained. The management of the changing complementarity between port and city, in this context, requires virtually continuous redefinition of that complementarity in today's terms and for the future.

Conclusions

The sequence of stages of cityport evolution and the common factors underlying cityport development from past to present help to explain similarities between modern cityports and the distinctiveness of individual locations. There is a tendency for modern ports and cities, acquiring similar attributes and fulfilling similar functions, to assume a similar layout and appearance, and for their revitalising waterfronts gradually to become essentially clones of comparable locations slightly further ahead in the redevelopment game. However, despite these tendencies, all modern cityports are anxious to enhance their local individuality, normally based on a subtle combination of location and heritage, while recognising that it is global forces which both promote and constrain their changing character. Three important consequences arise from this sequence. There is a need to re-examine the roles played by modern industrial and commercial ports in regional and national economies. The challenges posed by the decline of outmoded port areas require a sensitive and appropriate local response. And the time is now ripe for an enhanced degree of cooperation between all the actors involved in port-city management, planning and development.

The port-city interface today is a highly sensitive planning environment. Port and city authorities do not normally see eye to eye about what should be done. They often share problems of the abandoned doorstep, the revitalising waterfront, the displaced community, the restructured economy, but disagree about *how* renewal should take place. Bringing separated port and city back together again (if indeed that is the aim) is about *managing complementarity* – identifying and analysing interdependence, and building on it in appropriate ways. This may seem obvious, but in practice it is not easy. Fields of tension continue to abound. What are the new opportunities for port cities as their *transport* role changes in a context of intermodalism? How can port cities manage their environment so as to enhance the quality of *urban* life and serve the industrial/commercial needs derived from the *port* function?

The transformation of port-city inter-relationships during the past 150 years, reflecting particularly the technological and transport changes that created a field of tension between port and city, culminated in the late-twentieth century situation in which ports and cities became dissociated and the rise of logistics and teleports transformed spatial systems and concepts. Traditional cityports are no longer necessarily the most logical sites for the development of new electronic ports, the logistic hubs through which flows of goods are directed and co-ordinated. Merchants no longer congregate on a city's waterfront but in its downtown financial district. Cities and ports which once were intimately connected and finely balanced have grown apart, and both ports and cities have found new ways of adjusting to their new relationships. Whether these relationships can, or should, be maintained in perpetuity is an open question, for the recent transformation of the port function is such that, in the twenty-first century, ports of many kinds may come to have little to do with cities.

Relationships between port and city are thus variable, both spatially and over time, and the idea of interdependence between port activities and urban phenomena resurfaces repeatedly throughout history and around the world. The social, economic and political complexities of port cities are distinguished from those of other cities by the fact that a port city provides, through maritime trade, a window on a wider world. Multidirectional transport and trade through that window provides, in turn, widespread opportunities for the growth of diverse specialised communities – a spatial, socio-economic and political matrix within which Jews have figured prominently and controversially. Geographical perspectives can provide some useful ways of seeing and interpreting environments and frameworks within which the history, distribution, activities and inter-communal relationships of port Jews are set.

NOTES

1. William Shakespeare, *The Merchant of Venice* (London, 1600), Act 1, Scene 3, line 44.
2. Maurice Wolkowitch, 'Port Extension as a Factor in Urban Development: The Case of Marseilles', in *Cityport Industrialization and Regional Development: Spatial Analysis and Planning Strategies*, ed. by Brian Hoyle and David Pinder (Oxford: Pergamon Press, Urban and Regional Planning Series, Vol.24, 1981), pp.87–101.
3. Han Meyer, *City and Port: Urban Planning as a Cultural Venture in London, Barcelona, New York and Rotterdam: Changing Relations between Public Urban Space and Large-Scale Infrastructure* (Utrecht: International Books, 1999), p.376. Reviewed by Brian Hoyle in *Urban Studies* 37.4 (2000), 823–5.
4. Brian Hoyle, 'Port-City Renewal in Developing Countries: The Waterfront at Dar es Salaam, Tanzania', *Erdkunde* 56.2 (2002), 114–29.
5. Josef Konvitz, *Cities and the Sea: Port City Planning in Early Modern Europe* (Baltimore and London: Johns Hopkins Press, 1978), p.xi.
6. Brian Hoyle and David Pinder (eds.), *European Port Cities in Transition* (London: Belhaven Press, in association with the British Association for the Advancement of Science, 1992).
7. Shakespeare (see note 1), lines 20–21.
8. Brian Hoyle, 'Seaport Systems and Agricultural Exports in a Developing Regional Economy: The Sugarports of Queensland, Australia', in *Seaport Systems and Spatial Change: Technology, Industry and Development Strategies*, ed. by Brian Hoyle and David Hilling (Chichester: John Wiley & Sons, 1984), pp.361–89.
9. Jean-Louis Bonillo (ed.), *Marseille: Ville et Port* (Marseille: Editions Parenthèses, 1991).
10. Josef Konvitz, 'Port Cities and World War', paper presented to the Centre for Urban and Regional Research, University of Glasgow, May 1987, p.31.
11. Rinio Bruttomesso, *Waterfronts: A New Frontier for Cities on Water* (Venice: International Centre Cities on Water, 1993); Ann Breen and Dick Rigby, *The New Waterfront: A Worldwide Urban Success Story* (London: Thames & Hudson, 1996).
12. Brian Hoyle, David Pinder and Sohail Husain (eds.), *Revitalising the Waterfront: International Dimensions of Dockland Redevelopment* (London: Belhaven Press, 1988).
13. Brian Hoyle, 'The Port-City Interface: Trends, Problems and Examples', *Geoforum* 20.4 (1989), 429–35.
14. Yehuda Hayuth, 'The Port-Urban Interface: An Area in Transition', *Area* 14.3 (1982), 219–24.
15. Brian Hoyle, 'Cityport Industrialization and Regional Development in Less-Developed Countries: The Tropical African Experience', in Hoyle and Pinder (see note 2), pp.281–303.
16. Adalberto Vallega, *The Changing Waterfront in Coastal Area Management* (Milan: Franco Angeli, 1992).
17. Claudia Robiglio, 'Combined Transport in Italy: The Case of the Quadrante Europa, Verona', in *Cityports, Coastal Zones and Regional Change* ed. by Brian Hoyle (Chichester: John Wiley & Sons, 1996), pp.249–70.
18. Brian Hoyle and Jacques Charlier, 'Inter-Port Competition in Developing Countries: An East African Case Study', *Journal of Transport Geography* 3.1 (1995), 87–103.
19. Brian Hoyle and Richard Knowles (eds.), *Modern Transport Geography* (Chichester: John Wiley & Sons, 1998), 2nd edn.
20. Hayuth (see note 14).

21. Thierry Baudouin, Michèle Collin and Claude Prélorenzo (eds.), *Urbanité des Cités Portuaires* (Paris: L'Harmattan, 1997).
22. Brian Hoyle, 'The Transformation of the Port of Southampton', in *Ports et Mers: Mélanges Maritimistes Offerts à André Vigarié*, ed. by Jacques Charlier (Caen: Paradigme, 1986), pp.171–88.
23. Yehuda Hayuth and David Hilling, 'Technological Change and Seaport Development', in Hoyle and Pinder (see note 2), pp.40–58.
24. Wolkowitsch (see note 2).
25. Barrie Gleave, 'Port Activities and the Spatial Structure of Cities: The Case of Freetown, Sierra Leone', *Journal of Transport Geography* 5.4 (1997), 257–75.
26. Stefano Soriani, 'The Venice Port and Industrial Area in a Context of Regional Change', in Hoyle, *Cityports* (see note 16), pp.235–48.
27. David Hilling, 'Socio-Economic Change in the Maritime Quarters: The Demise of Sailortown', in Hoyle, Pinder and Husain (see note 12), pp.20–37.
28. Meyer (see note 3).
29. Ann Breen and Dick Rigby, *Waterfronts: Cities Regain their Edge* (New York: McGraw-Hill, 1993); Sir Peter Hall, 'Waterfronts: A New Urban Frontier', in Bruttomesso (see note 11), pp.12–19; Brian Hoyle, 'Global and Local Change on the Port-City Waterfront', *The Geographical Review* 90.3 (2000), 395–417.
30. Gregory Ashworth and John Tunbridge, *The Tourist-Historic City* (London: Belhaven Press, 1990).
31. David Gordon, 'Planning, Design and Managing Change in Urban Waterfront Redevelopment', *Town Planning Review*, 67.3 (1996), 261–90; and 'Managing the Changing Political Environment in Urban Waterfront Redevelopment', *Urban Studies* 34.1 (1997), 61–83.

Port Jews and the
Three Regions of Emancipation

DAVID SORKIN

In keeping with the venerable academic tradition of not leaving well enough alone, I would like to start with a qualification. At the same time that I heartily endorse and enthusiastically welcome the broader research project which this volume initiates, I would also hope that in the course of future research we will not dilute the historical specificity of the social type of the 'port Jew'. I propose to safeguard that social type by distinguishing between it and the concept of Jews in ports or port cities. Thus 'port Jew' would refer specifically to the Sephardi and Italian Jews in the early modern period (seventeenth–eighteenth centuries), but also shading into the nineteenth century, who primarily resided in the Mediterranean ports of Venice, Livorno and Trieste, the Atlantic ports of Bordeaux and London, Amsterdam and Hamburg, and the New World ports of Jamaica, Surinam, Recife and New Amsterdam. In contrast, the concept 'Jews in port cities' would be applicable anywhere at anytime. The distinction between these two concepts would leave that of the port Jew intact while identifying the phenomenon of Jews in port cities as a virtually unlimited subject with neither fixed geographical nor chronological boundaries.

My concern in not diluting the historical specificity of the social type of the 'port Jew' is to help us rethink our understanding of emancipation in Europe. Emancipation remains something of the problem child of modern Jewish history: it receives what seems like an inordinate amount of attention, but most of it is attention of the wrong kind. On the one hand, it continues to preoccupy historians of modern Jewry by serving as the symbolic point of departure, the great divide between 'tradition' and 'modernity' or the medieval and the modern world. On the other hand, it bears two significant burdens: the taint of an alleged responsibility for the dissolution of a cohesive and coherent 'autonomous' community and thus for the consequent ambiguities if not agonies of assimilation – despite the fact that historians have gone a long way in reassessing that process by separating ideological aspersions from historical actualities;[1] as well as the

burden of the supposedly negative verdict of history in the form of the
Holocaust, a malediction which no quantity of scholarly ink is capable of
exorcising. For these reasons the recent literature has focused more on
emancipation's consequences, that is, its social and economic impact, than
on the actual process.[2] In consequence, emancipation as a European
phenomenon has not received the sustained attention that it deserves.
Despite the explosive growth of scholarship on European Jewry in the last
few decades, there has not been a synthetic monograph devoted to the
subject in almost 30 years (Jacob Katz's *Out of the Ghetto* appeared in 1973).

Our current conceptions of emancipation suffer from a number of
glaring flaws.[3] We have no concept that is comprehensive, encompassing
all of Europe (or at least the bulk of it). Most conceptions omit one
section of Europe or another. Those schemes that cover western and
central Europe (England, France, Holland, Germany and Austria) omit
eastern Europe, while others focus on Germany and France but omit
other parts of western Europe (for example, England and Holland) as
well as eastern Europe. We also lack adequate categories to analyse and
classify various forms of toleration and emancipation. Similarly, we lack
classifications for various kinds of community structures: we are aware of
the extremes of the autonomous and the voluntary, but can neither
identify nor label the various gradations between them. A few prominent
examples of the extant scholarship should suffice to exemplify the
deficiencies.

The major book on emancipation, and probably the one most often
assigned, whether to undergraduates or postgraduates, is Jacob Katz's *Out
of the Ghetto*.[4] For my purposes it has two inescapable shortcomings.
Katz's book presumes the widely held notion of a bipartite East–West
divide by entirely omitting the eastern side, and thus the vast majority of
European Jewry. Eastern Europe simply does not figure in Katz's
conceptualisation. Katz limits his analysis to what he calls 'Western
Europe', by which he means Germany, Austria, Hungary, France,
Holland and England, and which he sees as a 'meaningful whole' that
followed 'a similar, if not identical, course'.[5] He distinguishes three
patterns of legal development: the revolutionary represented by France,
the reformist in Austria, and the combined revolutionary and reformist
of Prussia. Yet even by his own definition, this conceptualisation fails to
take account of Holland and England.[6] In addition, though Katz discusses
the Sephardim of western Europe episodically as the advanced guard of
acculturation and educational reform, they do not play an identifiable
role in emancipation itself.[7] Indeed, there is no recognition that the
countries in which emancipation was first achieved are precisely those
settled by New Christians or conversos. These two problems are

highlighted by Katz's chronology: his study covers the period 1770–1870. To take account of England, Holland and the Sephardim he would have had to begin his study at least a century earlier; to take account of eastern Europe he would have had to end his study at least half a century later.

Reinhard Rürup's important article focusing on German Jewry implicitly reinforced the bipartite East–West divide and the accompanying chronology. Rürup linked emancipation to the growth of civil or bourgeois society and saw two ways in which it was achieved: the revolutionary pattern in France, in which emancipation was granted in a stroke and the consequences were left to society, and the tutelary or reformist pattern in the German states, in which the state forcefully intervened in, and superintended, an incremental process, one that was complicated by the varied policies of the multiple polities. His article is limited to the period 1781–1870.[8]

Like Katz and Rürup, Pierre Birnbaum and Ira Katznelson, in the introduction to their recent volume, *Paths of Emancipation*, deal with 'the long century of emancipation': they hold to the axiom that the age of emancipation begins with the American and French revolutions.[9] In so doing they truncate the process, so that although their professed interest is in 'paths *to*, paths *of*, and paths *from* emancipation', they make it difficult to analyse the 'paths to' and 'paths of' emancipation.[10] Moreover, while they are concerned to restore 'confidence in the coherence and integrity of emancipation', and cover eastern Europe as well, the individual essays lack the common categories requisite to doing so in a coordinated manner. The essays teach us more of the consequences of emancipation ('paths *from* emancipation') than of the emancipation process itself.

What are the origins of the East–West divide and the truncated chronology characteristic of so many studies of emancipation? In a trenchant historiographical essay, Jonathan Frankel located the origins in what he called the 'East European school of Jewish history' of the first two-thirds of the twentieth century. Including such influential figures as Simon Dubnow, Raphael Mahler, Ben-Zion Dinur and Shmuel Ettinger, and informed by an impassioned nationalism, this school used 'dichotomies' or 'bipolar categories' to separate the positive from the negative forces in modern Jewish life. The negative forces were the Haskalah and emancipation, symbolised respectively by Berlin (1770s–1790s) and Paris (1789): these were thought to have wreaked havoc on Jewish life – in the form of assimilation, religious Reform and the *Wissenschaft des Judentums* – in 'western' Europe (extending from England to the Habsburg Lands) and, then, through an alliance with the Tsarist government, to have threatened East European Jewry as well. In

contrast, the positive forces that maintained the solidarity and vitality of
Jewish life were those of tradition, and these were represented by the
continuities in 'East' European Jewry. The period in which this
East–West divide emerged, and the negative forces did their damage, was
the century or more from 1770 to 1881. At that point, in the view of the
East European school, a Jewish nationalism arose that began to discredit
the ideals of emancipation and Haskalah and to indicate the correct path
towards a restored Jewish national life.[11]

Frankel argued that in recent years a 'revisionist' historical
scholarship has appeared which, by resisting the East European school's
'reductionist' black and white arguments, has offered a multi-hued
palette. Yet, significantly, this 'revisionist' scholarship has done so by
replacing the older concept of assimilation with that of 'acculturation'.
The focus has been on the consequences of emancipation. The concept of
emancipation itself has not received a similar reevaluation. How are we,
then, to achieve a new view of emancipation?

In his voluminous works Salo Baron sought to map an independent
alternative to the views of the two dominant strains of Jewish historical
scholarship in his day: the German school of Heinrich Graetz which
celebrated emancipation, and the East European school which rued its
effects. Emancipation was, then, the crucial issue of the modern period
for Baron's endeavour, and it was in regard to emancipation that in 1928
he used the now famous phrase, the 'lachrymose view' of Jewish
history.[12] In a suggestive essay published in 1960 Baron pointed a way
beyond the East–West divide and the focus on the century 1770–1870. He
offered a scheme based on the distinction between 'new' and 'old'
communities. He argued that the Jewish settlements of Holland,
England, France and the New World represented a fresh start:
unburdened by a medieval heritage of Jewry law, these 'newly arising
democratic societies' could attempt to 'solve their Jewish problem' (note
the anachronistic language: these communities did not have a Jewish
problem) by incorporating the Jews into society through the grant of
'equality minus certain specific disabilities'. In contrast, Russia,
Germany, Austria and Italy represented the 'old' communities. Russia
retreated from its earliest efforts to incorporate the Jews on a basis of
equality by subjecting them to special legislation, preeminently the
residential and economic restrictions of the Pale of Settlement. In
Germany, Austria and Italy emancipation was tied to the 'halting'
progress of democracy.[13]

Baron's article presents a number of seminal ideas. His scheme was
geographically comprehensive. He identified Holland, England and
France as a unit. He also distinguished Russia from Germany and

Austria. What we need to do is to elaborate this analysis. This elaboration can be accomplished in part by formulating categories to characterise the various legal statuses of Jewish communities. In formulating these categories I would hope to be able to describe the situation of European Jewry in the 265 years between 1654, when Jews were granted rights as burghers in Amsterdam, and 1919, when the Minority Rights Treaties were signed.[14] The various statuses of those centuries cannot be adequately grasped by simple dichotomies such as emancipated and unemancipated. It is necessary to identify finer gradations, allowing us to grasp a number of statuses as well as variations among them.

Before proceeding one proviso is in order, however. Legal decrees are in themselves insufficient to understand an historical situation. It is necessary to analyse how laws functioned in society, whether there was opposition that obstructed their realisation or whether they were administered with such zeal that the reality exceeded the law – that is, whether the law was implemented totally, in part or not at all. That legality alone is deceptive can be ascertained from any number of examples. In seventeenth-century Amsterdam Jews were admitted to municipal citizenship, yet that did not bring with it admission to guild occupations, and some historians have therefore assumed that those occupations remained closed to Jews. Yet in fact Jews managed to practice guild professions either by gaining special permission or by practising the trade among other Jews.[15] Here is a case in which the historical reality was better than the legal one. The reverse can be seen in Amsterdam after 1796. The 2 September 1796 edict of emancipation promised the Jews political equality, and that equality would appear to have been realised when Jews not only exercised the franchise but two Amsterdam Jews were elected to the National Assembly (Second) and a third became a member of the Amsterdam Municipal Council. Indeed, these events have often been heralded as the first elections of Jews to representative bodies in Europe. Yet the reality is that these delegates were quickly turned out of office and no Jews were subsequently elected. Jewish political equality remained a dead letter because the municipal and national establishment maintained a Protestant supremacy which systematically discriminated against, and barred, Catholics and Jews from political office. Thus in Amsterdam after 1796 political practice was inferior to the legal decree.[16]

As a provisional approach I would suggest that we distinguish four statuses, which were *not* chronologically or logically sequential. I have attempted to avoid a fixed teleology, instead recognising the twisted as well as the straight paths of history. Nevertheless, the statuses are arranged somewhat hierarchically. The first two are more of alternative points of departure; the latter two the means whereby emancipation was gained.

Toleration

This would represent the status of many Jewish communities that were part of the corporate society of early modern Europe, especially in central and eastern Europe. A specific Jewry law granted Jews privileges for a limited, specified period of time. The Jews constituted a quasi-corporation or estate that lived on sufferance, yet internally exercised a broad autonomy, such as their own courts, welfare, schools, and can thus be characterised as an 'autonomous community'.

In the Polish-Lithuanian Kingdom, for example, privileges granting Jews a particular status were issued for individuals, communities, regions and the entire country. As the central power of the monarchy began to decline in the sixteenth century (especially after the Constitution of 1539), the privileges for communities and individuals became increasingly important. In the seventeenth century, as royal and privately owned magnate towns sought new sources of population to offset the losses caused by war and dislocation, privileges were issued that permitted Jews to practice trades and crafts hitherto closed to them (and under the control of the guilds) as well as to produce, and trade in, alcoholic beverages. The Polish King also extended privileges to individual Jews who served him, releasing them from the jurisdiction of local Jewish courts as well as normal taxation. In general the privileges in towns granted Jews rights similar to burghers with respect to residence, ownership of immovable property and the practice of specific professions and trades but not municipal citizenship.[17]

An important variation on such forms of toleration emerged with the rise of state absolutism, especially in central Europe. In the name of consolidating power by means of centralising administration and levelling corporate bodies, the state began to intervene extensively in the autonomy of the Jewish community. This could take the form of the erosion of such powers as juridical competence, financial independence and self-governance. This situation often emerged in relationship to communities established around court Jews. These northern communities (such as Berlin, Koenigsberg, Dessau) were frequently more vulnerable by virtue of being new.[18]

Similar developments were in evidence in the Polish-Lithuanian commonwealth from the late-seventeenth century: the private towns where some three-quarters of the Jews in Poland lived were governed by a 'species of absolutism'.[19] There was a marked 'tendency of the magnates to try gradually to deprive Jewish communal institutions of autonomous functions and real power, while reinforcing their functioning as agents of the owner's interests'.[20] Magnates therefore consistently interceded in, or usurped, the workings of the communities and their rabbis, especially since the Jews' courts from the start belonged to, and were a subordinate part of, the magnates' court system.[21]

It is also important not to overlook the flip side of the absolutist coin: in addition to encroachment (for example, Frederick of Prussia), there was also the extension of privilege (for example, Joseph II and Catherine of Russia). These efforts will appear in subsequent categories.

Another way in which absolutist rulers intervened in the Jewish communities was to single out individuals or groups of individuals through a grant of extensive privileges. This variation also emerged in regard to court Jews, who were often vouchsafed freedom from jurisdiction of Jewish courts or the normal taxation, as well as free travel and release from the degrading 'body tax' (*Leibzoll*), all of which was intended to facilitate their ability to serve the sovereign.[22] The same phenomenon also emerged in Poland, as already mentioned.

An important point worth introducing at this juncture is the irreducible continuity between the terms of the Jews' admission and settlement and the nature of the ensuing path to emancipation. For tolerated communities to be emancipated, Jewry laws had to be abrogated and autonomous community structures dismantled. Such fundamental legal shifts could take place only if coupled with fundamental societal transformation as well – the emergence of democratic states or constitutional monarchies on the one side, the development of civil or bourgeois society on the other.

Civil Inclusion

I borrow this term from Lois Dubin to describe the situation of the port Jews: it is a new term to label a distinct status.[23] The term toleration is not adequate to describe their situation, as in 'toleration with trust and inequality' (Swetschinski), since this sort of additive formula does not accurately characterise the Jews' fundamental legal status.[24] At the same time, Baron's label of 'equality minus certain disabilities', while it conveys the essence of the situation, rests on the anachronism of 'equality', as Lois Dubin has argued: the port Jews lived in corporate societies based on privileges; the legal and administrative uniformity necessary for equality did not exist. Civil inclusion points to freedom from disabilities, or most disabilities, but not freedom for participation in politics or administration (that is, political inclusion).[25]

The case of the port Jews further bears out the relationship between the terms of admission and the nature of emancipation: since in London and Amsterdam, Bordeaux and Trieste, Jews were not subject to special Jewry laws and, in turn, did not constitute autonomous communities, emancipation was in large measure continuous with the existing legal situation. The authorities in Bordeaux admitted new Christians (*marchands portugais*) to the privileges of a merchant corporation who publicly emerged as Jews from the late-seventeenth century, their privileges as a merchant corporation being confirmed for them as Jews in 1723, in exchange for payment of a large sum.[26] Emancipation came in 1791 as the confirmation of their existing privileges and admission to the civic oath. Since the Whitehall Conference in London dissolved without making an official recommendation, the Jews were governed by a formal letter from the Secretary of State acknowledging their toleration (1664) and a royal order from James II that constituted a virtual declaration of indulgence (1685).[27] While some of the most prominent of the foreign-born Jews were endenizened, the native-born enjoyed basic commercial privileges.[28] Emancipation came through the gradual removal of such disabilities as exclusion from political office and the bar. In Amsterdam, individual Jews were granted citizenship as early as 1597, and in 1654 the city made a wholesale grant to safeguard trade. Citizenship for Jews was not transmissible, so that as permanent first-generation immigrants they were excluded from 'political, legal and military administration'.[29] Emancipation in 1796 (2 September) meant enfranchisement and the right to stand for political office, and some Jews were immediately elected to the Second National Assembly and the Amsterdam Municipal Council, though their tenure was admittedly brief (as we have seen, the Batavian Republic proceeded de facto to exclude Catholics and Jews from public office).[30] In Trieste the occupying French forces in the 1790s and again in 1809–13 found that the Jews' privileges virtually equalled emancipation. Equality came when the French allowed them to enter public service and to serve in the recently established municipal council.[31]

In each case, it should be noted, emancipation was also clearly linked to a transition in the larger society from a corporate to a civil society or constitutional monarchy.

Partial Emancipation

In this status an actual edict abolished Jewry laws to release the Jews from their former status, and granted some form of citizenship or rights but not all citizenship rights. Disabilities or inequalities remained and the Jews were either not citizens, or partial citizens (municipality but not state or vice versa) or second-class citizens. Such a status was characteristic of many German states and the Habsburg lands, including large parts of Italy, in the nineteenth century. Two distinct variants are discernible:

• Individuals could be granted partial emancipation. In the German states this took the form of municipal rights that did not entail, and were distinct from, state citizenship. There were numerous instances of individuals who received municipal rights beginning in the late eighteenth century as a grant from the territorial ruler or town council, for example, Upper Silesia, Schleswig-Holstein, Prussia (1791), Palatinate (1798–99).[32] Similarly, in the province of Posen, which Prussia had acquired through the partitions of Poland, the Ordinance of 1833 allowed for naturalisation on an individual basis.[33]

• Communities were granted some rights but not all rights. This held for the Jews in Prussia after 1812, who were given municipal enfranchisement (1808) and state rights (1812), but who lacked other rights (access to civil service). The status of Judaism and the Jewish community also remained inferior to that of Christianity and Christian communities. But more importantly, many Prussian Jews were not covered by the new legislation and continued to live under older Jewry laws, while administrative practice eroded many of the rights the 1812 edict had granted.[34] In the case of Baden, Jews were given general emancipation (1849) and only subsequently attained municipal rights (1862). In Bavaria the Jews were given citizenship (1813) but the infamous *Matrikel* limited the number allowed permanent residence (repealed in 1861).

The extension of privileges under late eighteenth-century absolutist regimes resulted in a similar situation. In the Habsburg lands and much of Italy Jews were governed by Joseph II's *Toleranzpatent* until 1848 or in some cases 1867. It represented a form of partial emancipation since it was combined with various Jewry laws limiting rights. The *Toleranzpatent* for Bohemia (October 1781) opened occupations and schools but left special taxes and a cap on the number of families (*Familiantengesetz*) in place. The *Toleranzpatent* for Vienna granted freedom of vocation, access to schools and universities and the ability to purchase real estate, but denied the Jews citizenship and, at least initially, prohibited the establishment of an official community or the building of a synagogue (the Seittenstettengasse synagogue was built in 1825–26).[35]

In Italy conditions varied widely, but they were best where Josephine legislation remained in place. Joseph II's *Toleranzpatent* (30 May 1782) applied in Lombardo-Venetia after 1815: Jews were given many political rights, such as entrance to militia, some public offices, practice of law, Assembly of Taxpayers and city council, but were expressly excluded from government administration.[36] In Piedmont after 1815 the Jews enjoyed occupational freedom and the right to own property outside the Ghetto but were still required to reside in the Ghetto until emancipation in 1848.[37]

Another variation on the status of partial emancipation was that in which Jews gained political rights prior to civic rights. This was the case in revolutionary Vienna in 1848 – where Jews not only manned the barricades (Adolf Fischhof, Joseph Goldmark) and were also elected to the Austrian National Assembly (Isak Mannheimer, Barukh Meisels) but still were deprived of civic rights – and also in the German states (Riesser in Frankfurt; Johann Jacoby and Raphael Kosch in the Prussian Assembly).[38] A similar situation held in Russia after the revolution of 1905 and the convocation of the Duma: Jews were able to exercise political rights and serve as deputies in the Duma yet were second-class citizens without civic rights.[39]

What was the difference between partial emancipation and civil inclusion? Was civil inclusion not also a form of partial emancipation? To be sure, civil inclusion was often a form of partial emancipation, yet the starting point between the two was essentially different. Civil inclusion in the first instance represented the extension of privilege in a corporate society. Under changing circumstances, either revolution or the gradual emergence of civil society, those privileges became the equivalent, or were transformed into, full equality or emancipation. In contrast, the starting point for partial emancipation was an autonomous or semi-autonomous community governed by Jewry laws. Partial emancipation arose from legal decrees which put the Jews in a situation in which other groups in society were fully emancipated or enjoyed greater equality than they did.

Another dimension of the difference between the two statuses lay in the process itself. Emancipation for the port Jews was largely continuous with civil inclusion. Emancipation for those Jews who had been tolerated under distinct Jewry laws was discontinuous, at least in narrow legal terms.

The abrogation of Jewry laws did represent an historic transition. Whether it also entailed a shift of similar dimensions in the Jews' daily lives – occupations, residence, social patterns – depended upon a host of factors in the larger society. For example, in Alsace emancipation had little impact on the Jews as long as their village life and economy remained – which was the case until the middle of the nineteenth century (1840s and 1850s).[40] In Holland the overwhelming poverty of the majority of Jews, and the perpetuation of a variety of forms of occupational discrimination, meant that the legal enactments brought little social or economic change.[41] Emancipation was not the universal panacea to Jewish afflictions, even if it was frequently touted as such. Rather, emancipation was the great enabler which allowed Jews to benefit if circumstances were favourable, such as an expanding economy.

Full Emancipation

Like partial emancipation, full emancipation could be granted to individuals. In France 15 letters of naturalisation were issued before 1789 to practising Jews (Jews had become eligible for naturalisation in theory once they were subsumed under the category of foreigners). The 15 included six families from Carpentras (1759); the banker Calmer Liefman (1769); the Paris merchant Israel Bernard (1770); the merchant Cerf Berr (1775) and the brothers Homberg and Lallement (1775); and some Bordeaux Jews (Jacob Perpignan, 1776; Moise Castro Soler, 1776).[42] In Prussia the Itzig family was naturalised in 1791, Israel Jacobson was granted full civic equality in Brunswick in 1804, and Jacob Kaulla achieved a similar status in Württemberg in 1806.[43]

In Russia there was a phenomenon of selective emancipation of individuals. Alexander II enacted numerous ordinances which granted categories of individuals the privileges and rights of their non-Jewish peers according to estate, including residence outside the Pale: university graduates (1861); artisans and mechanics (1865); all graduates of institutions of higher education, including pharmacists, dentists and midwives (1879). Jews were also permitted to become lawyers and judges (1864).[44] On this basis new communities emerged in such cities as St. Petersburg.

The notion that full emancipation was achieved at the stroke of a pen is deceptive: it, too, was a process which could extend over prolonged periods of time. Take the key example of France. When was the emancipation process finished? With the decrees of 28 January 1790 and 3 September 1791? Or with the end of the Napoleonic chapter, which ran from the convocation of the Assembly of Notables in 1806 to the lapsing of the so-called infamous decrees (17 March 1808) in 1818?[45] Or was emancipation still incomplete until rabbis received government salaries (1831), as was the case for the other confessions, and the Jews' oath (*more Judaico*) was abrogated (1846)?

One might ask the same of Germany. The edicts of 3 July 1869 (North German Confederation) and 22 April 1871 (Emancipation in Bavaria) removed the last barriers to political participation and holding office. Yet was emancipation complete? The Jews' status in regard to appointments in two key areas, education and the judiciary, remained unresolved because these were caught in the constitutional tension between a 'secular Empire' and Christian states (some of which defied the law openly, indeed gleefully).[46] In this sense full emancipation was achieved only with the establishment of the Weimar Republic.

Building on the distinctions between civil inclusion, partial emancipation and full emancipation, I would now suggest in place of the bipartite East–West divide a scheme of three regions of emancipation: western, central and eastern Europe.

In western Europe, consisting of England, Holland and France, and including a city such as Trieste, the scope of the emancipation process was limited since extensive privileges were granted in the seventeenth and eighteenth centuries as part of the process of resettlement, including such basic rights as citizenship as well as freedom of residence, occupations, religious observance and property ownership. Moreover, these Jews lived in voluntary communities: having arrived as professing Catholics (Bordeaux) or conversos (Amsterdam, London), or being an invited merchant community (Trieste), they were not subject to distinct Jewry laws and did not constitute autonomous communities. Full emancipation came either through a revolutionary act (France, Holland, Trieste) or a gradual abrogation of disabilities (England), but in either case the scope of the emancipation process was narrow and the transition between the two statuses was marked more by continuity than rupture (with the obvious exception of Alsace). This pattern, associated with the social type of the port Jew, represented a direct path from civil inclusion to full emancipation.

In central Europe, comprising the German states, the Habsburg empire, and Italy, emancipation was comprehensive in scope and protracted in duration. It entailed the abrogation of Jewry laws as well as the dismantling of the autonomous community (in many instances already in a much reduced state). This process occurred incrementally under the supervision of the tutelary state: in a quid pro quo of regeneration for rights, the Jews attained piecemeal rights beginning with Joseph's Toleration edict (1782) and the partial emancipation in Baden (1809), Prussia (1812) and other states. Full emancipation was finally granted with the simultaneous achievement of constitutional monarchy and national unification (Germany, Italy) or the restructuring of the Empire (Austria-Hungary). In central Europe, then, a state-supervised reformist process of rights for regeneration produced a long transition period from toleration through various forms of partial emancipation to full emancipation.

In eastern Europe the emancipation process had fundamental affinities to that in central Europe but also significant differences: Czarist policy oscillated between emancipatory legislation and coercive regeneration. As in central Europe, the process was comprehensive, encompassing the full gamut of rights, and the duration was protracted, beginning with the first Partition (1772) and the public debates in Poland (1780s). Yet in contrast to central Europe, full emancipation was deferred, except for selected individuals, being achieved only with the collapse of the Czarist regime. While the Czars embraced policies typical of absolutist states – conditional emancipation or the quid pro quo of rights for regeneration – there was a significant difference in application from central Europe, since there was a greater emphasis on regeneration, which was often applied in a coercive fashion (for example, military conscription, compulsory education). On the one side Catherine the Great's initial policies granted Jews some of the most extensive privileges available to them anywhere in Europe, and Alexander II introduced a highly selective emancipation in the 1850s–1860s based on criteria common to the central European regimes (education, wealth, useful versus non-useful labour) as well as a general emancipation in Congress Poland (1862–63). On the other side, while there were hints of the Jews being treated in an anomalous manner once their status was fixed as 'aliens' (*inorodtsy*; 1835), which put them in the same category as Siberian and central Asian peoples (such as the Kirghiz, Bahkirs and Yukagirs), they truly became anomalies in 1881–82 with the promulgation of discriminatory administrative measures (May Laws).[47] In eastern Europe, including Russia and Poland, the process of emancipation was comprehensive and the duration was protracted, yet because the emphasis was on regeneration, with partial rights being granted only selectively to a tiny fraction of the Jews, full emancipation was first achieved with the establishment of a democratic regime following the February revolution (1917) or with the signing of the Minority Rights Treaties in the successor states.

In conclusion, while the analysis of three regions of emancipation that I have offered is provisional and clearly requires elaboration, it nevertheless does establish the incontrovertible utility of the concept or social type of the port Jew. The port Jew is integral to a geographically comprehensive scheme which recognises diverse legal statuses and differing paths to emancipation. Above all, developments in western Europe are simply incomprehensible without it.

NOTES

1. For an important volume in this regard see *Assimilation and Community in European Jewry, 1815–81* ed. by Jonathan Frankel and Steven Zipperstein (Cambridge: Cambridge University Press, 1992). For an illuminating discussion of the view the 'East European school' (Dubnow, Mahler, Dinur, Ettinger) developed of emancipation's consequences see Jonathan Frankel, 'Assimilation and the Jews in Nineteenth-century Europe: Towards a New Historiography?', 10ff.
2. This is certainly true of the essays in *Assimilation and Community in European Jewry, 1815–81*, in which 'acculturation' serves as the conceptual bridge beyond the East–West divide.
3. One indication of emancipation's inferior status as an historical subject is that there is

no volume devoted to it in the *Essential Papers* series published by New York University Press.

4. The article on emancipation in a recent handbook relies heavily on Katz. See David Weinberg, 'Jewish Emancipation', in *The Modern Jewish Experience: A Reader's Guide*, ed. by Jack Wertheimer (New York: New York University Press, 1993), pp.95–101.

5. Jacob Katz, *Out of the Ghetto: The Social Background of Jewish Emancipation, 1770–1870* (New York: Schocken, 1978), pp.3–4. The major documentary anthology on modern Jewish history also reinforces the East–West divide by placing the few documents on the emancipation of eastern European Jewry in the separate section devoted to that subject rather than in the section on emancipation. See Paul Mendes-Flohr and Jehuda Reinharz, *The Jew in the Modern World: A Documentary History* 2nd ed. (New York: Oxford University Press, 1995), pp.432–33, 437–39.

6. Katz, *Out of the Ghetto* (see note 5), pp.166–69.

7. Ibid., pp.9, 22–23, 34, 37, 43, 83, 126, 146, 168. For a sustained analysis of the view of the Sephardim in Jewish historiography see Yosef Kaplan, *An Alternative Path to Modernity: The Sephardi Diaspora in Western Europe* (Leiden: Brill, 2000), pp.1–13.

8. Reinhard Rürup, 'Jewish Emancipation and Bourgeois Society', *Leo Baeck Institute Yearbook* 14 (1969) 67–91. See Rürup, 'The Tortuous and Thorny Path to Legal Equality: 'Jew Laws' and the Emancipatory Legislation in Germany from the late Eighteenth Century', *Leo Baeck Institute Yearbook* 31 (1986) 3–33.

9. *Paths of Emancipation: Jews, States and Citizenship* ed. by Pierre Birnbaum and Ira Katznelson (Princeton: Princeton University Press, 1995), pp.20, 36.

10. Ibid., p.24.

11. For the east European school see Jonathan Frankel, 'Assimilation and the Jews in nineteenth-century Europe: towards a new historiography?' One of the best analyses of the East–West divide from its end point in the twentieth century is to be found in Ezra Mendelsohn, *The Jews of East Central Europe Between the World Wars* (Bloomington: Indiana University Press, 1983). Mendelsohn discerned two types of communities on the basis of socio-economic, demographic and cultural factors. Political status was not an explicit determining issue, but certainly hovered in the background. The 'eastern European type' 'was characterized by the relative weakness of acculturation and assimilation, the preservation of Yiddish speech and religious Orthodoxy ... and a lower-middle-class and proletarian socioeconomic structure'. In contrast, the western European type 'was characterized by a high degree of acculturation, aspirations toward assimilation, and a general tendency to abandon both Yiddish and Orthodoxy... From a socioeconomic point of view, such Jewish communities tended to be middle class; from a demographic point of view, they were highly urbanized'. (pp.6–7).

12. For Baron's overall contribution see the excellent monograph by Robert Liberles, *Salo Wittmayer Baron: Architect of Jewish History* (New York: New York University Press, 1995).

13. Salo W. Baron, 'Newer Approaches to Jewish Emancipation', *Diogenes* 29 (Spring 1960) 56–81.

14. See Raphael Mahler's excellent anthology, *Jewish Emancipation: A Selection of Documents* (New York: American Jewish Committee, 1944).

15. Daniel M. Swetschinski, *Reluctant Cosmopolitans: The Portuguese Jews of Seventeenth-Century Amsterdam* (London: Littman Library, 2000), pp.20–22.

16. Jozeph Michman, *Dutch Jewry During the Emancipation Period, 1787–1815: Gothic Turrets on a Corinthian Building* (Amsterdam: Amsterdam University Press, 1995), pp.23–53.

17. Jacob Goldberg, 'The privileges granted to Jewish communities of the Polish Commonwealth as a stabilising factor in Jewish support', in *The Jews in Poland* ed. by Chimen Abramsky, Maciej Jachimczyk and Antony Polonsky (Oxford: Blackwell, 1986) 31–54, and *Jewish Privileges in the Polish Commonwealth: Charters of Rights Granted to Jewish Communities in Poland-Lithuania in the Sixteenth to Eighteenth Centuries* (Jerusalem: The Israel Academy of Sciences and Humanities, 1985).

18. For the newer settlements see Steven M. Lowenstein, 'The Social Dynamics of Jewish Responses to Moses Mendelssohn', in *Moses Mendelssohn und die Kreise seiner Wirksamkeit* ed. by Michael Albrecht, Eva J. Engel and Norbert Hinske (Tübingen: J.C.B. Mohr, 1994), p.342. For the resettlement of central Europe in general see Jonathan Israel, 'Central European Jewry during the Thirty Years War', *Central European History* 16 (1983) 3–30.

19. Gershon Hundert, *The Jews in a Polish Private Town: The Case of Opatow in the Eighteenth Century* (Baltimore: Johns Hopkins University Press, 1992), p.136.

20. M.J. Rosman, *The Lords' Jews: Magnate-Jewish Relations in the Polish-Lithuanian Commonwealth during the Eighteenth Century* (Cambridge, MA: Harvard, 1990), p.198.

21. Ibid., pp.56–8. For a case of the magnate suspending self-government because of alleged abuses see Hundert (note 19), p.136.

22. Selma Stern, *The Court Jew* (Philadelphia: Jewish Publication Society, 1950).

23. Louis C. Dubin, *The Port Jews of Habsburg Trieste: Absolutist Politics and Enlightenment Culture* (Stanford: Stanford University Press, 1999), pp.198–225, esp. 223.

24. Daniel Swetschinski characterises the situation in Amsterdam as an intermediate stage between earlier examples of 'toleration with disapproval' and later examples of 'emancipation with equality'. See Swetschinski (note 15), p.52.

25. Dubin, *The Port Jews of Habsburg Trieste* (see note 23), p.222.

26. Frances Malino, *The Sephardic Jews of Bordeaux* (Tuscaloosa: University of Alabama Press, 1978).

27. David Katz, *The Jews in the History of England, 1485–1850* (Oxford: Oxford University Press, 1994), pp.142–3, 149–51.

28. Ibid., 242; and Todd Endelman, *The Jews of Georgian England, 1714–1830* (Philadelphia: Jewish Publication Society, 1979), pp.20–25.

29. Swetschinski (see note 15), pp.8–25. See also, Miriam Bodian, *Hebrews of the Portuguese Nation: Conversos and Community in Early Modern Amsterdam* (Bloomington: Indiana University Press, 1997), pp.53–63.

30. Michman, *Dutch Jewry During the Emancipation Period, 1787–1815* (see note 15), pp.27–30.

31. Dubin (see note 23), p.220.

32. Jacob Toury, 'Types of Jewish Municipal Rights in German Townships: The Problem of Local Emancipation', *Leo Baeck Institute Yearbook* 22 (1977) 55–80.

33. Stefi Jersch-Wenzel, 'Legal Status and Emancipation', in *German-Jewish History in Modern Times* ed. by Michael Meyer, 4 vols (New York: Columbia University Press, 1996–98) II, pp.43–44.

34. For 1816 Rürup cites 68,023 enjoying equality and 58,500 living under older laws. See, 'The Tortuous and Thorny Path to Legal Equality' (note 8), p.17.

35. Wolfgang Haeusler, 'Toleranz, Emanzipation und Antisemitismus. Das oesterreichische Judentum des buergerlichen Zeitalters (1782–1918)', in *Das oesterreichische Judentum: Vorassetzungen und Geschichte* ed. by Nikolaus Vielmetti (Munich: Jugend und Volk, 1974) pp.83–89; Jersch-Wenzel (see note 33), pp.16–17.

36. Mario Rossi, 'Emancipation of the Jews in Italy', in *Emancipation and Counter-Emancipation* ed. by Abraham Duker and Meir Ben-Horin (New York: Ktav, 1974), p.212.

37. Dan V. Segre, 'The Emancipation of Jews in Italy', in *Paths of Emancipation* (see note 9), pp.217, 222.

38. Salo Baron, 'The Impact of the Revolution of 1848 on Jewish Emancipation', *Jewish Social Studies* 11 (1949); Haeusler, 'Toleranz, Emanzipation und Antisemitismus' (see note 35), 97–103.

39. Michael Stanislawski, 'Russian Jewry, the Russian State, and the Dynamics of Jewish Emancipation', *Paths of Emancipation* (see note 9), p.280.

40. Paula Hyman, *The Emancipation of the Jews in Alsace* (New Haven: Yale University Press, 1991).

41. Karina Sonnenberg-Stern, *Emancipation and Poverty: The Ashkenazi Jews of Amsterdam, 1796–1850* (Basingstoke: Macmillan, 2000).
42. Peter Sahlins, 'Fictions of a Catholic France: The Naturalization of Foreigners, 1685–1787', *Representations* 47 (Summer, 1994) 96–102.
43. Rürup, 'The Tortuous and Thorny Path to Legal Equality' (note 8), pp.11–12.
44. Hans Rogger, *Jewish Policies and Right-Wing Politics in Imperial Russia* (London: Macmillan, 1986), pp.12–13; Benjamin Nathans, 'Mythologies and Realities of Jewish life in Pre-revolutionary St. Petersburg', *Studies in Contemporary Jewry* 15 (1999) 107.
45. It is worth noting that in Prussia's territories along the Rhine these decrees remained in force until the 1840s.
46. Peter Pulzer, *Jews and the German State: The Political History of a Minority, 1848–1933* (Oxford: Blackwell, 1992), p.34.
47. John Klier, 'The Concept of "Jewish Emancipation" in a Russian Context', in *Civil Rights in Imperial Russia* ed. by Olga Crisp and Linda Edmondson (Oxford: Clarendon Press, 1989), pp.121–44; Michael Stanislawski, *Tsar Nicholas I and the Jews: The Transformation of Jewish Society in Russia, 1825–1855* (Philadelphia: Jewish Publication Society, 1983); and Stanislawski, 'Russian Jewry, the Russian State, and the Dynamics of Jewish Emancipation', *Paths of Emancipation* (see note 9), pp.262–83; Benjamin Nathans, 'Mythologies and Realities of Jewish Life in Pre-revolutionary St. Petersburg', *Studies in Contemporary Jewry* 15 (1999) 107–48; Arnold Springer, 'Enlightened Absolutism and Jewish Reform: Prussia, Austria, and Russia', *California Slavic Studies* 11 (1980) 237–67; Hans Rogger, 'The Question of Jewish Emancipation: Russia in the Mirror of Europe', in Rogger, *Jewish Policies and Right-Wing Politics in Imperial Russia* (see note 44), pp.1–24; Michael Aronson, 'The Prospects for the Emancipation of Russian Jewry during the 1880s', *Slavonic and East European Review* 55.3 (1977) 348–69; Artur Eisenbach, *The Emancipation of the Jews in Poland, 1780–1870* (Oxford: Blackwell, 1991).

Researching Port Jews and Port Jewries: Trieste and Beyond

LOIS DUBIN

*...to order affairs according to the
principles followed in other civilised
mercantile centres...*

Intendant Schell, Trieste, 1766

Jews in cities and Jews with money are subjects with long pedigrees. The
concept of *port Jews* is a variation on those themes. *Port Jews* were Jewish
merchants who lived in dynamic port cities and who, along with other
merchants, were valued for their engagement in the international
maritime trade upon which such cities thrived.

The concept of port Jews arose in the late 1990s. While writing my
book *The Port Jews of Habsburg Trieste: Absolutist Politics and Enlightenment
Culture*, I coined the term 'port Jews'. Through our ongoing conversations,
David Sorkin and I became aware that a new category was needed for
acculturated Jewish merchants in port cities whose path towards
integration in early modern Europe was distinctive.[1] The term *port Jews*
seemed apt and arresting. For it highlights both the location and function
of Jews in port cities engaging in international maritime commerce. And,
port Jews rhymes with *court Jews*, the well-known merchant-financiers who
served seventeenth-century Central European rulers. In his articles, Sorkin
referred to Italian port Jews in the Mediterranean, but he focused mainly
on Sephardic Jews in western European ports such as Amsterdam,
Hamburg, London and Bordeaux, and defined *port Jews* as predominantly
Sephardic. He drew sharp contrasts between the port Jews of Atlantic and
Mediterranean Europe and the Ashkenazic court Jews of northern and
Central Europe as a means of comparing their respective societies and
cultures. As Tullia Catalan later noted, the play on words works well in
German too: *Hafenjuden* and *Hofjuden* for port Jews and court Jews
respectively.[2]

My book extensively analyses one port Jewry, the Ashkenazic–

Sephardic–Italian Jewish community in the eighteenth-century Free Port of Trieste at the crossroads of Central Europe, Italy and the eastern Mediterranean. I have found the concept *port Jewry* equally as necessary as *port Jew* or *port Jews*, for it highlights a type of Jewish *community* in port cities and not only a type of Jewish *individual*. *Port Jewry* thus stresses the communal dimension so important in Jewish history, certainly in the early modern period.

In this essay, I focus upon the concept of utility – a concept fundamental to the *port Jew* phenomenon – and examine its construction in the eighteenth-century Free Port of Trieste. How were the port Jews of Trieste seen as useful by their contemporaries? And how does their perceived utility help us better understand the discourse and dynamics of eighteenth-century Enlightenment, reforming absolutism and Haskalah? I contend that *port Jews* provide a concrete setting for seeing these in action, and moreover, an unusual one in which the typical Enlightenment critiques of Jewish society and calls for Jewish self-improvement did not obtain. The study of port Jews in Trieste focuses the mind on the key eighteenth-century nexus of commerce, utility and culture, while at the same time it helps us better understand perceptions of other port Jews and their paths towards integration.

Towards the end of this essay, I contend that the full historiographical value of the concept *port Jew/port Jews/port Jewry* can be realised only if we broaden the purview to identify and analyse port Jews in other locations, such as Livorno, Salonika, Odessa and cities in the New World and the Far East. Study of port Jewries in different locales and periods would allow us to engage broadly in comparative Jewish history, and, in so doing, to raise general questions about the interrelations of economy, society and culture in Jewish history. Thus, I seek to demonstrate both the utility of the phenomenon of *port Jews* in their own societies and the utility of the concept of *port Jews* for current historiography.

How Were the Port Jews of Trieste Seen as Useful to the Reforming Absolutist State?

Early in the eighteenth century, the small and sleepy town of Trieste was declared a free port when its Habsburg rulers deemed maritime commercial development essential to state-building. By century's end, Trieste had become a major seaport and commercial entrepot of international significance.

Commerce defined and structured modern Trieste. The new port and surrounding free zone were developed as a separate administrative entity outside the old municipality, which they eventually absorbed. The various names of the new entity – Commercial Intendancy, later Imperial Commercial Province – proclaimed commercial interest paramount. Towards that end, the first free port patents invited persons of 'any religion or nationality' to settle and trade in Trieste; later, local officials noted the 'insufficiency and inexperience of the native merchants' and argued for luring foreign merchants – particularly Greek Orthodox and Jews – with privileges of settlement and freedom of commerce.[3] Under the aegis of the otherwise notoriously intolerant Maria Theresa, an explicit policy of toleration and corporate standing for religious-ethnic minorities was developed in Trieste. Thus the new port city was forged by governmental officials and a polyethnic, multilingual and religiously diverse mercantile elite working in tandem. A government almanac of the 1780s contained 'useful and pleasing notices for Roman Catholics, Lutherans, Calvinists, non-Uniate Greeks, Jews, Turks'.[4]

Jews thrived in the new free-port city. The Jewish population increased dramatically, from just under 100 at the beginning of the eighteenth century to approximately 1,250 in 1800 (then c. 5–7 per cent of the total population. When the Jewish community of Trieste was renegotiating its privileges in 1770, they claimed that they deserved to be 'considered as summoned and invited, rather than tolerated'.[5] Indeed, they were accurately tracing their historical development. First, Jews had been included in the general calls for merchants to the new free port. Later, Jews were specifically invited by means of legal corporate standing for their community and extensive privileges for all Jews residing in the city. Local officials working on regulations for Jews in the late 1760s consulted their counterparts in the celebrated Tuscan free port of Livorno since they wanted 'to order affairs according to the principles followed in other civilised mercantile centres'.[6] They had the sense that well-ordered port-cities play by their own rules, according to which commercial need and aptitude might outweigh religious or ethnic affiliation.

Triestine authorities prized Jewish commercial expertise. In 1761, a leading official Giuseppe Pasquale Ricci echoed the arguments employed earlier by Simone Luzzatto, Menasseh ben Israel, and John Toland on behalf of Jews: 'The Jewish nation has accumulated great riches through commerce... commerce is the only nourishment...of this nation... its dispersion and settlement in all parts of the world have made it *an experienced participant in all the world's commerce* (my emphasis).'[7] The valuable Theresian Privilege of 1771 explicitly expressed Jewish commercial aptitude, utility, desirability and invitation – some of the defining elements of a port Jewry:

We Maria Theresa...have not spared...effort...to further the dual
purpose of making [external] commerce prosper especially in Trieste,
and of improving the condition of merchants...who have established
themselves in that Port... *The Jewish Nation, especially suited to
commerce, invited* (my emphasis) by the general patents of Our Most
August Parent and recognized with individual Privileges from His
most glorious predecessors, arouses Our most merciful particular
reflections, all the more since on the one hand the settlements of the
Nation itself in Trieste already constitute a formal community, and
[since] on the other, some of its Individuals who belong to the
Mercantile Exchange *contribute by means of work and counsel to the
growth of Commerce and Navigation for the common benefit of the
merchants and of the marketplace* (my emphasis). We therefore wish to
give...a solemn demonstration of our Sovereign approval for the
purpose of *attracting more such families and individuals* (my emphasis)
who would make themselves worthy of the City and State by
establishing new commercial firms and by engaging in wholesale
Trade.[8]

Because of their perceived utility, Jews in Trieste were proffered an
unusual range of liberties, including ownership of real property, and free
and equal engagement in maritime and inland commerce, manufacturing
and artisanry. The mainstay of the community was international
commerce and its related businesses of brokerage, shipping and
forwarding, finance and insurance. The wealthiest Jewish wholesalers
held seats on the *Borsa mercantile* (Mercantile Exchange) from its very
inception in 1755; to accommodate them, it met on weekdays rather than
Saturdays. In the early 1780s, Jews comprised 14 per cent (6 of 42
members) of that important institution.

In official eyes, the logic of the free port as a 'civilised mercantile
centre' dictated significant degrees of similarity and parity among
merchants. Business experience and its utility had nothing to do with
religion or ethnicity, argued Chancellor Heinrich Cajetan Blümegen in
Vienna in 1780 when urging that Jews be made eligible for leadership
positions in the *Borsa*:

> no well-founded reason presents itself why in a free seaport, in which
> there is otherwise no difference among the nations, Jewish merchant
> houses should practically be excluded from such a merchants' managing
> board, for which the practical knowledge and discernment of the
> aforesaid are just as good and useful as those of members of the other
> religions.[9]

Further, similarities among merchants were perceived to rest not only on their practical knowledge but also on their utility, which was understood also in cultural and moral terms. The nexus of commerce, utility, culture and morality – one is tempted to say the amalgam – is evident in remarks made by Triestine officials in 1786:

> Concerning the Jewish community of Trieste it is in any case well known that they mostly earn their livelihood respectably through trade and other decent occupations, and also that they distinguish themselves from other Jewish communities by virtue of the morality of their behavior.[10]

What is the equation here? Quite simply, that when commercial activity is successful, it is useful and respectable, its purveyors *ipso facto* honest and honourable, and their behaviour moral. Economic and social utility are equated with morality and virtue.

The cultural component of the nexus emerges especially clearly in a report penned by Chief of Police Pietro Antonio Pittoni in December 1786:

> It has been a long time – since the declaration of the Free Port – that the populace has been composed of diverse nations and religions... Since then the City has united these in business activities, which require knowledge and skills. This traffic in business and knowledge has made the City well-off and rich. The City has witnessed that the non-Catholic can be and is an honest man, that morality is the same, that he has learned the customs of the others, and felt their same needs... this brotherly sharing of knowledge, of customs, and of reciprocally useful needs has rendered the City not only tolerant, but friendly.[11]

In other words, the kind of interaction that occurs in the port, the marketplace and the *Borsa* leads to significant acculturation in speech, habits and behaviour, and contributes to a non-denominational morality shared by productive, useful merchants. The perception of Triestine Jewish acculturation and morality was reinforced by the community's ready establishment of a Josephinian normal-school – one of whose purposes was precisely to inculcate a non-denominational civic morality – and by its Italian Jewish traditions of speaking the vernacular and of relative cultural openness.

Thus, merchants of different religious-ethnic communities could prove themselves similarly useful through commerce, conduct themselves according to similar norms of behaviour, and be treated in similar ways. By the crucial measures of utility, behaviour and culture, the port Jews of

Trieste were deemed comparable to the city's other merchants. And this perception had direct bearing on their legal status. When Joseph II's Toleration proposals reached Trieste, Governor Karl von Zinzendorf thought most of them unnecessary because the Jews there already enjoyed 'almost all the privileges and equalities with the rest of the people'. [12] And these same measures of utility, behaviour and culture also led Habsburg officials to distinguish the Jewish merchants of Trieste from Jews of other places who were not merchants. Officials grouped Triestine Jews with the Sephardic Jews of Amsterdam and of Livorno – that is, with other port Jews – since, as they put it, these all shared a similar life-style and should thus be exempted from the usual restrictions imposed on Jewish merchants visiting Vienna. [13]

The essentials of the port Jewry of Trieste can thus be discerned. Jewish merchants were invited or welcomed because of their presumed commercial expertise which was deemed of prime value to the port city. They were seen to have demonstrated their economic and social utility both in the past and present. Commerce and culture fused as secular virtue, as their behaviour, morals and culture were seen as all of a piece with their utility. Proving their utility and virtue meant continuing along the path they were already on; they did not have to prove them for the first time.

The construction of utility in Trieste has broader implications for our understanding of late eighteenth-century reforming absolutist discourse and practice. 'To make the Jews more useful to the state' – many have tended to hear this famous phrase of Joseph II's Toleration proposals with post-Kantian ears as overly instrumentalist for its apparent treatment of people as means rather than ends in themselves. However, the example of the port Jewry of Trieste shows that the phrase need not be thus construed. First, the tone is mitigated when utility is treated as a demonstrated and ongoing fact rather than as a demand for future transformation. Second, utility contained a moral dimension. Perceptions of the utility of late eighteenth-century port Jews in Trieste melded older mercantilist notions – those who build up commerce are useful to the state – with later Enlightenment-tinged absolutist and cameralist concepts – to be productive and to serve society and state with a sense of civic duty are ways of expressing virtue and humanity. For Joseph, utility became increasingly a civic and moral concept: Giving all subjects without regard to religion or nation opportunities for productive service was to provide a path of inclusion within the state and within humanity. Utility was the yardstick by which all of Joseph's subjects were measured and prodded, and for many, internalising this new ethos involved great and wrenching transformation. But for port Jews, the demand 'to be useful' which lay at the core of Josephinian centralisation and rationalisation was not experienced as a bludgeon of transformation, but rather as continuity and the basic condition of a broader favourable programme of civil inclusion.

The example of the port Jewry of Trieste helps reveal the moral dimension of utility within reforming absolutism and enlightenment, and, in certain circumstances, its positive potential as a way-station between abstract Enlightenment ideals of common humanity and concrete social reality. Many Enlightenment thinkers saw the common humanity of Jews as something existing only in potential, to be regenerated only in the future after thoroughgoing transformation of woefully deficient present Jews. But port Jews provided a concrete basis for partially actualising Enlightenment ideals of inclusion since they fit the regnant constructions of utility, morality and humanity. With port Jews, the transaction was not future rights in exchange for future regeneration and proof of humanity but rather present rights in exchange for already demonstrated utility and humanity. With their humanity acknowledged in the present tense, the Enlightenment promise of rationalist inclusion of Jews could be translated from potentiality to actuality. The mediator was in fact utility.

How Were Port Jews Useful for Maskilim and Was Haskalah Useful for Port Jews?

Port Jews captured the imagination of *maskilim* in Central Europe, serving as inspiring examples or models of acculturated, productive and esteemed Jewries. Hartwig Wessely had long admired the educational system of the Sephardim in Amsterdam. In 1782 he praised the Jews of Trieste, positing a connection between their far-flung mercantile activities and their broad cultural horizons: 'Your customs have always been wise, consistent with respect for living beings and peace among humankind. In addition, trade in your lands is with the large states of Europe, Asia, and Africa, and you get to hear of the customs of areas distant from you.'[14] Wessely's view was that merchants who shipped goods to distant places would naturally be interested in the people and customs of those distant places. Was he not suggesting that the sea opens minds as well as wallets and holds of ships? Indeed, commercial entrepots often function as centres of exchange for people, as magnets for immigrants, and as sites for cultural mixing. Wessely's sense of the open-mindedness of port Jews was reinforced when Triestine Jewish leaders rounded up support for him and adjusted their Talmud Tora to fit Josephinian normal-school prescriptions.[15] In the late 1780s, Isaac Euchel wrote admiringly of the acculturated language, dress and behaviour of the

Jews of Livorno – another port Jewry – and the security and esteem in which they dwelled: 'There is no difference between their dress and that of the [other] inhabitants. They speak the language of the people correctly and eloquently... They pursue every occupation and business their hearts desire... I am proud to see my brothers living securely amidst the Gentiles.'[16]

Thus, for *maskilim,* port Jews exemplified some of their own cultural, economic and political goals. While they could not press fellow Jews in non-maritime settings to be productive in exactly the same way as port Jews were, they could urge them to emulate their behaviour, mentality, and above all, strivings for utility. In sum, *maskilim* certainly did find port Jews useful.

Now, to pose the question in reverse: Did port Jews find the ideology of Haskalah useful? Did port Jews, like owners and employees in Central European business and manufacturing enterprises, form a constituency for Haskalah?

Triestine Jews responded positively to Wessely's basic message – that Jewish education provide a measure of practical and general knowledge and civic morality so that Jews could contribute usefully to state and society – and they urged other Italian Jews to do the same. Thus, this port Jew community offered a sympathetic ear for Haskalah, functioning as a point of reception, consumption and transmission. But Trieste did not provide an example of the creation, generation, or production of Haskalah. As I have argued elsewhere, their partially Sephardic-influenced Italian Jewish tradition now converged with Haskalah, but was not identical to Haskalah nor an instance of it.[17] With a fundamentally harmonious view of Torah and human culture, heirs of this tradition saw no need to argue for the legitimacy of human culture or engage in *Kulturkampf* to assert its rights.

But something besides cultural tradition, whether Italian or Sephardic, was at work, namely, the structural and existential realities of port Jews. David Sorkin has nicely explained an important connection between social-structural conditions and the cultural production of Haskalah. He argues that Haskalah was generated in northern Central Europe in part from the tensions that arose when states attempted to 'graft mercantilist, commercial policy onto primarily agricultural societies', and that, in contrast, Haskalah was not generated in commercial societies or port cities.[18] My analysis of Trieste supports this view. Though port Jews might well support Haskalah if it came their way, they did not create or generate Haskalah because they did not need an explicit ideology of transformation in order to make the vernacular, secular studies or acculturation part of their everyday life; through a different route, their socio-economic realities and cultural behaviour already reflected the core Haskalah goals of utility and acculturation. Thus, in forcing us to realise again that acculturation and appreciation of secular studies and general knowledge are not necessarily synonymous with Haskalah, the example of port Jews helps us better contextualise and reconceptualise Haskalah.[19]

The Historiographical Utility of the Concept Port Jew/Jews/Jewries

David Sorkin has argued that consideration of port Jews in early modern Europe will lead to new conceptualisations of Jewish paths to modernity.[20] Indeed, we gain new insight into these processes once we include the experiences of these acculturated Jewish merchants in developing commercial centres, and take seriously their non-ideological paths of acculturation and their attainment of significant liberties by way of Old Regime privilege before formal political emancipation.[21] To the usual concentration on German-Jewish intellectuals and court Jews, we thereby add some important new foci: Sephardim and Italians, merchants, integration of Jews in commercial societies, socio-economic factors rather than ideological pronouncements, gradual processes of change rather than sudden legal transformation. Port Jews provide a concrete example and testing-ground for Salo Baron's claims about the decisive importance of early modern capitalism and of socio-economic forces more generally in modern Jewish history.[22]

However, the concept of port Jews may be useful not only for the analysis of early modern European Jewish history. I contend that we should look for port Jews and port Jewries not only in the seventeenth and eighteenth centuries and not only on the Atlantic and Adriatic. We should be prepared to identify and analyse port Jews in places such as Livorno, Salonika, Odessa and beyond Europe in the New World and the Far East. Because the phenomenon of port Jews cuts across geographic, ethnic and chronological boundaries at least from the sixteenth through nineteenth centuries, the concept is of broad historiographical import and provides a useful tool for comparative historical analysis in Jewish history of the sort advocated by Todd Endelman.[23] For example, the concepts *port Jews* and *port Jewries* can help us compare different kinds of Jewish individuals, merchants, communities, cultures and integration in surrounding societies. If we find the port Jew phenomenon in other eras, then the concept may prove a useful tool for comparing Jewish experience not only in different places but also across different chronological periods.

A broad view of port Jews and disciplined comparative analysis can help us begin to address some thorny issues in new ways. Sorkin and I both tried to generalise about port Jews from particular cases, but it has become clear that it is a complex task to distinguish between the specific features of one set of historical circumstances and the common structural factors of the port Jew situation. For example, about Trieste, I still wonder: Which aspects were due to the specific Italian cultural tradition and which were due to port Jew conditions? I suggest that a similar question be posed about early modern western Sephardim: Sorkin identified voluntaristic communities and religious laxity, heterodoxy and individualism as characteristic features, but how much was due to the wrenching adjustments of former New Christians and how much was due to port Jew status? The cases of the western Sephardim and Trieste suggest that port Jews were not creators or producers of Haskalah. Will comparative analysis of port Jewries in very different milieux sustain this generalisation? Odessa with its active and creative Haskalah movement of the late nineteenth century provides an obvious counter-example. What fostered this production of Haskalah in the midst of a port Jewry: Ashkenazic cultural struggles or the social and political conditions of Russian Jewry? These are examples of the kinds of problem that the heuristic concept of port Jewries can help us investigate. By studying comparatively several port Jew examples, we may discern commonalities and divergent specificities that will enable us to distinguish better between economic and social factors on the one hand and cultural traditions and political circumstances on the other. Using the concept of *port Jews* to refine our generalisations about merchants, open-mindedness, acculturation and cosmopolitanism will help us better understand the interaction of economics, society, politics and culture in Jewish history.

To do so most effectively, however, we need to consider *port Jews* in the plural or *port Jewry* in the collective as well as *port Jew* in the singular. When we look beyond the early modern western Sephardic examples to consider ones such as Livorno, Trieste, Salonika, Istanbul and Odessa, we find port Jews living in autonomous Jewish communities that held some corporate privileges. Thus, we ought to consider port Jews not only as a social type of Jewish individual but also as a type of Jewish community or Jewry, for that collective dimension is essential in the study of cultural and communal traditions. Keeping in mind both individual and collective dimensions, and concentrating on each as appropriate, we can more fully exploit the utility of the concept of *port Jews* for comparative historical analysis, and for the clarification of the roles of economy, society and culture that it can yield.

We can, I believe, engage in specific studies of port Jewries in different times and places and also proceed to broad comparative analysis. The multiplication of examples will enrich our understanding of the realities of port Jews; broadening the range of the concept *port Jew* need not dilute or weaken it. We can analyse *port Jews* and *port Jewries* comparatively while still maintaining a firm grasp of their key role in early modern Europe and without sacrificing the historical specificity of whichever port Jews – early modern or other, European or other – that we investigate. Comparison is an essential part of the promise of the *port Jew* concept.

ACKNOWLEDGEMENTS

I presented earlier versions of this paper at the Second International Seminar for Research on the Jewish Enlightenment: New Approaches and Insights in Haskalah Research in the 1990s, held at Bar-Ilan University, Israel, 9–10 April 2000, and at the Port Jews Symposium, held at the AHRB Parkes Centre for the Study of Jewish/non-Jewish Relations, University of Southampton, England, 28–29 June 2001. I'd like to thank conference participants for their helpful responses. I am also grateful to Jay Berkovitz for his comments on the written version. All translations from primary documents in German and Italian are my own.

NOTES

1. Lois C. Dubin, *The Port Jews of Habsburg Trieste: Absolutist Politics and Enlightenment Culture* (Stanford: Stanford University Press, 1999). The term 'port Jews' first appeared in print when David Sorkin referred to my usage of the new term in his article 'Enlightenment and Emancipation: German Jewry's Formative Age in Comparative Perspective', in *Comparing Jewish Societies* ed. by Todd M. Endelman (Ann Arbor: University of Michigan Press, 1997), pp.89–112, see pp.104–5 and nn.49–50, pp.111–12. There, as well as in his interpretive survey 'Into the Modern World', in Nicholas De Lange, *The Illustrated History of the Jewish People* (New York, San Diego, London: Harcourt Brace, 1997), pp.198–253 (especially pp.205–9, 403), he contrasted port Jews with court Jews as part of a broader comparison of different Jewish societies. In his article 'The Port Jew: Notes Toward a Social Type', *Journal of Jewish Studies* 50.1 (1999): 87–97, Sorkin defined the concept further through comparative analysis of predominantly western Sephardic port Jews.
2. Oral comment by Tullia Catalan, author of *La comunità ebraica di Trieste: Politica, società e cultura (1781–1914)* (Trieste: Lint, 2000), at International Conference, 'Between Trieste, Salonica and Odessa: Historicising Balkan and Related Jewries 1492–1918', Simon-Dubnow-Institute for Jewish History and Culture at the University of Leipzig, 4–6 Nov. 2000.
3. Dubin, *Port Jews* (see note 1), pp.13–14.
4. Ibid., p.201, and n.6, p.288.
5. Archivio di Stato di Trieste, Cesarea Regia Suprema Intendenza Commerciale per il Litorale in Trieste, busta 78, f. 168v; and Kofkammerarchiv, Oesterreichisches Staatsarchiv, Kommerz Littorale, rot 502, f. 177, discussed in Dubin, *Port Jews* (see note 1), p.56 and n.59, p.245.
6. Archivio di Stato di Trieste, Cesarea Regia Suprema Intendenza Commerciale per il Litorale in Trieste, b. 78, f. 14r, discussed in Dubin, *Port Jews* (see note 1), p.62 and n.81, p.247.
7. Dubin, *Port Jews* (see note 1), p.14.
8. Ibid, pp.45–7, and n.18, p.242.
9. Hofkammerarchiv, Oesterreichisches Staatsarchiv, Kommerz Littorale, r. 617, 16. ex Jan. 1780, ff. 349v and 351r, Blümegen private letter 22 Jan. 1780, discussed in Dubin, *Port Jews* (see note 1), p.35, and n.104, p.240.

10. Archivio di Stato di Trieste, Cesareo Regio Governo in Trieste, b. 620, N. 1998 (8 Apr. 1786), discussed in Dubin, *Port Jews* (see note 1), p.115.
11. Dubin, Port Jews (see note 1), p.201, and nn. 5 and 6, p.288.
12. Zinzendorf report of 17 Aug. 1781, Archivio di Stato di Trieste, Cesareo Regio Governo in Trieste, b. 83, Ad N. 1412, discussed in Dubin, *Port Jews* (see note 1), pp.76–9 and nn.44–45, p.252, and also pp.218–20. For further analysis of this phrase and the political thinking embedded in it, see my article, 'Between Toleration and 'Equalities': Jewish Status and Community in Pre-Revolutionary Europe', *Yearbook of the Simon-Dubnow-Institute* 1 (2002) (in press).
13. Dubin, *Port Jews* (see note 1), pp.46 and 62, and nn.20 (p.242) and 83 (p.247).
14. Hartwig Wessely (Naftali Herz Weisel), *Divrei shalom ve-emet*, vol. 2: *Rav tuv le-vet Yisrael*, discussed in ibid., pp.120–1 and nn.9–10, p.265.
15. See ibid., chs. 4–5, and 'Trieste and Berlin: The Italian Role in the Cultural Politics of the Haskalah', in *Toward Modernity: The European Jewish Model* ed. by Jacob Katz (New Brunswick, NJ and Oxford, UK: Transaction Books 1987), pp.189–224.
16. Euchel, 'Iggerot Meshullam ben Uriyyah ha-Eshtamoi', in *Ha-Meassef* 6 (1789–90): 173–4; discussed in Dubin, *Port Jews* (see note 1), p.134, and 'Trieste and Berlin' (see note 15), p.206. For more on images of Italian Jews held by German Jewish modernisers, see also my essay 'The Rise and Fall of the Italian Jewish Model in Germany: From Haskalah to Reform, 1780–1820', in *Jewish History and Jewish Memory: Essays in Honor of Yosef Hayim Yerushalmi* ed. by Elisheva Carlebach, John M. Efron, and David N. Myers (Hanover, NH and London: University Press of New England [for Brandeis University Press], 1998), pp.271–95.
17. Dubin, *Port Jews* (see note 1), chs. 4–5, and 9, pp.213–16.
18. Sorkin, 'Enlightenment and Emancipation' (see note 1), pp.104–5, and 'Port Jew' (see note 1), p.94.
19. On recent research and new approaches, see *New Perspectives on the Haskalah* ed. by Shmuel Feiner and David Sorkin (London and Portland, OR: Littman Library of Jewish Civilization, 2001), especially the editors' Introduction, pp.1–7, and Shmuel Feiner, 'Towards a Historical Definition of the Haskalah', pp.184–219. I think that Sorkin's fine analysis of the structural situations of port Jew communities may reduce the temptation to use notions of Haskalah – whether proto-Haskalah (Salo Baron), or 'Haskalah that did not mature' (Yosef Kaplan), or Haskalah *avant la lettre* – to characterise their cultural profiles. See Sorkin, 'Port Jew' (see note 1), pp.92–4, and especially nn.29–30, and Dubin, 'Trieste and Berlin' (see note 15), p.211, and n.105, p.224, and *Port Jews*, p.137, for discussions of these terms. Sorkin likes the phrase *Haskalah avant la lettre* while I prefer not to use it; when I raised it in my 'Trieste and Berlin' article, I did so in order to argue against it. For the cultures of port Jews, I think we need characterisations that do not point so teleologically towards eighteenth-century Enlightenment and Haskalah, but rather treat mercantile cultures on their own terms.
20. Sorkin, 'Port Jew' (see note 1), especially pp.88, 96–7.
21. See Dubin, *Port Jews* (note 1), ch.9, Conclusion: Civil Inclusion of a Port Jewry in a Reforming Absolutist State, pp.198–225, and 'Between Toleration and 'Equalities'' (note 12); cf. Sorkin, 'Port Jew' (note 1), pp.96–7. Michael Silber first raised the issue of Old Regime privileges as a means towards significant improvement of Jewish status, especially in his unpublished paper 'Jewish Equality before Egalité? The Policy of Joseph II towards the Jews, 1781–1790', presented at the Tenth World Congress of Jewish Studies, Jerusalem, August 1989. I am indebted to him for many stimulating conversations on this theme.
22. See, for example, Salo W. Baron, 'Modern Capitalism and Jewish Fate', in *History and Jewish Historians: Essays and Addresses* (Philadelphia: Jewish Publication Society of America, 1964), pp.41–55, and *A Social and Religious History of the Jews*, 3 vols (New York: Columbia University Press, 1937), vol.2, pp.164–90.
23. See the call for comparative Jewish history, that is, comparisons of the historical development of different Jewish communities, in Endelman, ed., *Comparing Jewish Societies* (note 1).

Portmanteau Jews:
Sephardim and Race in the
Early Modern Atlantic World

JONATHAN SCHORSCH

The significance of ports and ships as conveyors of people, goods and ideas has quickly become a staple of recent historiography dealing with the newly-forged category of Atlantic studies or Atlantic history, a rubric centred appropriately enough around an ocean. The new 'hybrid' category – assuming, justifiably, the importance of movement, transmission, reflexivity and simultaneity – has been of great use in the study of regions deeply affected by the colliding of worlds proverbially said to have begun in 1492. This has been especially true for certain minority groups, especially the Africans forcibly removed from their continent and their descendants, hitherto foreigners in both European and American history. The appearance of Paul Gilroy's *The Black Atlantic: Modernity and Double Consciousness* in 1993, Jeffrey Bolster's 1997 *Black Jacks: African American Seamen in the Age of Sail* and a 1998 anthology of the earliest slave narratives from the Enlightenment era, all evoke and promulgate the hermeneutic tool of the port.[1] Here one sees that which was previously marginalised and denigrated held aloft to trump its abusers: mobility, in-betweenness.

When dealing with the Sephardic populations of the Atlantic world – in places such as Bordeaux, Amsterdam, London, Recife, Surinam, Curaçao or Kingston – an emphasis on the importance of ports and maritime intercourse justifies itself with equal ease. While the majority of the Sephardic population (even in wealthy Amsterdam) continued to be poor, what R. David de Rephael Meldola wrote about Amsterdam Jewry in the mid-eighteenth century applies as well to their seventeenth-century counterparts:

> Here in the city of Amsterdam most of the wealthy and the Gentlemen have all of their monies abroad, for from early times they placed all or most of their wealth in another kingdom to bear interest or to trade with overseas, and these funds never saw this country [Holland].[2]

Not all Sephardic communities maintained such extensive overseas activities, but Meldola's characterisation catches the gist of the entrepreneurial endeavours of their upper and often middle classes. Not for nothing did the enlightenment philosopher Naphtali Herz Wessely, who had visited Amsterdam in 1755, and had more travel experience than most of his fellow Ashkenazim, look to the Sephardim as late as the 1790s as exemplars of urbane cosmopolitanism: 'And moreover you trade in your country with the great imperial powers in Europe, Asia and Africa and are informed of the customs of regions distant from your own.'[3]

The focus of my research has been on the racial imagination of the Atlantic Sephardim.[4] Few faces of culture in the early colonial Atlantic world can be said to have been as international as the imagination or construction of race. It is especially noticeable that the Sephardic ideas about Black Africans and their descendants participated to a high degree in the collective improvisation of the *sistema de castas* – the racial caste system – forged under the experiments of European overseas expansion, colonial administration and proto-industrial plantation slavery. This patchwork discourse of race was hammered out in the transmigration of people and ideas between colony and metropole, between dominant and subaltern populations, between 'high' culture and 'everyday life'. The Sephardic racial imagination provides an excellent case study of these processes. Here I will explore two sets of source material: textual and what we might today call social engineering.

Our point of departure comprises two texts from seventeenth-century Amsterdam, written by Catholics Jewish background who returned to Judaism. The writings of these former *conversos* indicate the interpenetration of the Iberian racial imagination within both Catholic and Jewish Iberian communities. As I hope to show, the Sephardic racial imagination developed firmly within the world of Sephardic cultural and commercial contacts.

Menasseh ben Israel published his work on the soul, *Nishmat Hayyim*, in 1652. Within its variegated themes, Ben Israel treated the powers of sorcery. As evidence that sorcerers can indeed transform themselves into the shapes of animals he cites 'the sages of the nations', who testify to this effect in 'many stories that occurred in the world'. Menasseh points to the works of several authorities on witches and witch-hunting, most prominently Jean Bodin's *De la démonomanie des sorciers*.[5]

Perhaps not surprisingly, given the international array of textual and eyewitness support, Ben Israel describes at length the magical prowess of Black African sorcerers.

And in Guinea, the city which is in Africa, the blacks strike their
fingers with a small knife between the flesh and the nail and remove
by means of a certain horn of a male goat some blood and write with
it on a board how they submit themselves to a demon and work great
wonders. Among them are some who transform their shape into that
of a cat or goose or other animal and they enter the houses and kill
the small children and they say that after their deaths the sorcerers go
to their burial place and cut out their hearts and sacrifice them to
demons. Among them are some who travel by magic, making a
journey of many days in but a few. And there are some who go
levitating in the air between heaven and earth, as happened to one
black. And all types of sorcery are found there because they are blacks
and their souls are from the side of the unclean [מסטרא דמסאבא].[6]

That Ben Israel devotes so much attention to these Black sorcerers reflects
the common contemporary view of Blacks as nefarious, barely civilised
people. If one is discussing black magic, what better topos could be
found? Indeed, much of his language comes straight out of Portuguese
and Spanish travel accounts. As part of the sum of this valuable
contemporary currency, Ben Israel cites a story he was told by 'a reliable
man of our nation who settled among them for some forty years'. To
point out that this circulation of discourse regarding Black Africans to
and from Menasseh ben Israel was in no small part made possible by
maritime navigation would be to state only the obvious.

The writer Daniel Levi (Miguel) de Barrios (Spain, Brussels,
Amsterdam; 1635–1701), who shuttled back and forth between
Christianity and Judaism, wrote in his 1683 history of the Jews of
Amsterdam, *Triumpho del govierno popular*, that the first people to fail
to honour wisdom and, by implication, lack the fear of God, were
certain descendants of the biblical Kush. These De Barrios opposed to
the God-fearing supporters of Solomon, who conquered them. De
Barrios linked these Ethiopian scorners of wisdom and religion with
unreason or insanity, calling them '*locos*'.[7] This particular work of De
Barrios comprises an amazing hodgepodge of genealogical and other
efforts to glorify the Jewish descendants of Shem. Noah acclaimed God
the creator, who was 'not [the God] of Iamphet, nor of Cham, but
rather of Sem, because Sem conveyed his true knowledge to the
Hibrim', the Jews. Elsewhere in this work De Barrios exerted himself
in refuting genealogical linkage between the Jews and the Indians or the
Ethiopians.[8] Here De Barios was writing against authors such as the
Mantuan Jesuit Antonio Possevino (*ca.* 1533–1611), who had cited
Prester John as an authority for the fact that the Abyssinians in general

originated from Solomon and their aristocracy from Abraham.[9] Bernardo José Aldrete (1565–1645), canon of the church at Cordoba, had argued that ancient Hebrew had (d)evolved into Ethiopian after the exile of the Jews to that locale.[10] Ancient writers such as Sulpicius Severus (ca. 360–ca. 425) had argued that the barbarian nations, such as the Parthians, Medes, Indians and Ethiopians, descended from the Jews.[11] But these early modern writers, including De Barrios, were influenced instead by the appearance in the sixteenth century of the first Spanish translations of the Ethiopian royal chronicles, the *Kebra Nagast*, which detailed the Solomonic ancestry of the Christian kings of Ethiopia.[12] De Barrios' distancing of Jews from Ethiopians was no mere genealogical exercise, then, but part of vividly contemporary Iberian polemics.

These two textual sources could be multiplied with ease; but all show that Sephardic racial imaginings stemmed from the cosmopolitan milieu of their authors. When one examines the anti-Black social engineering of some of the Atlantic Sephardic communities, the same conclusion becomes even more apparent.

In the mid-seventeenth century the 'Portuguese' Jewish community of Amsterdam instituted several communal ordinances which reflected and constructed the desired 'ethnic' transformation of the Jews into 'whites'. Archival records in the GemeenteArchief Amsterdam reflect the perception that of the first few Blacks who lived in Amsterdam, most belonged to 'Portuguese Jews'.[13] The *takanot* passed in response to the problematic presence of Blacks within the *naçao* adumbrate the process through which Whiteness became an operative principle in the organisation of Jewish communal life in Amsterdam.

Perhaps the first exclusionary practice emerged in 1627, when an ordinance was passed restricting access to burial at the community's cemetery, officially opened only in 1618. The ordinance read, in part:

> No black person nor mulato will be able to be buried in the cemetery, except for those who had buried in it a Jewish mother. None shall persuade any of the said blacks and mulatos, man or woman, or any other person who is not of the nation of Israel to be made Jews.[14]

While the prohibition intended all foreigners, the specification of Blacks and mulattos reflected both the reality of their presence as slaves or servants in the Amsterdam Jewish community as well as the degree to which they were seen to draw negative attention. An ordinance passed in 1614 with the initial purchase of the Ouderkerk cemetery had already established a separate section 'intended especially for the burial of slaves, servants and 'Jewish girls, who are not of our Nation'.[15] Though the motivation in 1627 still was *halakhic*, the language had in 12 years become explicitly 'racial'.

Other exclusionary ordinances soon followed within the seventeenth-century Amsterdam Sephardic community. All drew on similar ordinances from the Iberian Catholic colonial world, and reflect trends beginning to appear as well in the north-European Protestant colonial orbit. In 1640, the Amsterdam Sephardic communal board ordered that Black and mulatto girls be allowed to sit in the synagogue's women's gallery only from the eighth row and farther back. At the same time the *Mahamad* decreed that the doors to the women's section of the sanctuary were not to be opened before six in the morning, in order to prevent the congregating of these slave women and other servants on the street.[16] Four years later the men of the communal board decreed that 'circumcised Negro Jews' were not to be called to the Torah or given any honorary commandment to perform in the synagogue, 'for such is fitting for the reputation of the congregation and its good government'.[17] Dutch Protestant planters in Brazil had been making it difficult for their slaves to attend church services, as early as if not earlier than a 1636 report to that effect by a Dutch Protestant pastor.[18] In 1647, a separate section of the Sephardic cemetery was established for 'all the Jewish Negroes and mulatos'. Exceptions were limited to those 'who were born in Judaism, [their parents] having [been married] with *quedosim* [with *kiddushin*, that is, properly, according to Jewish law], or those who were married to whites with *quedosim*'.[19] In other words, *very* few if any Blacks or mulattos would have qualified for burial in the Jewish cemetery proper. That so many Blacks and mulattos *did* receive burial in the segregated section of the Jewish cemetery after this ordinance reflects a communal rift when it came to treatment of slaves. While the *mahamad* wished to terminate the inclusion of Blacks and mulattos in Jewish life, individual owners clearly saw fit to continue including them. In 1658, the *mahamad* decided that mulatto boys would no longer be admitted for study in the Amsterdam *yeshiva* of the Sephardim.[20] Based on a view expressed in the Talmud, some early medieval rabbis, as well as Maimonides, prohibited the teaching of Torah to one's slave and ruled that such knowledge did not cause his liberation. These seventeenth-century mulattos were not identified as slaves, however; the issue was their background. Such an exclusion of Others considered unworthy had other general precedents. The Jesuit College of St. Peter and St. Paul in Mexico City, founded in 1582, had included in its constitution a clause expressly forbidding the admission of Blacks and mulattos.[21] Indeed, since the mid-1500s, full-blooded American Indians and Blacks were not allowed to receive holy orders or hold sacerdotal office in the Viceroyalties of Mexico or Peru.[22]

By the early seventeenth century, exceptions aside, the Jesuits and other religious orders working in the Congo and Angola 'refused to admit either blacks or mulattos to their own ranks, though they did train them at [their] colleges to enter the secular priesthood'.[23]

Though only one Sephardic community apart from Amsterdam, Surinam, produced ordinances with similarly explicit exclusions, it seems that most such communities in the Americas followed them in practice, as will be shown below.[24] By the eighteenth century, Surinamese Sephardim at Jodensavane had promulgated similar legislation limiting the participation of coloured Jews. The Sephardim of Curaçao had, from the beginning of the community, refused entry to non-whites. Like their non-Jewish peers throughout the Dutch and English colonies, Jews for the most part kept their religion from the great majority of their slaves.[25]

The ritual absorption of slaves into the Jewish community, which remained the traditional modus operandi in Mediterranean communities well into the eighteenth century, faded away in the face of the regnant western *sistema de castas*. The 1649 *haskamot* [communal ordinances] of Recife explicitly addressed the issue of circumcising slaves. No doubt, as in Amsterdam, these *haskamot* proceeded from a specific local cause; scholar Jonathan Israel mentioned, without citing a source, that in early Dutch Brazil 'a few of the Jews were mulatto half-castes'.[26] Instead of banning conversions of slaves (and not slaves alone) the *mahamad* attempted to control them:

> No person shall – except with the permission of the Gentlemen of the Mahamad – circumcise a stranger or admit a strange woman to the Theuilah, under penalty of being separated from the nation and fined 50 florins. And if that person be a slave, he shall not be circumcised without first having been freed by his master, so that the master shall not be able to sell him from the moment the slave will have bound himself [to Judaism].[27]

The last provision constitutes a nimble response to the specific exigencies of the Brazilian slave economy, in which Jewish merchants routinely possessed enormous numbers of slaves temporarily before selling them off. Yet *halakhic* reasoning had long before permitted the temporary possession of uncircumcised slaves. The provision ensured the potential convert – slaves belonging to Jewish masters, urban and rural – that their conversion will guarantee manumission, but effectively penalised any master who circumcised his slaves. Whether protective of the slave's interest or exclusively for the sake of the Jewish community, the provision went directly contrary to the *Shulkhan Arukh* and would have placed a hardship on observant masters in a slave economy such as Brazil. Within a year, a nearly identical ordinance was passed in Amsterdam. This 1650 ordinance of the *mahamad* ordered an end to the circumcision or ritual immersion of Blacks and mulattos other than those who narrowly and incorrectly were considered *yelidei bayit*, slaves born into the master's household. For these latter, the *mahamad* left the decision to circumcise/immerse or not in the hands of the individual master.[28] The spirit of this particular Sephardic ordinance paralleled, and may have derived from, certain results of the 1618 Synod of Dordt. The leaders of the Reformed Churches gathered there had failed to reach a conclusion on the issue of 'whether slaves born in Reformed households should be baptised and of whether baptism would free them', since the latter case would 'discourage slave-owners from allowing [baptism]'. Ultimately, in the face of disagreement over the consequences of baptism for the slave and master, the Reformed sages 'favoured leaving the discretion on whether to baptise to the head of household'.[29] Similarly, from the outset of English colonisation on Barbados (1625) slaves (Africans), but not servants (Europeans) faced 'exclusion from the Christian church', language that I assume included baptism.[30]

It seems highly unlikely that the Sephardim of Curaçao routinely absorbed their slaves into the community. Both Protestants and Jews 'mostly had their slaves christened as Catholics'.[31] Like the Protestant population, the Jewish community 'would not recognize colored persons as members'.[32] Jacob Rader Marcus was correct in thinking that the Jews of Curaçao did not circumcise their male slaves.[33] The attitude towards the circumcision of slaves among Caribbean Sephardim can probably be accurately gauged from Rabbi Selomoh Levy Maduro's 1768 *Brit Yitshak*, a compendium of texts to be read the night before a circumcision and guide to the order of the ceremony, which contains the blessings for circumcising a slave, but prefaces it with the heading: 'The order for circumcising and immersing a slave *at the time the Temple was in existence.*' The ceremony's first instructions reiterate this declaration: 'A Jew in buying a slave *used to be obligated* to bless.'[34] Levy Maduro made this commandment obsolete,[35] despite the fact that many Sephardic rabbis held that the laws of slavery continued to be operative, and that responsa from Amsterdam make it clear that some Jews even in 'the West' continued to own slaves according to the *halakhic*, and not just social, nomenclature and category. He evidently held views like those Sephardic rabbis who argued that the laws relating to Canaanite slaves no longer obtained. The author could not have been unaware of the social fact of Jewish slave-owning; the book's final pages consist of a list of *mohelim* in the colonies of Curaçao and Surinam, among other

Sephardic habitations. A connection probably exists between Levy Maduro's stance on the circumcision of slaves and his belonging to a family boasting prominent members in Curaçao, where male slaves were not circumcised.[36] Indeed, a Selomoh L. Maduro, no doubt our author, appeared in contemporary records as the owner of an unnamed plantation in 1722.[37]

Primary sources make it seem unlikely that the Jews of Surinam regularly circumcised their slaves.[38] I have so far been unable to locate any circumcision registers from Surinam, however, which might help resolve the question of whether slaves were circumcised. But the generalisation of circumcision seems doubtful for many reasons. A 1794 letter written by some of the Sephardic leaders to the colony's governor attempted to explain their position regarding recent controversies involving the group of Jewish mulattos (congregation *Darhe Jesarim*) who desired rights equal to those of the White Jews. Describing the genesis of this mulatto group, they write:

> Several among the Portuguese Jewish Nation, out of private affection begot children with some of their female slaves or mulattos. Out of particular love for the Jewish Religion the boys were properly circumcised and the girls instructed by a teacher, as were their descendants.[39]

I infer from the language used here that only these children of 'private affection' were circumcised, not every slave. (Though the language, at least of the translation, leaves unclear whose private affection acted here.) If these Sephardic settlers followed the communal ordinance from Zur Israel in Recife, the circumcisions would have been performed only *after* manumission. Certainly the majority of the slaves belonging to Surinamese Jews were not circumcised or converted to Judaism. The mulatto children brought about through relations with their slave women constituted the only Jewish slaves or former slaves in the colony, and not even all such mulatto offspring became Jewish. One can infer from this that the community considered only these mulatto slaves born to Jewish fathers to be *yelidei bayit* (houseborn) slaves according to Gen. 17:13 and *halakhic* principle, as opposed to *every* child born of one's slaves, and that in Surinam only these slaves with Jewish fathers received circumcision, though I have not come across any explicit statement that such was the community's policy. I have also not found any *halakhic* precedent for this understanding. Such a practice would, if calculated generously, yield a total of perhaps 200 circumcised slaves (contemporary documentation recorded only 27 coloured Jews of both genders in 1762 and nearly 100 in 1788), compared with the well over 10,000 uncircumcised slaves who belonged to Surinamese Jews during the seventeenth and eighteenth centuries, that is, under two per cent.

The religious dynamics pertaining to the slaves of Jewish masters in Surinam would seem to have run no differently than with those of Christians. Rosemary Brana-Shute calculated that only eight per cent of the 1,346 slaves nominated for manumission from 1760 to 1828 'indicated any experience of, education in, or commitment to Christianity'.[40] The *Historical Essay* (1788), produced by leading members of the Sephardic Surinamese community, made distinctions between Jewish and non-Jewish slaves. Speaking of the losses incurred on a 1749 expedition against the Maroons, the authors mentioned 'Abm. de Britton, a mulatto Jew, and three or four good slaves.'[41] The latter, that is, had not been converted, as must have been true of the overwhelming majority of the slaves of these Jews.

If so few male slaves were circumcised in Surinam, it could not have been due to ignorance. Surinam was not a completely isolated hinterland when it came to religious culture. For example, a 1739 list of the Hebrew books held in the Ets Hayim school at Jodensavane makes it clear that enough *halakhic* sources existed in Surinam from which to draw a proper picture of duties regarding slaves.[42] People with rabbinic knowledge and training lived in the colony as early as 1642 and throughout the eighteenth century.[43]

Slaves in the colonial territories, then, remained unconverted, but, more importantly, due to their high numbers and concomitantly increased social segregation they constituted a significant class of people for the most part no longer admissible into the community. In 1793 the London rabbinic court reported receiving a letter from the Jewish congregation in Philadelphia, Mikveh Israel, asking 'how to proceed in the matter of a *Yahid* [member] who wishes to have converted, so that he may marry her, a servant with whom he has lived and by whom he has begotten children. The [London] Mahamad discreetly advised the Beth Din that it is impolitic to give instructions in such a case.'[44] Note the distance between this response – so sensitive as to require behind-the-scenes treatment – and the perfectly explicit and *halakhic* reactions of earlier and Mediterranean rabbis to marriages between former servants and free Jews. Other cases of conversion to Judaism had occurred by 1793 in England and its colonies; was the *mahamad*'s discretion due entirely to political fears about converts in general?

Jews do not seem to have manumitted their slaves, other than in their wills, according to *halakha*. The wills met *halakhic* criteria as the intention of the master expressed therein was considered legally binding on any heirs.[45] In the ideal case wills bore the signatures of two witnesses, making them valid for confirmation by a *beit din* (rabbinic court). I have not found any indication of the existence of a *beit din* or an equivalent anywhere in the Caribbean, staffed by rabbis or other qualified laymen, which performed the functions ordained by *halakha* in the liberation of slaves. I have not come across any mention that owners granted slaves a *get* (contract of emancipation) or that manumitted slaves were brought to the *mikve* for ritual immersion; presumably unconverted slaves possessed outside the framework of *halakha* needed no such rituals. In 1780, requirements of manumission and declaration of paternity were established by the *parnasim*, the Surinamese Sephardic community leaders, as mentioned by Robert Cohen, but he failed to provide their content.[46]

As in the Mediterranean world, manumissions of slaves by colonial Jews conformed closely to local practices. Of the manumissions committed to writing, only a rare few occurred before the death of the owner. Wills often contained a clause reverting the possession of inherited slaves to other relatives should the heir die without children of their own.[47]

The last such stipulations indicate the economic value of slaves, but may also show that those who insisted on inserting these clauses into their testaments believed that slaves *must* be passed down by Jewish law. If so, here we see at work not some eternal Jewish view, but the functional and self-interested invocation of a particular earlier *halakhic* opinion, (re)constructed for new times. As mentioned previously, this view had many adherents among the Jews of the Mediterranean region. Such, too, was the opinion of Rabbi Abraham Gabay Yzidro (eighteenth century), who served various communal functions in Surinam and then Barbados.[48] In his verse rendition of the 613 commandments according to Maimonides, published in 1763, Gabay Yzidro explicitly juxtaposed the freeing of a Hebrew slave with the eternal employment of a non-Jewish slave:

And the slave of my holy people [i.e., a Jewish/Hebrew slave]
Sustain on his going free,
But forever with the Kushite
Work at the task.[49]

Joanna Westphal found an intriguing entry relating to the manumission of slaves in the Barbados congregation's minute book. In 1800, a woman named Judith Pereira was removed from the pension list for 'having endeavoured to emancipate her negro woman'. The *mahamad* preferred that she donate the slave to the congregation or sell her and donate the profits. She evidently promised to comply, as six months later Pereira was reinstated on the list, on condition that she 'gives a deed to her nieces for her negro slave'.[50] Control over the manumission of slaves constituted a common strategy in societies with numerous slaves. As of 1713, masters in the French Caribbean islands needed written permission from the governor general in order to free a slave.[51] Perhaps the actions of the Sephardic leaders on Barbados in the case of Judith Pereira reflected the positing of a positive commandment of eternal servitude of non-Jewish slaves. Yet the invocation of this attitude out of *halakhic* sources served as little more than a homegrown justification for the imitation of the de facto racialised practices of Caribbean Christian slaveholders.

In short, the language conveying the exclusionary legislation of Sephardic Amsterdam stands as another instance of the international logic of anti-Black thought. The Amsterdam ordinances could have excluded '*avadim*/slaves' of questionable *halakhic* status, rather than '*negros*/Blacks' or '*mulatos*/mulattos'. The texts' use of the 'racial' term assumed that it already has come to replace the term 'slave'. The giving of honours in the synagogue to Black Jews 'does not befit the reputation of the Congregation', read the statute of 1644. So also ran a 1664 Maryland law forbidding 'ffreeborne English women' to marry 'Negro slaves', an act seen to be 'to the disgrace of our Nation'.[52] The 1703 ordinance implementing yet another special row in the cemetery stated that it was for 'Black Jews and other people who appear unworthy of being buried in an ordinary row'. These Sephardic ordinances embodied a discourse larger than, or between, ruling groups (a *langue*) uttered this time by certain Jews with their own inflection and context, their own intention (*parole*). The origins of the behaviour and thought described here spanned Jewish *and* non-Jewish discourses. The reluctance to convert slaves in western colonies, for instance, had parallels, as did each of the Sephardic ordinances under discussion. Jewish behaviour was analogous as well as influenced, had internal as well as external causes. The series of Amsterdam Sephardic ordinances did nothing less than instantiate a miscegenation of *halakhic* worries and the 'pigmentocracy' reigning throughout the Iberian, Dutch, English and French worlds.[53]

Mobile, circulating *conversos* and Jews indeed served as one of the conveyors of Iberian racialised discourse and social engineering into the expanding northern European colonial sphere. Not only did these Jews reside in and depend on ports for their economic and cultural life, they in essence acted as trans-shippers of culture. When it is said, therefore, that Jewish slaveholders did things 'Jewishly', we see that this often signified far less than such a statement purported. Despite religious differences distinguishing them from their surrounding host populations, Sephardic Jews in the Atlantic colonies behaved towards their slaves in noteworthy concert with their sociological setting.

NOTES

1. Paul Gilroy, *The Black Atlantic: Modernity and Double Consciousness* (Cambridge: Harvard University Press, 1993); Jeffrey W. Bolster, *Black Jacks: African American Seamen in the Age of Sail* (Cambridge: Harvard University Press, 1997).

2. "רוב העשירים וגבירי מתא כל מעותיהם וממון שלהם הוא חוץ למדינה שממון קדמון נתנו כל ממונם או רובו" [...]
     "לרבית במלכות אחרת או לשאת עמהם בברכי הים ומעולם לא ראה פני המדינה פה בעיר אמשטרדם.

    David de Rephael Meldola, *Sefer Divrei David* (Amsterdam: Hirsch Levi Rofe, 1753), p.141a (responsum no.54). All translations are mine unless otherwise noted.

3. Cited in J. Melkman, *David Franco Mendes: A Hebrew Poet* (Jerusalem and Amsterdam: Massadah/Joachimsthal's Boekhandel, Uitgevers- en Drukkerrijbedrijf, 1951), p.13.

4. This essay reworks material from Jonathan Schorsch, 'Jews and Blacks in the Early Modern Mediterranean and Atlantic Worlds, 1450–1800' (PhD Dissertation, University of California-Berkeley, 2000). A revised version will be published by Cambridge University Press (forthcoming 2003).

5. Menasseh ben Israel, *Nishmat Ḥayyim* (Amsterdam: Shmuel Abravanel Soeiro, 1652), p.136a-b (3rd art., ch.24).

6. Third article, ch.23: ובגיני העיר אשר בחלקת האפריקה [....] שמכחישין פמליא של מעלה. ואמרו למה נקראו שמם כשפי [....]
   השחורים עם סכין קטן מכ' אבצעותיה'! בין הבשר והצפורן ומוציאין בתוך קרן א' של תיש איזה דם ועמו כותבים על לוח איך מוסרים עצמם
   לשד ופועלים נפלאות גדולות. יש מהם שמשתמנים צורתם בצורת חתול או אווז או בעל חי אחר ונכנסים בבתים והורגים הילדים הקטנים
   ואומרים שאחר מיתתם הולכים לבית קבורתם וחוזקים מהם הלבבו! ומקרבים אותם לשדים. ומודים שכאשר מרפאים בעל כרחם איו' ילד
   שכשפו מחוייבים להמית אחר במקומו לפיס את השטן. ויש מהם שעושים קפיצת הדרך ומהלך כמה ימים מועטים. ויש מהם שבין
   השמים והארץ הולכים תלוים באויר כאשר קרא לאיזה שחור אשר חזו עליו שימות מנשיכת עקרב ועם כל זה לא יכול להציל את נפשו כי ניצל
   מאחד הפחתי' ולא נצל מהעקרבי' ופתע פתאום פגע בו עקרב ומת מנשיכתו. ויש מהם שזורעים בחלקת שדותיהם את הקשאים אבטיחים בצלים
   ושומים וכי ישלח איש את בערו ובעד ובישר בשדהו מיד שנגנבת הבהמה בתחום שאינו שלו נופלת לארץ ורוח אין עוד בנה עד שבחבלים יוציאוה.
   ויש מהם שאם נגנב באו להם וירבחו בהחבא אם לא ימצא הגנב לוקחים מעפור מדרך כף רגלו נדפס בחול אשר פתח הבית ובמבטא שפתם כל
   מקום שהגנב הוא שם יחוג וינוע כשכור ולא יכול עוד לצאת ולבא ולהרחיק את נדודו עד ימצא. ויש מהם שמניחים את פירותיהם על פני הארץ
   כהפקר לכל. ואם אחד בא ושולח את אמתו לאכול את ליקח מהם ומיבש ידו אשר שלח אליו עד בואו ובעל ומתיר לכשווו. וכל מיני הכשופים
   נמצאים שם כי הם שחורים ונשמתן מסטרא דמסאבא. והם קורים עוד היום לשדים גינים. ונראה לי שהוא השם שקוראים להם בהרבה מקומות
   בזוהר זיני בישין בחלוף ז' בג' אשר הם קרובים במבטא. וספר לי איש נאמן מבני עמנו אשר נתיישב בינינו כארבעי' שנים איף פעם א' היה
   מהלך בדרך רוכב על סוס. ויהי באמצע הדרך העבד העובר לפניו הפך פניו לנגדו לראות מה יקרה לו ותכף הסוס אשר רכב עליו נעכב
   במקומו ותעמוד מלכת. ואף שהכה אותו מכת מות לא הועילה השתדלותו כלום עד שהעבד הגיע ותפס אותו מן הרסן והעבירו מן המקום ההוא.
   ואז שם לדרך פעמיו בלי איחור ועכוב. ויהי בלילה והנה זה מספר לרעהו משכשף כמהו אשר לבית אדני אתו בבית את כל אשר קרהו ואת
   פרשת הדרך אשר עליו היו בג' גינים עומדים ואיך כאשר ראם ויאמר מחנה שדים זה הפך פני לאדוניו לראות מה יהיה לו ואיך הסוס הוכה
   בתמהון. ואתה הקורא אל תתמה מזה כי הבהמות רואות מה שאין האדם רואה"

7. '[Y] los temerosos de Dios, fundan el palacio de la Sabiduria, en los cimientos del temor, por no haver ciencia como temer el Divino castigo; ni delirio como despreciarlo con las presunciones de excederlo: los primeros que no la preciaron fueron los que el noticioso Aldrete llama *Evileos*, descendientes de *Chus*: y los que temen à Dios son, los que con Salomon dominan à los Evileos, *Evelim*, (Locos) *Temor del Señor es principio de Sabiduria: Ciencia, y castigo los locos despreciaron*' (Daniel Levi [Miguel] de Barrios, *Triumpho del govierno popular, y de la antiguedad holandesa* [n.p., n.d. (1683)] p.66).

8. De Barrios, *Triumpho*, pp.48, 54–8.

9. Antonio Possevino, *Bibliotheca Selecta de Ratione Studiorum* (n.p., 1607 [orig. 1603?]), bk.15, ch.19.

10. Bernardo José Aldrete, *Varias antigvedades de españa africa y otras provincias* (Amberes: A costa de Iuan Hasrey, 1614), p.165.

11. Arno Borst, *Der Turmbau von Babel: Geschichte der Meinungen Über Ursprung und Vielfalt der Sprachen und Völker*, 4 vols. in 6 parts (Stuttgart: Anton Hiersemann, 1957–63), II, p.406.

12. See, for example, Enrique Cornelio Agrippa, *Historia de las cosas de etiopía* (Toledo,

1528) and Manuel Almeida (1580–1646), *Historia de Etiopía*, the latter not published in its entirety.

13. Ernst van den Boogaart, 'Colour Prejudice and the Yardstick of Civility: the Initial Dutch Confrontation with Black Africans, 1590–1635', *Racism and Colonialism: Essays on Ideology and Social Structure* ed. by Robert Ross (The Hague: Martinus Nijhoff, 1982), p.45, n.37; Eli Faber, *Jews, Slaves, and the Slave Trade: Setting the Record Straight* (New York: New York University Press, 1998), 16, citing Johannes Menne Postma, *The Dutch in the Atlantic Slave Trade, 1600–1815* (Cambridge: Cambridge University Press, 1990), p.10.

14. 'Libro dos termos da ymposta da naçao', 20 Tamuz 5387 (1627), Archive of the Portuguese Jewish Community of Amsterdam, GemeenteArchief Amsterdam (hereafter GAA), sec.334, no.13, fol.42.

15. Robert Cohen, *Jews in Another Environment: Surinam in the Second Half of the Eighteenth Century* (Leiden: E.J. Brill, 1991), p.161.

16. Escamoth (undated [1640]), GAA, sec.334, no.19.

17. 'Livros dos Acordos da Nacao e Ascamot', GAA, sec.334, no.19, fol.173.

18. B.N. Teensma, 'The Brazilian Letters of Vicent Joachim Soler', in *Dutch Brazil*, vol.1, *Documents in the Leiden University Library* (Rio de Janeiro: Editora Index, 1997), p.61.

19. 'Livros dos Acordos da Nacao e Ascamot', 24 Nisan 5407 (1647), GAA, sec.334, no.19, fol.224.

20. 'Livros dos Acordos da Nacao e Ascamot', 9 Sh'vat 5418 (1658), GAA, sec.334, no.19, fol.426; cited also in Yosef Kaplan, 'The Portuguese Community in Amsterdam in the Seventeenth Century: Between Tradition and Change (Hebrew)', *Reports of the Israeli National Academy of Sciences* 7, no.6 (Jerusalem: Israeli National Academy of Sciences, 1986), p.168.

21. Colin A. Palmer, *Slaves of the White God: Blacks in Mexico, 1570–1650* (Cambridge: Harvard University Press, 1976), p.54.

22. In 1555 the first Mexican Ecclesiastical Provincial Council declared Indians, mestizos, mulattos, descendants of Moors, Jews and persons sentenced by the Inquisition 'inherently unworthy of the sacerdotal office'. The Third Provincial Council (1585) relaxed this somewhat, admitting 'Mexicans who are descended in the first degree from Amerindians, or from Moors, or from parents of whom one is a Negro'. By implication, full-blood Indians and Blacks remained unacceptable for admission. All from C.R. Boxer, *The Church Militant and Iberian Expansion, 1440–1770* (Baltimore: Johns Hopkins University Press, 1978), pp.15–16.

23. Ibid., p.9.

24. The communal ordinances of the Sephardic congregations in Morocco, for instance, made no mention of issues related to the burial or ritual participation of slaves. See *The Taqanot of the Jews of Morocco: A Collection of Communal Ordinances from the 16th to 18th Century as found in 'Kerem Hemer' II by Avraham Ankawa* ed. by Shalom Bar-Asher (Jerusalem: Zalman Shazar Center/Hebrew University, 1977).

25. On the segregation of Calvinism and slaves, see Cornelis Ch. Goslinga, *The Dutch in the Caribbean and on the Wild Coast, 1580–1680* (Assen: Van Gorcum, 1971), pp.368–69; R.A.J. van Lier, *Frontier Society: A Social Analysis of the History of Surinam* (The Hague: Martinus Nijhoff, 1971), pp.72–74; Rosemary Brana-Shute, 'The Manumission of Slaves in Suriname, 1760–1828' (Ph.D. diss., University of Florida, 1985), 256–58.

26. Jonathan Israel, 'Menasseh ben Israel and the Dutch Sephardic Colonization Movement of the Mid-Seventeenth Century (1645–1657)', in *Menasseh ben Israel and His World*, ed. by Yosef Kaplan, Henry Méchoulan and Richard H. Popkin (Leiden: E.J. Brill, 1989), p.106.

27. *Haskamah* 32 [dated 5409/1649]; translated in Arnold Wiznitzer, *The Records of the*

Earliest Jewish Community in the New World (New York: American Jewish Historical Society, 1954), p.69.

28. 'Reformation of the *escama* [ordinance] of the year [16]39 which treats the circumcising of *goyim* [non-Jews]. The Gentlemen of the *Mahamad* declare that the same penalty of *herem* [one of the three forms of excommunication] [will apply] to any who circumcise blacks or mulatos and also any who immerse them ritually or any who act as a witness for them, seeing them bathe, or any other Man or woman who is not of our Hebrew nation. The Gentlemen of the *Mahamad* [declare] that a slavewoman, having some occasion of [the birth of] a son or daughter by a Jew, who will come to the bathhouse [to bathe the child] or [a child?] from Portugal who should be born in his house by his [concubine?] may do as he sees fit / Reformassaõ da escama de an 39: que trata sobre o sircunsidar goim declaraõ os SSres. do Mahamad que a mesma Pena de herem [illegible word] em quem sircumsidar negros ou mulatos e tambem quem os Banhar ou ser testigo de os ver banhar ou qualquer outra Pessoa ou mulher q naõ ser de nossa nassaõ hebrea. os SSres. do Mahamad q Escrava [?] avendo algua oCaziaõ de algun filho ou filha de judeu q venga de abanha ou De portugal [?] que se Criasse em sua Caza Com seu intimo [?] poderaõ dispor Como lhe paraser' (Livro dos Acordos, 24 Shvat 5410 [1650], GAA 334, no.19, fol.281).

29. Robin Blackburn, *The Making of New World Slavery: From the Baroque to the Modern, 1492–1800* (London: Verso, 1997), p.64. Robert C.-H. Shell, Blackburn's source, framed this step in a manner that well illuminates the trajectory of the Jewish discourse under discussion, 'Baptism, a public imperative for the Catholic church, became a household choice for the Reformed Christian' (Robert C.-H. Shell, *Children of Bondage: A Social History of the Slave Society at the Cape of Good Hope, 1652–1838* [Hanover, NH: Wesleyan University Press/University Press of New England, 1994], p.334).

30. Gary A. Puckrein, *Little England: Plantation Society and Anglo-Barbadian Politics, 1627–1700* (New York: New York University Press, 1984), p.23.

31. J. Hartog, *Curaçao: from Colonial Dependence to Autonomy* (Aruba: De Wit, 1968), p.148.

32. Isaac S. and Suzanne A. Emmanuel, *History of the Jews of the Netherlands Antilles*, 2 vols. (Cincinnati: American Jewish Archives, 1970), I, p.146.

33. Jacob Rader Marcus, *The Colonial American Jew, 1492-1776*, 3 vols. (Detroit: Wayne State University Press, 1970), I, p.200.

34. My emphasis; Selomoh Levy Maduro, *Brit Yitshak* (Amsterdam: Gerard Johann Janson/House of Mondui, 1768), pp.15b–16a.

35. He did so by conflating the cessation of Canaanite slave laws with the time universally assigned to the end of *Hebrew* slaves, the point at which the jubilee year supposedly was no longer observed (because of the destruction of the Jerusalem Temple, the absence of the 12 tribal representatives, etc.). Levy Maduro's view went counter to that of Maimonides, who specifically distinguished between the laws pertaining to Hebrew slaves – dependent on the Temple, the jubilee – and the 'eternal' laws pertaining to Canaanite slaves (*Mishneh Torah*, Laws of Slaves, V, p.17).

36. On the Maduros of Curaçao, see Isaac S. Emmanuel, *Precious Stones of Curaçao: Curaçaon Jewry 1656-1957* (New York: Bloch Publishing Co., 1957), pp.209–13.

37. Emmanuel, *Jews in the Netherlands Antilles* (see note 32), II, p.653.

38. Unfortunately, I have been unable yet to find any pertinent evidence from seventeenth- century Surinam.

39. Cohen, *Jews in Another Environment* (see note 15), p.159.

40. Brana-Shute, 'Manumission of Slaves' (see note 25), p.260.

41. *Historical Essay on the Colony of Surinam, 1788*, ed. by Jacob R. Marcus and Stanley F. Chyet, trans. Simon Cohen (Cincinnati/New York: American Jewish Archives/

KTAV Publishing House, 1974), p.71. The name is probably a mistake for De Britto, a prominent Sephardic planter family.

42. Among the library's holdings: the talmudic tractates Kidushin, Gitin, Ketubot and Yebamot (among others); a commentary on the *Shulkhan Arukh* (though in bad condition [mal tratado]); and, perhaps most crucially, three different multi-volume editions of the *Shulkhan Arukh* itself (Records of Jurators of Surinam; Portuguese Jewish Communion [sic] / Archief der Nederlandsch-Portugeesch-Israelietische Gemeente in Suriname, Algemeen RijksArchief, The Hague, no.25 = American Jewish Archives [hereafter AJA] microfilm reel 67h, fols.48–49).

43. P.A. Hilfman, 'Notes on the History of the Jews in Surinam', *Publications of the American Jewish Historical Society* 18 (1909), 185, provided a list of the rabbis serving in Surinam until 1750.

44. Richard D. Barnett, 'The Correspondence of the Mahamad of the Spanish and Portuguese Congregation of London during the Seventeenth and Eighteenth Centuries', *Transactions of the Jewish Historical Society of England* 20 (1959/1961), 17.

45. Maimonides, *Mishneh Torah*, Laws of Slaves, 6.4; Karo, *Shulkhan Arukh*, Yoreh De'ah, sec.267:77–78.

46. Cohen, *Jews in Another Environment*, p.305, n.39. I have not yet found this crucial document.

47. The 1713 codicil of Daniel Ulloa stated that if his daughter 'has no children, the slaves are to revert after her death to Sarah's siblings and their heirs and assigns' (Bertram Wallace Korn, 'Barbadian Jewish Wills, 1676–1740', in *A Bicentennial Festschrift for Jacob Rader Marcus*, ed. by Bertram Wallace Korn [Waltham, MA/New York: American Jewish Historical Society/Ktav, 1976], p.306), while the 1733 will of Miriam Arobas specified that should any of her children 'die before reaching the age of twenty-one and without issue, the slaves bequeathed to that child are to be divided equally among the other children named, and their heirs and assigns' (Ibid., 307). Similar clauses can be found among Surinamese Jews as well, for instance, in the will of Abraham da Costa (12 August 1768; Records of Jurators of Surinam; Jurator Isaac Nassy, Minutes, 1763–74. Jurator Jacob de Barrios, Minutes and registered acts, 1779–80 / Archief der Nederlandsch-Portugeesch-Israelietische Gemeente in Suriname, no.784 = AJA microfilm reel 67a, frame 777).

48. Yzidro had been in Surinam since at least 1735 or so, when his name was mentioned as a teacher in the Jodensavane community (AJA microfilm reel 67h, frame 143). He had been born in Spain, fled to England and studied in Amsterdam with David Israel Athias, before leaving for the Caribbean. His wife came from the Sephardic community of Bayonne, *Jews in the Caribbean: Evidence on the History of the Jews in the Caribbean Zone in Colonial Times* ed. by France (Zvi Loker [Jerusalem: Misgav Yerushalayim, 1991], p.83, n.1–2).

49. Abraham Gabay Yzidro, *Yad Avraham. ve-Hu Ḥibur ha-Azharot* (Amsterdam: Leib b. Moshe Zusmans/Jan Janson, 1763), p.4b. My translation ignores the rhyme scheme: "ועבד עם קדשי/תעניק בצאת חפשי/ולעולם בכושי/תעבוד במשרה". Yzidro substituted, no doubt based on his experience in plantation slave societies, the traditional term 'Canaanite' slave with 'Kushite'.

50. Entries of 22 September 1800 and 10 March 1801, Minute Book of the Mahamad and Adjuntos 1791–1808 (MS 328), Lauderdale Road Synagogue, London; cited in Joanna Westphal, 'Jews in a Colonial Society: The Jewish Community of Barbados, 1654–1833', unpublished MA thesis (London: University College, London University, 1993), p.54.

51. David Brion Davis, *The Problem of Slavery in Western Culture* (Ithaca: Cornell University Press, 1966), p.263.

52. Cited in Alden T. Vaughan, *Roots of American Racism: Essays on the Colonial Experience* (Oxford: Oxford University Press, 1995), p.170.

53. The term 'pigmentocracy' was first used by the Chilean Alejandro Lipschütz, *El indoamericanismo y el problema racial en las Américas*, 2nd ed. (Santiago de Chile, 1944), p.75 and passim, then picked up by Magnus Mörner, *Race Mixture in the History of Latin America* (Boston: Little, Brown & Company, 1967), p.54, whence it entered the scholarly vocabulary. It was later used by Boxer, *The Church Militant* (see note 23), p.38.

Germany's Door to the World: A Haven for the Jews? Hamburg, 1590–1933

RAINER LIEDTKE

Hamburg, Germany's dominant port city for centuries, also contained one of the largest, richest and culturally most productive Jewish communities of the German-speaking lands. This essay asks whether the supposedly cosmopolitan and open environment of this major German entrepot also created favourable living and working conditions for its Jews. Thus at the centre of the investigation is the question of how Jewish–non-Jewish interactions developed between the settlement of the first members of the minority in the late sixteenth century and the onset of the Nazi period.[1] In order to provide answers I will first give a brief overview over the historical development of the city of Hamburg, with emphasis on its economy, the importance of its port and its political as well as religious make-up. Then I will outline the historical experience of Hamburg Jewry from the seventeenth to the early twentieth century. Finally, I will advance a number of theses that draw from the results of the first two sections, enquire into minority–majority relations and address the issue of toleration.

The Historical Development of the City

Hamburg is located where two smaller tributaries, the Alster and the Bille flow into one of Europe's great rivers, the Elbe, approximately 100 kilometres before it reaches the North Sea. Already in the thirteenth century the city, which had originally been founded as the seat of a bishop, had begun to make use of its favourable geographic location by building a harbour and engaging in North German and later North European transit trade. For most of its long-standing history, Hamburg has been not only a city but also an independent state with its own government, postal system, flag and mint. Hamburg conducted its own foreign policy, mainly by signing bilateral commercial treaties all over the world. Through politics of strict neutrality, it managed to maintain its independence against the pressures of much more powerful neighbours, especially Denmark and later Prussia. Hamburg also underwent territorial changes, particularly in the nineteenth century, which are too complicated to discuss in detail in this essay.

The biggest Free Imperial City within the Holy Roman Empire of the German Nation, Hamburg was occupied by Napoleonic troops from 1806 to 1814 and incorporated into the French Empire. After the Congress of Vienna it was one of four free cities of the German Confederation, next to the other 34 sovereign states. In 1867 it forcibly became part of the Prussian-led North German Confederation and four years later a constituent of the German Empire. Only then did it lose its long-standing autonomy and had to relinquish the insignia of independence. Today, Hamburg is one of 16 states of the Federal Republic and Germany's second biggest and richest city.

By the time of the French Revolution Hamburg had well exceeded a population of 100,000 inhabitants. Wars and the Napoleonic occupation slowed the city's development but during the nineteenth century a steady if not dramatic population increase set in, reaching a quarter of a million in 1860.[2] Population gains from the Middle Ages to the middle of the nineteenth century were mainly a result of immigration from Lower Saxony. Only in the first half of the seventeenth century was there more immigration from further away, in particular from people who were persecuted because of their religious beliefs. Dutch who would not change their allegiance to Catholicism were forced by the Spanish to leave the Netherlands and came to Hamburg in larger numbers from 1685. They were very similar to the indigenous population and many had old established trade contacts. These immigrants integrated quickly and at all social levels and they were also put on an approximately equal legal footing, including the right to acquire real estate.[3] Foreign merchants, especially the Dutch but also Portuguese, French, Italians and Sephardic Jews from Portugal and Spain, were allowed to settle because they brought important stimuli for trade and commerce, and not least because they brought contacts and also new techniques and methods with them.[4]

Hamburg was and still is Germany's most important commercial city. Until the early sixteenth century, Lübeck, Germany's pre-eminent Baltic port, was more significant because of the dominance of trade among North and Baltic Sea locations. Then Hamburg profited from the emergence of Spain and Portugal as major players in the European economy. However, because the German lands had no colonies and were economically comparatively weak, Hamburg still focused on transit trade, especially linking Scandinavian and Baltic destinations with the Atlantic economy. American independence allowed the city to build up its first direct commercial connections overseas, to be followed in the eighteenth century by strong links with the newly independent states of South and Central America. In the seventeenth century trade and shipping were the backbone of the city's economy, but other sectors such as sugar refining, train oil manufacture and financial services began to gain ground.[5] Hamburg was also the main place of transhipment for grain exports from Eastern Europe. Its harbour remained largely natural until the middle of the nineteenth century and only then it was enlarged and modernised through the building of basins, quays and warehouses.[6]

In the 40 years leading up to the First World War, Hamburg rapidly developed into a modern metropolis and was firmly established as one of Europe's foremost commercial centres. If transit trade had been the mainstay of the city's economy until the middle of the nineteenth century, Hamburg's harbour now became truly the door to the world of a rapidly industrialising Germany which, from the 1880s, also demonstrated its colonial ambitions and assumed its place as one of Europe's great powers.[7] From the middle of the nineteenth century, Hamburg developed as a regional consumer centre. Its diversity of businesses and occupations was evidenced by the existence of numerous small workshops in the city centre employing skilled artisans, retailers and street-hawkers as well as agents, auctioneers and brokers. In the closing decades of the century chemical and electrical industries, the manufacture of clothing and furniture, food processing and the building industry contributed increasingly to the diversification of Hamburg's economy. In the last year before the First World War, 42 per cent of German imports and 38 per cent of its exports passed through Hamburg where the sector's trade and transportation (39.9 per cent) and industry and manufacturing (36 per cent) were of similar proportions.[8]

As a republican city state with a long-standing civic tradition, Hamburg was run by a self-conscious, independent bourgeoisie. When it lost the title of Free Imperial City in 1806, it assumed the name 'Free Hanseatic City', only to lose that freedom half a year later with the French occupation.[9] After the liberation from Napoleon's troops the official name became 'Free and Hanseatic City', which is still used today.[10]

The city government changed in many details over the centuries but its basic structure can be outlined as follows. The city was run by a council, called 'Senate' from 1860, which was composed of merchants and lawyers. The duration of membership varied, but practically all posts were filled by co-option. The council was controlled by a lower house, the 'Bürgerschaft', in which the propertied middle-class was represented. The two bodies were very often at odds, since they represented different interests. Political participation was mainly based on the ownership of property. It has been estimated that, in about 1800, 3000–4000 citizens could participate, that is, could vote and be voted into office, but since most were not interested in spending time in politics, the city was run by on average 400 individuals, who were supported by a small number of professional bureaucrats. Less than 10 per cent of those entitled to political office actually participated.[11]

The population was graded according to political status. Only full citizens had complete freedom of trade and could use the stock exchange. A second group – scholars, artists and artisans – held a 'minor citizenship' (Kleines Bürgerrecht). The next group were the 'protected dwellers' (Schutzverwandte), who had the right of settlement and of work. Last came the 'strangers' (Fremde). In 1759, 9000 burghers were counted, comprising the first two classes, with 4000 Schutzverwandte and 3300 Fremde (all males with families). Only 15–20 per cent of the population had full civic rights, which could only be acquired by males of Lutheran faith. But because relatives were included, about 70–80 per cent of the population were included.[12] Most important for political participation was wealth and ownership of landed property. Academic merits and certain offices were other prerequisites, but also these usually required wealth.[13]

Religion mattered in Hamburg. The city constitution of 1603 stipulated that adherence to the Lutheran faith was binding for all citizens and that it was the obligation of the state to protect and further this single faith. In the absence of a university until the early twentieth century, the church also had a virtual monopoly on scholarship and education. Religion and politics were inextricably linked and over the next centuries religion was constantly instrumentalised to justify political decisions. In contrast to its neighbouring city of Altona, under Danish rule until the 1860s, Hamburg did not allow non-Lutherans to build their own places of worship or practise their faith openly. Religious minorities were only allowed to live and work within the city under special legislation. The Lutheran clergy particularly used sermons as a strong instrument of the dissemination of their ideas and convictions and could thereby mobilise a strong following for their political aims at any time.[14]

After the Restoration, non-Lutheran Christians were emancipated. This concerned members of the Reformed Church, Mennonites and Catholics, who could become senators, but not members of the civic councils (Bürgerliche Kollegien) since these required adherence to the Lutheran faith.[15] Despite the existence of several religious minority groups, it is important to stress that Hamburg was and still is not a religiously diverse city. In 1910, 91.6 per cent of the inhabitants identified themselves as Protestants – the vast majority Lutheran. By that time, Catholics had become the largest minority, numbering approximately 5 per cent, closely followed by the Jews.

These religious disabilities, suffered by Christians, speak strongly against the existence of a liberal and open environment, which tolerated 'otherness' only partially and when it furthered trade and commerce. A further sign of the closeness and political backwardness of Hamburg can be seen in the way the city handled freedom of trade (*Gewerbefreiheit*). In Prussia and many other states, full freedom of trade was instituted while Napoleon dominated Europe. In Hamburg it came in 1864, although in 1816 a number of sectors close to industry were deregulated.[16] Hamburg depended on free trade for its wealth, but inside the city, economic conditions were by no means regulated by the market economy. It is befitting that the closing of the gates was also abolished only in 1860.[17] Where the mercantile bourgeoisie felt its ability to do business was not threatened, it gave way to the particularistic interests of the petty bourgeoisie.

One could argue that there are other indicators which do point to the existence of a liberal spirit within the city state. Freedom of speech and the press, for example, was comparatively tolerated in Hamburg, especially if compared to other German states. In the eighteenth century there was censorship by the senate but this was usually quite lax. Because of the comparatively free political information it disseminated, the *Hamburgischer Correspondent* became Germany's most influential newspaper in the second half of the eighteenth century.[18] However, even this may be seen as ultimately serving a particular aim, since this partial freedom was in tune with the republican tradition of a polity dependent on the quick dissemination of accurate information in order to be economically viable.

The Historical Experience of Hamburg Jewry

A continuous Jewish presence in Hamburg is documented since 1590, when Sephardic Jews, whose ancestors had left the Iberian Peninsula in the late fifteenth century, had found their way to North Germany, via the south of France and the Netherlands. Hamburg's registry of resident merchants of 1610 lists about 100 'Portuguese', including dependants. Although the immigrants were officially considered Catholics, it was never a secret that they were really Jews. Throughout the seventeenth century their situation was precarious. Most of the Sephardic Jews were working in close conjunction with Spanish and Portuguese merchant houses, an important area of commerce for the city of Hamburg. Many also had important connections to high officials in the Spanish government. Needless to say, they were not allowed to practise their religion or worship in public. They buried their dead in a plot of land they had acquired in Danish Altona. The *Bürgerschaft* and the Lutheran clergy, who also instigated random acts of violence against the Jews, made repeated efforts to have them expelled. The Senate defended their right to dwell in the city and do business. It constantly warned that an expulsion would have a damaging effect on trade. In the 1650s, when the number of the Sephardim had reached 600, the Senate also gave in to their petitions to consecrate a synagogue, not least because it feared that if this were constantly denied they would look elsewhere for a more tolerant location for their business. To ensure their unmolested existence, the Sephardic community also administered self-censorship. No Hebrew books were printed that would upset Hamburg's clergy; ostentatious dress or luxurious festivities and even sleigh rides were forbidden or limited in order not to attract any attention from non-Jews. However, when in 1697 a heavy special contribution and annual taxes were demanded from the 'Portuguese', a number of influential families began to leave Hamburg for Amsterdam. This exodus marked the beginning of a continuous decline of the Sephardic community, which by the time of the French occupation numbered only 200 people, most of them of modest financial means. The community never again flourished, and it was finally completely destroyed in the Nazi period.[19]

Ashkenazim first settled in the early seventeenth century in Altona, which was under Danish control. Until well into the nineteenth century, they were *Schutzjuden* [protected Jews] who, against payment of a special annual tax, were granted the right to settle, work and practise religion. From the start, many Jews from Altona went to do business in neighbouring Hamburg, and from the middle of the seventeenth century some gradually managed to settle there. Like the Sephardim, they were only allowed to worship in private gatherings. A law of 1710, the so-called 'Jew regulation', determined in 23 articles the rights and status of Ashkenazic and Sephardic Jews in Hamburg until well into the nineteenth century. In the middle of the eighteenth century most Ashkenazim were economically active in trade and money-lending or early forms of banking. The spectrum included peddlers as well as immensely rich merchants dealing in large-scale imports and exports. Apart from that there were a few Jewish artisans in crafts not limited by guilds, and a larger group of Jews who provided services for the community. Whenever Jews were openly attacked by what contemporary sources characterise as 'the rabble' of the city, they resorted to demanding and obtaining protection from the state, and troublemakers were commonly sentenced by the city courts.[20]

During the brief French interlude in the early nineteenth century, when Hamburg contained Germany's largest Jewish community with approximately 6,000 people, the Jews had obtained equal rights, and some had even begun to engage in municipal politics. After the liberation of the city in 1814, however, Jewish emancipation was immediately revoked and the 'Jew regulation' of 1710 reinstated. It has to be borne in mind that the lack of civic rights involved more than a denial of political participation. It meant that Jews could not own businesses in their own name or acquire real estate as individuals. Only as members of their corporations (Gemeinden) could they claim legal privileges. The absence of civic rights thus impacted on every aspect of Jewish economic and social existence.

A feature that accompanied the struggle to achieve equal rights was Reform Judaism, and Hamburg was one of its cradles. Inspired by Berlin predecessors, the New Israelite Temple Association (Neuer Israelitischer Tempel-Verein) was founded in 1817. It incorporated into the services a German sermon and some prayers in the vernacular. Initially, less than 10 per cent of Hamburg Jewry, approximately 100 families, were attracted by the new institution. They came predominantly from the Jewish middle class of the city, whereas the 'old wealth' of the community shunned the Tempel-Verein, at least in its early years. Religious forms closer to Christian worship would, as some Jews hoped, also promote their quest for civic equality.[21]

On a practical level, the issue of emancipation was revived in 1833 when a group of Hamburg Jews formed a committee which prompted the community to petition the government for an alteration of the 'Jew laws'. A governmental review of the conditions of the Jews came to nothing. Only in the 1840s, and in particular after the great fire of 1842 which destroyed much of Hamburg's city centre, did the Jews experience some improvements in their situation, albeit in a piecemeal fashion. A decisive change occurred only with the Revolution of 1848, which was non-violent in Hamburg and was determined mainly by outside events. The Hamburg government would not accept the 'basic rights' of the Frankfurt National Assembly but insisted in passing its own law, the Provisional Decree of 1849. When the revolution collapsed a year later and all laws passed in Frankfurt were annulled, Hamburg had a decree guaranteeing religious equality in its constitution and did not attempt to revoke it. While the Jews obtained rights as individuals, which enabled them among other things to acquire citizenship, the legal position of their corporations was left untouched. Finally, in 1860 a new constitution disconnected all civic rights from religion, and the protracted emancipation process of Hamburg Jewry was finally achieved. Only then was the nightly gate closure abolished, which enabled wealthier Jews, who had settled predominantly in one part of the city centre (the Neustadt) to buy houses in the newly accessible districts of Eimsbüttel, Rotherbaum, and Harvestehude.[22]

Once the Jews had attained civic emancipation, the city government intended to radically reform the structure of the Jewish communities. A law in early 1865 abolished compulsory community membership, and the Gemeinden were relived of the duties to uphold their own poor welfare, sick care and schools. However, on the part of the communities, there was no desire to abolish the structure that for centuries had held Jews together and cared for their needs. A most innovative and radical compromise evolved. One communal organisation continued to exist which was still responsible for schools, welfare and burials, yet within it two independent associations were instituted. The Reform association, *Tempelverband*, was joined by an Orthodox association, the *Synagogenverband*. Communal institutions were run in a way that did not offend the Orthodox element, and marriages, burials, and circumcisions were usually conducted according to Orthodox rites.[23]

Throughout the nineteenth century Hamburg Jewry grew at a steady pace, though increments were never dramatic. The proportion of Jews among the city's inhabitants declined, since the non-Jewish population grew faster than the minority which became increasingly middle-class and accordingly followed a specific demographical pattern. At the beginning of the First World War approximately 19,000 Jews lived in Hamburg, a community by then soundly eclipsed by the Jewry of Berlin, the capital. Eastern European Jewish immigration did not add significantly to this number, although the issue was of special significance to Hamburg's Jewish and also non-Jewish citizens. It illuminates further the comparatively uneasy existence of the minority in the city.

Hamburg was, next to Bremen, Germany's main centre of Eastern European transmigration, especially between 1870 and 1914 when over 2.3 million people passed through Hamburg and its harbour on the way to North and South America and a number of other destinations. A large proportion of the migrants were Jews from various Eastern European countries; however, exact figures are difficult to obtain. One estimate is that in the four years preceding the First World War, 130,000 Jewish travellers departed from Hamburg alone. In the context of this volume, it is important to stress that most inhabitants of Hamburg had little or no contact with this huge number of foreigners. The migrants arrived by train in specially built reception areas at the harbour and most of them remained there for a few days before their ships were ready to leave. In the vicinity of the harbour, many private pensions (boarding houses) offered somewhat more comfortable accommodation for those migrants who could afford it. The number of migrants who stayed on in Hamburg was extremely small. In the case of the Jews, the 1910 census classified as foreigners just over 3000 individuals who constituted 16 per cent of Hamburg's Jews, and by no means all of them were from Eastern Europe. The community supported the city wholeheartedly in its effort to keep the number of immigrants as low as possible.[24] It is thus fair to say that immigration did not contribute to a cosmopolitan environment.

Minority–Majority Relations and Toleration

For most of its existence, Hamburg was an independent political entity. Hamburg's relation to the Jews was obviously influenced by the politics of other German states, but ultimately the politically active class of the city were responsible for the treatment of the minority. Thus, Hamburg is a case in which a mercantile and maritime environment can be studied that was, for much of its history, not part of a larger political entity which provided its legal framework or one that merely communicated political decisions.

Hamburg was dependent on trade and good contacts with the outside world. Its politics were strongly dominated by mercantile interests. Germany's door to the world despatched and received goods to and from all continents and its merchants corresponded with the entire world. The question is: did these factors create an open, liberal and cosmopolitan environment? The ultimate test case to answer such a question is the treatment of non-dominant religious groups. Therefore it needs to be asked whether Hamburg was tolerant towards the Jews and whether it was a good place to live in if you were a Jew. These two questions, although they sound complementary, need to be answered separately.

First of all, Hamburg was by no means tolerant towards the Jews nor, for most of its history, towards any other religious minority. Sephardic settlers were admitted purely because of their economic utility, and on numerous occasions the city council had to defend their presence against the conflicting interests of the church and a large part of the middle class. The emancipation process was as protracted in Hamburg as in nearly all other German states, and civic equality came to the Jews as a by-product of general political changes and not because Hamburg's citizenry was keen on changing the status of the minority. Sporadic anti-Jewish violence, although not in an organised form, was a regular occurrence of early modern times and until well into the nineteenth century. Anti-semitic parties managed to gain some ground in the late nineteenth and early twentieth century, and were just as successful or unsuccessful as in other German locations of comparable social structure.

Apart from reasons based on general Jew-hatred or anti-semitism, Hamburg had difficulty accepting a minority such as the Jews because of two circumstances: (1) the long-standing tradition of an independent republican city state run by a closed oligarchy of birth and property that was practically impenetrable; and (2) the strong position of the Lutheran church which influenced politics and society well beyond the time of disestablishment, which also made it difficult to impossible for non-Lutheran Christians to become part of Hamburg's establishment.

But was Hamburg a good place for Jews to live? Perhaps yes. A city that so emphasised commerce and trade necessarily provided a good environment for those many Jews who engaged in commercial activities and who thus not only contributed significantly to the economic well-being of the city but also became well off and in some instances immensely wealthy. In the middle decades of the nineteenth century, parallel to the process of formal emancipation, the majority of the Jews joined the middle class. If one therefore defines an open and tolerant environment as one that generated a stable legal framework which protected economic interests for everyone, regardless of creed or religion, then Hamburg was a perfectly tolerant place. For a Jew who did not aspire to political participation but was mainly interested in quietly furthering his business, Hamburg was certainly a good place to live, even before the age of emancipation. If, however, 'tolerance' is meant to encompass not only mutual respect and understanding of non-conformist lifestyles, and religious belief and practice that deviates from the majority, but also the deconstruction of legal and political barriers based on such differences, then Hamburg was certainly an intolerant city that did not provide a congenial living environment for Jews.

The dual facts that Hamburg was Germany's largest Jewish community in the early nineteenth century, and the predominantly middle-class makeup of Hamburg Jewry from the middle of the nineteenth century, indicate that adherents to the minority voted with their feet to declare the city a desirable environment. Yet, while Jews were accepted as part of the Hamburg mercantile group, they were not accepted or tolerated as a religious minority, let alone were they integrated on any level but the economic, be it politically, culturally or socially. Two examples of this partial and selective integration are arguably Hamburg's most successful and high-profile Jewish businessmen in the late nineteenth and early twentieth centuries: Albert Ballin, the director of the HAPAG shipping line, and the banker Max M. Warburg. Both these well-honoured citizens based their social lives largely on Jewish circles and were on numerous occasions made aware of their social inferiority based on their religious allegiance – this despite the fact that Ballin had virtually no interest in Jewish matters and had a non-Jewish wife, while Warburg only involved himself in community affairs for reasons that could be characterised as noblesse oblige.[25]

Thus the question whether the port city of Hamburg was also a haven for the Jews is not all that easy to answer. One could develop the thought further. Is tolerance in the sense of wholeheartedly accepting 'otherness' really so decisive for the flourishing of a minority? Is even the absence of tolerance in the sense of equal opportunities in the political or economic spheres an insurmountable obstacle for the thriving existence of a religious minority? Doubts to an affirmative answer may be entertained if one regards the great cultural productivity of Eastern European Jewry in the nineteenth and early twentieth centuries, when this minority was most harshly oppressed in numerous spheres of everyday life. True, many Eastern European Jews voted with their feet and left for a more 'tolerant' climate overseas, although, some may argue, that also came at a price.

NOTES

1. Developments after 1933 will not be regarded but may be included in a further contribution of the 'Port Jews' project.
2. Gerhard Ahrens, 'Von der Franzosenzeit bis zur Verabschiedung der neuen Verfassung, 1806–1860', in Werner Jochmann and Hans-Dieter Loose (eds.), *Hamburg: Geschichte der Stadt und ihrer Bewohner*, Vol.I, pp.415–90 (p.484).
3. Hans-Dieter Loose, 'Das Zeitalter der Bürgerunruhen und der großen europäischen Kriege, 1816–1712', in Werner Jochmann and Hans-Dieter Loose (eds.) (see note 2), pp.259–350 (pp.265–6); Jürgen Ellermeyer, 'Zu Handel, Hafen und Grundeigentum Hamburgs im 17. und 18. Jahrhundert', in Jürgen Ellermeyer and Rainer Postel (eds.), *Stadt und Hafen. Hamburger Beiträge zur Geschichte von Handel und Schiffahrt* (Hamburg, 1986), pp.58–79 (p.60).
4. Loose (see note 3), p.311.
5. Ibid., p.328.
6. Ahrens (see note 2), p.463–4.
7. Antje Kraus, *Die Unterschichten Hamburgs in der ersten Hälfte des 19. Jahrhunderts. Entstehung, Struktur und Lebensverhältnisse* (Stuttgart, 1965), pp.20–21.
8. Rainer Liedtke, *Jewish Welfare in Hamburg and Manchester, c. 1850–1914* (Oxford: Oxford University Press, 1998), p.23.
9. Franklin Kopitzsch, 'Zwischen Hauptrezeß und Franzosenzeit, 1712–1806', in Werner Jochmann and Hans-Dieter Loose (eds.) (see note 3), pp.351–414 (p.357).
10. Ahrens (see note 2), p.431.
11. Kopitzsch (see note 9), pp.359–60. Richard Evans, in his masterly study of the cholera outbreak of 1892, has argued strongly that an incompetent municipal government was largely responsible for the epidemic reaching catastrophic proportions. Richard J. Evans, *Death in Hamburg: Society and Politics in the Cholera Years 1830–1910* (London: Penguin, 1987), especially pp.372–402.
12. Loose, (see note 3), p.266.

13. Kopitzsch (see note 9), pp.367–9.
14. Loose (see note 3), pp.335–6.
15. Ahrens (see note 2), p.435
16. Ibid., p.450.
17. Ibid., p.485.
18. Kopitzsch (see note 9), pp.352, 408.
19. Günter Böhm, 'Die Sephardim in Hamburg', in Arno Herzig (ed.), *Die Juden in Hamburg, 1590–1990* (Hamburg: Dölling und Galitz, 1991), pp.21–40.
20. Günter Marwedel, 'Die aschkenasischen Juden im Hamburger Raum (bis 1780)', in Arno Herzig (ed.) (see note 19), pp.41–60.
21. Michael A. Meyer, *Response to Modernity: A History of the Reform Movement in Judaism*, (Oxford: Oxford University Press, 1988), pp.53–61.
22. A detailed account of the emancipation controversy can be found in Moshe Zimmermann, *Hamburgischer Patriotismus und deutscher Nationalismus* (Hamburg, 1979).
23. Ina Lorenz, *Identität und Assimilation: Hamburgs Juden in der Weimarer Republik*, (Hamburg: Dölling und Galitz, 1989), pp.xxiv–xxxv.
24. For a more general appreciation of the reaction of organised German Jewry to the immigration and transmigration issues see Jack Wertheimer, *Unwelcome Strangers: East European Jews in Imperial Germany* (Oxford: Oxford University Press, 1987), especially pp.162–75.
25. A more detailed analysis, in particular of Warburg's community relations, which became somewhat more animated towards the end of the Weimar Republic see Rainer Liedtke, 'Zur mäzenatischen Praxis und zum kulturellen Selbstverständnis der jüdischen Wirtschaftselite in Deutschland. Die Hamburger Warburgs im ersten Drittel des 20. Jahrhunderts', in Dieter Ziegler (ed.), *Großbürger und Unternehmer: Die deutsche Wirtschaftselite im 20. Jahrhundert* (Göttingen Vandenhoeck & Ruprecht, 2000), pp.187–203.

A Tale of Two Port Jewish Communities: Southampton and Portsmouth Compared

TONY KUSHNER

Did Portsmouth and Southampton contain port Jewries? At a basic and obvious level, the two south coast of England towns are ports and both have had and continue to have a Jewish presence. The rise of Jewish settlements in these Hampshire towns in the eighteenth and early nineteenth centuries was directly or indirectly connected to their spectacular developments as ports: one naval, the other commercial. Were they, however, Jews who lived in ports or port Jews? The concept of 'port Jewry' or 'port Jews' has been developed by Lois Dubin in her classic study of Habsburg Trieste and by David Sorkin more thematically as a 'social type'. Dubin has made a plea to expand the geographical scope in the understanding of the cultural, religious and political dynamics of European Jewry at the dawn of the modern era: 'we need not a tale of two cities, Berlin and Paris, but one that includes a third city, Trieste, or perhaps a third and fourth city in tandem: Trieste and Vienna'.[1] Sorkin has also attempted to shift the historiographical focus more broadly, working against what he refers to as the '"ashkenazification" of modern Jewish history'.[2] Yet in spite of these inclusive tendencies, the concept of port Jew they have constructed ultimately remains elitist, confined by place, period, social type and intellectual achievement. Sorkin, for example, defines the social type of port Jew by five characteristics, limiting them to a Sephardi trade network coming out of the expulsion in 1492. They flourished, he argues, in specific ports, representing 'a particular experience of early modern Europe and a particular path to modernity'.[3]

Under these rules of entry, it is clear that neither of the Hampshire ports qualifies for membership of this elite club. They do not, for example, have their origins in the early modern period nor, in spite of the presence of some individuals of Spanish and Portuguese origin, could they be described in essence as Sephardi communities. Indeed, it was argued by the Anglo-Jewish historian, journalist and communal activist Lucien Wolf that the attempt by the Corporation of London in the 1670s and thereafter to keep out poor Jews of Ashkenazi origin 'gave an impulse to the formation of provincial communities, especially at Portsmouth and Hull': in this sense Portsmouth in Wolf's analysis was a counter-port Jew community.[4] Fundamentally, the studies of Dubin and Sorkin are about elite Jews operating at a sophisticated commercial, intellectual and cultural level, one that the Jews of Portsmouth and Southampton rarely attained. And yet I will argue that they offer valuable insights into the concept of the port Jew, but one that has to be extended to cover a later chronology and within it issues of class, ethnicity and the notion of permanence against fluidity in the modern Jewish experience.[5]

Communities such as Portsmouth and Southampton suffer a quadruple marginality. First, they are part of the history of the Jews in Britain which has until recently been regarded within Jewish studies as an intellectual and cultural backwater.[6] Second, they suffer the intellectual snobbery of so-called mainstream historians of Britain who have not regarded immigrants and minority groups, including Jews, as worthy of attention. As David Cannadine, director of the Institute of Historical Research in London, has put it, assimilating the patronising approach of Jewish studies but adding to it a British historiographical sneer, 'In the context of international Jewry, the history of British Jewry is neither very interesting, nor very exciting. In the context of British history, it is just not that important.'[7] Third, within British Jewish studies they are subsumed in importance due to the understandable but still limiting concentration on London. Although a maximum of two-thirds of the British Jewish community since the readmission have lived in the capital, the work of local historians has still not changed the assumption that for the United Kingdom read London. There is a need in British Jewish studies for the equivalent of Norman Davies' The Isles, which both brings what has been seen and treated as the peripheral regions of Britain into the mainstream of historical narrative and puts the British history firmly into the European experience.[8]

The fourth and final aspect of marginalisation relates to the second and third. Local studies are regarded as the poor relations of British historiography with an informal hierarchy of kudos evolving, in growing order of importance and prestige, from the local to the national and finally, the global.[9] Sadly, however, until recently local studies have followed the national example and ignored ethnic and racial diversity. It is ironic that Leicester, the home of English local studies at university level, has totally ignored minority history in a city that is predicted to be the first in Britain to have a non-white majority.[10]

Single, double, triple or even quadruple marginality is, of course, no proof on its own that the subject matter is worthy of study. On the surface, a case can be made for Portsmouth Jewry having a degree of importance if not precisely in the Dubin-Sorkin model then with echoes of it. Post-readmission, it was probably the oldest and initially most substantial British Jewish settlement outside London (itself a Sorkin-approved 'port Jewry'),[11] dating from the 1740s as a formal community.[12] By the mid-nineteenth century it had a Jewish population of some 300, making it the fourth largest provincial community in the country.[13] It had a close and important relationship with the Royal Navy and has a particular though unnoticed significance in that it provided the intellectual and cultural background to produce the Moss sisters, Cecile and Marion, and Katie Magnus – some of the earliest Jewish women novelists and historical writers on a world stage, whose work will be explored briefly later in this article.[14]

On the religious level, Portsmouth was unique in Britain in having its own college 'for the training and maintenance of young men...as Jewish divines on Orthodox principles'. It was the inspiration of Lewis Aria who was 'of humble Portsea parents and was one of several enterprising Portsmouth Jews who emigrated to the West Indies possibly influenced by the Navy's connections with that part of the world'. Aria made his money as a Jamaican merchant and left part of his wealth to set up the college which opened in 1874. While there is little evidence that any of the rabbis trained at Aria College became great religious thinkers, the geographical range of the positions they were occupying by the end of the nineteenth century *was* remarkable and fitting given the international connections of Portsmouth. By 1900 Aria-trained ministers were at work in South Africa (two), Jamaica, and Australia as well as in Britain itself in Liverpool and London. Aria, if of poor pedlar and probably German origin, was in a sense a latter-day port Jew of the Dubin-Sorkin mode, with his New World mercantile wealth, attachment to his place of birth and desire to help the advancement and public welfare of world Jewry through the products of his college.[15] Moreover, Michael Galchinsky, in his study of Victorian Jewish women writers, goes as far as describing the Moss sisters as 'the unacknowledged Mendelssohns of England'.[16] Yet it would be wrong to push such analogies to the early modern port Jewries too far. If Portsmouth's Jewish minority has a deeper significance as a collectivity, it has to be beyond some of the remarkable characters associated with it.

Indeed, a similarly elite exercise in the case of Southampton would fail to create any particular justification for the study of its Jewish community, established formally in the 1860s and with an estimated Jewish population of 75 in 1850.[17] Apart from being one of the ports in which the Jews were expelled from medieval England in 1290, and, according to David Katz, even with a connection to the 'unofficial' Jewish community of the sixteenth century, when Christopher Fernandes acted as its 'intelligence service' by meeting 'the Portuguese spice ships stopping at Southampton and Plymouth to give the Marranos information about the current political and religious climate which would await them in Antwerp',[18] its only major claim to fame in standard narratives of early readmission Anglo-Jewish history was its status as the town in which a Jew was first elected in Britain as a councillor – in 1838.[19] In the late nineteenth century through to his death in the 1930s, Claude Montefiore was loosely connected to the Southampton Jewish community as he resided nearby – the only Jew in Britain to create a new form of formal Jewish religious identity, Liberal Judaism.[20]

It would be distorting to dismiss these elite connections of great men and women in the cultural and religious sphere and to ignore the often remarkable contribution of the Jews locally, nationally and globally to political, economic and civic life. Yet such a top-down approach has dominated the limited interest in these towns from the scholars that typified Anglo-Jewish history in the late nineteenth century and the first half of the twentieth century, Lucien Wolf and his protegé, Cecil Roth. Both saw their potential in portraying Jews in a positive light – as loyal contributors to the defence of the realm and to local society. Roth, in a paper on 'Jews in the Defence of Britain' published in 1940, which featured the role of Portsmouth Jews in Nelson's ships, started by saying it was necessary for him 'to point out that to consider the military ability of the Jew negligible is not only erroneous but is in diametrical opposition to the facts'.[21] Such defensiveness continued as late as 1989 in Geoffrey Green's award- winning *The Royal Navy and Anglo-Jewry* which concluded that after the Napoleonic Wars, especially through the role of Portsmouth Jewry, this naval contribution was rewarded in the granting of civic equality:

> By 1820 a tradition of Jewish service in, and trading with, the Royal Navy had been established. One important result was that a small number of relatively poor Jews had come into direct and continuous contact with the wider indigenous population. A small contribution had been made by the Jews in their connections with the Royal Navy towards the wider aspirations of the Anglo-Jewish community. The beginning of the quest for emancipation of British Jewry was not far away.[22]

The apologetic approach of British Jewish historiography and its focus on great men (and the occasional great woman) will generally be avoided here. Instead, I want to offer the case studies of Southampton and Portsmouth as, in essence, history from below, providing a contrast to the potential exclusivity associated with what might become the classic port Jew study. In the two examples chosen, communities were largely founded and maintained by Jews of poor itinerant status, some of whom progressed into the lower middle and middle classes and were joined by an even smaller number of elite Jews operating on the outside edges. I want to suggest, however, that in spite of their humble origins, the Jews of Portsmouth and Southampton had something in common with their earlier and more magnificent predecessors in the ports of Europe and the New World (and even with earlier Jewish communities in the ports of antiquity and the Middle Ages).[23] In short, rather than being two among many of the small, neglected Jewish communities created in towns by Jews of central and then eastern European Jewish origin during the eighteenth and nineteenth centuries in Britain and beyond, their port connection is important, perhaps even vital, in explaining their very nature. They are not, I will argue – returning to the question raised at the start of this article – simply Jews who happen to live in ports but communities whose lives and identities were shaped by the ports, even when they wanted to escape such identification.

My approach has been influenced by those such as Bill Williams in his history of Manchester Jewry who places that experience firmly within the wider history of the city. As Williams emphasises, 'in no sense can the Jewish community be regarded as "alien" to Manchester. It was not a late addition to an established pattern of urban life, but an integral part of the pattern itself'.[24] It has also, however, been deeply influenced by historical geographers such as Doreen Massey and their work on place and identity. In the past, local studies were justified by how typical or not they were in representing larger, but essentially national tendencies. The historical profession with its metropolitan bias has been prejudiced against such studies, no matter how good the attempt to argue that what happened at Nether Wallop was in fact true of the country as a whole. While almost all of the religious, cultural, social and political trends in wider British Jewish history can be illustrated through the specific prisms of Portsmouth and Southampton from the mid-eighteenth century to the present day, this is not the approach I will generally be adopting.

In newer, multi- and inter-disciplinary approaches to local studies within geography, such narrow constraints of meeting what might be termed the typicality challenge are less severe. As Doreen Massey and Pat Jess argue,

'Places' – their character and the differences between them – continue to matter: they matter to capital which exploits the different characteristics of place – in other words, uneven development; and they matter to people because of our senses of belonging and identification, and the quality of our geographical imaginations.[25]

Moreover, the importance of the *typicality* rather than the *significance* of place breaks down when an exclusive national perspective is problematised. Massey emphasises that the 'local uniqueness' of places 'is always already a product of wider contacts; the local is always a product in part of "global" forces, where global in this context refers not necessarily to the planetary scale, but to the geographical beyond, the world beyond the place itself.'[26]

Massey' concludes that 'The attempt to align "us" and "them" with the general concepts of "local" and "global" is always deeply problematical. For in the historical and geographical constructions of places, the "other" in general terms is already within. The global is everywhere and already, in one way or another, implicated in the local.'[27] I want to tentatively argue at this stage that in the case of Southampton and even more so initially but increasingly far less so, Portsmouth, local Jewish identities were shaped by the attempt to avoid the label of the 'global' other. Yet no matter how 'well-behaved', integrated and civically minded, these Jewish communities could not avoid an association of cosmopolitanism that all seaport communities possessed in Britain.[28]

W.H. Hudson, one of the leading travel writers and naturalists in Victorian and Edwardian Britain, whose book *Hampshire Days* (1903)[29] continues to be republished by Oxford University Press and the local heritage industry,[30] shows the potential of this othering process to exclude. In the book Hudson, a close friend of many British 'race scientists',[31] identified 'four distinct Hampshire types', descended he believed from ancient peoples from the neolithic tribes through to the Danes who came to the county. His ethnographic study, however, was limited to the 'true natives of the soil'. He added that 'There was little profit in looking at the townspeople. The big coast towns [of Southampton and Portsmouth] ha[d] a population as heterogeneous as that of the metropolis.'[32] It should be added that Hampshire itself has a deeper significance in constructions of British national identity. According to the leading travel writer of inter-war Britain, H.V. Morton, Winchester, its county town, was the place to look 'for the germ of the British empire. The princes of this city emerged from their long war with the Danes as the Kings of Wessex, who later became the Kings of England; ...it was the royal city of Winchester which was truly the very heart of England.' Morton's best-selling *In Search of England* was, as he put it, the pursuit 'of a common racial heritage'. He thus contrasted the essentially quiet and unchanging Winchester, where 'a thrush was singing in the cathedral limes', with the disquieting, grey and noisy port of Southampton with its streets thronging with steerage passengers huddled together with their meagre possessions, 'Irish, English, Jews and Italians' looking 'like a herd of scared cattle'.[33]

Morton was not alone. Another writer described Hampshire's history and landscape as representing 'the most *English* of English counties' and 'the cradle of our race'. Yet crucially the mongrelised town of Portsmouth with its naval connection, and Southampton with its commercial port, remained outside such essentialised constructions. The same commentator, writing as late as 1940, put it succinctly: 'There is not much Hampshire in Southampton. Voices from every corner of the globe, but few, very few from Hampshire.' Southampton, he concluded, was simply 'not Hampshire' because 'it [was] cosmopolitan'.[34]

For much of the nineteenth century, Jews in Portsmouth carried this stigma. Here is a description from 1846, but relating to an earlier period, of its principal and notorious dock area where most of the local Jews lived and traded:

The Point was...famous for the dwellings of those kind-hearted children of Israel who supplied the wants of the seamen at the moderate interest of about five hundred per cent. Talk of your London Jews – keen as they are – a Point Jew would have cheated a dozen of them in an hour. The sea-line of this neck of land was prepared as a fortification, and its semicircular arches used to remind me of an enormous mouse-trap.[35]

Another account of the same district from 1844 by when it had changed markedly, and significantly by an author not unsympathetic to the Jews, indicates how much taken for granted and unchanging such associations had become. A guidebook description of the streets of Portsea broke off into verse without comment:

In line with [the streets] is found the busy hive
Where Israel's sons their various traffic drive
And many a gazing passenger is caught
With treasures rich as those from Egypt brought.[36]

And yet it would be wrong to conclude that such imagined cosmopolitanism was merely negative. For others, there was a freedom and excitement of port 'mongrelisation'. It was expressed most infamously by the novelist Howard Spring writing in 1939 about his memories of Butetown, the sailortown part of Cardiff, before the First World War:

> There was a fascination in the walk through Tiger Bay. Chinks and
> Dagos, Lascars and Levantines slippered about the faintly evil by-ways
> that ran off from Bute Street. The whole place was a warren of
> seamen's boarding houses, dubious hotels, ships' chandlers smelling of
> rope and tarpaulin...children of the strangest colours, fruit of frightful
> mesalliances, staggered half-naked about the streets... It was a dirty,
> smelly, rotten and romantic district, an offence and an inspiration and
> I loved it.[37]

The disreputable Tiger Bay was clearly the 'respectable' city of Cardiff's
geographical and ethnographic 'other', representing more generally in
British society the fear and danger of 'race mixing'.[38]

Images of Southampton and Portsmouth by the start of the twentieth
century were somewhat less racialised than Tiger Bay which had gained
a national and international infamy for its alleged vice and violence.
Indeed, it could be argued that within the towns there seems to have been
some acceptance of diversity, although such a positive assessment needs
to be treated cautiously – in 1919, for example, there was intermittent
violence against Southampton's Lascar seamen, though nothing to
compare to the murderous racist riots that swept some of Britain's other
seaports that year, especially Cardiff and Liverpool.[39] Nevertheless, a
tantalising glimpse of everyday acceptance was provided by a description
from a visitor to Southampton in 1909: 'In the streets near the docks a
rare medley of peoples, races, and languages are to be met with. Lascars,
Norwegians, Japanese, and many others jostle one another, and pass
unnoticed – too familiar a sight here to excite remark.'[40] But alongside the
essential ambivalence towards diversity in towns such as Portsmouth and
Southampton – made up of the fear and fascination that emerged from
racialised constructions on the one hand and, on the other, the more
mundane reality where people of different backgrounds met on an
everyday level – was the nitty-gritty of political economy.

Not surprisingly, Southampton, which expanded massively in the
second half of the nineteenth century as a modern dock, was a town that
was naturally drawn to the free movement of goods.[41] As the
Southampton Times put it in 1905: 'Everyone who desires that
Southampton should remain steadfast and true to the principles of Free
Trade. Protection means ruin'.[42] As the century drew to a close, it
benefited increasingly not just from commercial trade in goods but also
from the international movement in people – emigrants from Britain as
well as transmigrants from southern and eastern Europe hoping to
improve their lot in the New World. Its response to the many thousands
of aliens who were present in its midst was also ambivalent.

Transmigrancy was a lucrative business but the aliens were not necessarily desirable in themselves. The response from the 1890s through to the 1920s, the point at which immigration controls in the West brought transmigrancy to a halt, was for the town, often in combination with the American authorities who had an important status through the locally stationed consul, as well as the shipping companies, to segregate the aliens and to make sure they were medically monitored and kept out of contact with the surrounding population.[43] Yet in the 1900s both Liberals and Conservatives in the area opposed the aliens legislation for fear of damaging the local economy, sometimes in the process revealing a sensitivity to those escaping foreign oppression: 'God forbid that they should refuse help to such a man as that in distress' as one Southampton Liberal put it.[44]

The situation in Portsmouth as a naval town was perhaps slightly different. Protectionism and nationalism at the turn of the twentieth century onwards may have made the town less sympathetic to the free movement of peoples – there was, for example, a more powerful anti-alien/anti-semitic movement in the town in the inter-war period with links to the naval presence.[45] Yet any anti-alienism before 1914 certainly did not stop the increase in the town's Jewish population which doubled in the years from the 1870s through to the start of the First World War – some 200 families approximating to 500 in total by the turn of the century. Hundreds of tailors were recruited from the East End of London as Portsmouth boomed, a result of the escalating naval race between Britain and Germany.[46]

By 1914, therefore, two different types of port Jew communities developed between the rival close neighbours of Southampton and Portsmouth. The settled Jewish community of Southampton was much smaller, roughly 100, and only a handful of east European Jews at the turn of the century settled there – in contrast to Portsmouth it had few openings in the classic immigrant trades such as tailoring and furniture making. It was, for the large part, a community of small shopkeepers, a few professionals and a small (but relatively prominent given its overall size) presence of Jewish aristocrats from the Montefiore, Rothschild and Swaythling families. The contribution of the last mentioned group to the local community was financial rather than through involvement in everyday social and religious life. Its minister remarked in 1895 that these upper-class Jews rarely if ever attended the synagogue and thus could 'hardly be called Southamptonians'.[47] What it did have, however, was a huge presence of Jewish transmigrants in the town and its close vicinity – numbering at any one time several thousands from the 1890s through to 1914. For example, in a two-month period in 1904, just under 8,000 aliens passed through the port, the majority of them being east European Jews.[48] In the 1920s the movement of transmigrants was still important in the port but the problems associated with this essentially fluid presence were exposed when some 1000 Jews got caught by American restrictionism in 1923 and remained interned near the town for up to seven years unable to move on, go back 'home' or stay in Britain.[49]

Yet, in spite of their very different origins and development, both Jewish communities at the level of authority, largely though not exclusively defined through the synagogue and synagogue-related committees, were united by a craving for respectability and acceptance from the society around them. In response and in contrast to the somewhat colourful life of some of its co-religionists in the town before, during and after the Napoleanic wars, it has been suggested that 'in the Portsmouth Synagogue all was exemplary – decorum reigned supreme. No one was allowed to talk, or to leave his seat'. Nor was good behaviour limited to the synagogue. Trading with Navy boats on the Sabbath was subject to huge self-imposed fines. In a town such as Portsmouth, manifestation of loyalty to the crown was crucial, especially against the allegations that Jewish traders were swindling 'innocent' patriotic sailors. Its minister in 1907, Reverend I.E. Meisels, was struck by the severity and comprehensiveness of his synagogue's rules and regulations 100 years earlier. As he suggested, duty, the need to avoid a profanation of the Name of God and the desire 'to preserve the name of Jew pure and unsullied' was 'the pivot round which everything else [in the late eighteenth and early nineteenth century] turn[ed]'.[50]

As the port Jewish hawkers and pedlars increasingly settled down after the Napoleonic Wars and became small shopkeepers, or simply left the town as its boom period ended, many to make their fortunes in the furthest reaches of the British empire and America (when the Jewish community of Ohio was formally established in 1824, half its committee had come from Portsmouth),[51] a more settled community emerged obsessed not only with its current respectability but also its earlier reputation. Such concerns about the past were not without foundation. The rapid transformation of Portsmouth Jewry from a transient and somewhat rough and tough trading community at the turn of the nineteenth century into model, industrious citizens post-1815 was not always matched by contemporary imagery. For example, the immensely popular naval author, Captain Marryat, composed his successful and much reprinted novel, *Peter Simple*, in 1834. Set in the Napoleonic era, it featured 'a Jew of Portsmouth' who swindles a sailor by selling him a gold seal which proved to be copper and other stereotypical Jews exploiting those on board a navy ship.[52] Even more virulent descriptions of the Jews relating to the Napoleonic War, but published several decades later, occurred in William Robinson's *Jack Nastyface, the Memoirs of an English Seamen* (1836) and Matthew Barker's *Jem Bunt* (1841), continuing a hostile tradition evident in naval ballads and other forms of popular culture. Taken together, in such representations 'The Jew was blamed for excessive prices on faulty goods, and outlandish interest on money lent, a butt for the authorities keeping the seamen in low pay and not allowing them ashore for fear of desertion.'[53]

It is thus perhaps no coincidence in the light of such specific imagery and the ongoing national debate about civic emancipation that Portsmouth was to produce in the Moss sisters, authors of *The Romance of Jewish History* (1840) and *Tales of Jewish History* (1843), the first Victorian Jewish women's writers. Their apologetic approach 'tended to associate Jewish women with heroic national liberation...historicizing the suffering Jewess' in a manner designed to gain sympathy from general society.[54] Their representations of the Jewish past were thus the reverse of those of the effeminate, untrustworthy port Jews which circulated contemporaniously at a national level, or indeed of Portsmouth's most famous son, Charles Dickens, and his creation of the diabolic Fagin (literary descendent of the most infamous anti-semitic representation of the port Jew, Shylock) in *Oliver Twist* (1838).[55] At a local level, Jews were involved in more mundane literature, subscribing to the publication of Henry Slight's *Chronicles of Portsmouth* (1828) which in contrast to earlier sensationalism, limited mention of the Jewish community to a description of the synagogue, doing so in a sober, matter-of-fact manner, and assimilating it within an account of the architecture of all the religious buildings of Portsmouth and Portsea.[56]

The battle over the reputation as well as the imagery associated with Portsmouth Jewry is well-illustrated by the progress of two parallel Emanuel families of German Jewish origin who, it has been suggested, 'dominated the Anglo-Jewish scene in Portsmouth for almost the entire nineteenth century'.[57] Abraham Leon Emanuel, JP, was elected to the town council in 1883 and became Portsmouth's second Jewish mayor in 1894. 'Respect for him was such that during the terminal illness of his wife, Julia, the Commanders in Chief of both arms of the Services gave instructions that no guns were to be fired from either garrison or ships in the port.'[58] In contrast, his ancestor, Samuel Emanuel, was the sole survivor of a tragedy in 1758 when 12 Jewish traders drowned trying to enter a man-of-war, the *HMS Lancaster*, in a small sailing boat – a disaster that hit the local Jewish community hard but hardly merited any contemporary attention from the wider world. From sellers of cheap trinkets and old clothes to the sailors, through to established pawnbrokers and jewellers with shops of their own in Portsmouth, and

then professionals such as artists and lawyers, the descendants of Samuel
Emanuel represent not so much a story of progress from rags to riches
but passage from the dangerous margins of society to full bourgeois
respectability.[59]

The rise of Emanuel Emanuel was not quite so spectacular but was
nevertheless impressive. Moses Emanuel was a purchaser who settled in
London from Bavaria, moving to Portsmouth in 1819. His son Ezekiel
ran a silversmith, jewellery and watchmaking shop on Portsea Hard.
The younger son, Emanuel, first came to prominence in 1825, charged
and fined for assaulting Lewis Lazarus, 'a respected pawnbroker and
Licensed Navy agent', also of Portsea and ironically given Emanuel's
later role, an elder of Portsmouth Hebrew congregation.[60] Such violence
was more typical of the rough Portsmouth of the Napoleonic era in
which the Jewish traders were both victims and perpetrators. It was,
ironically, by fighting an image of Portsmouth as disreputable, unruly
and unseemly that Emanuel Emanuel made his political reputation,
transforming the town by the time of his death in 1888 beyond
recognition.

If the violence for which the 17-year-old Emanuel was found guilty
could be excused through youthful male aggression, his energy and the
ability to take risks was typical of his adult life. How relevant, however,
was his Jewishness in his career? In 1900, Portsmouth's paper, the
Hampshire Telegraph, published an illustrated history of the town by
William Gates to mark its centenary. A chapter was devoted to 'The Jews
at Portsmouth' which was a eulogy to the community, its local
patriotism, civic and religious achievements. It started by explaining the
community's earlier 'ghetto' tendencies through the absence of
emancipation, the granting of which had been mutually beneficial:

For nearly two hundred years Portsmouth has been the abiding
place of a numerous Jewish colony, which has ever maintained the
most friendly relations with the other townspeople and cheerfully
borne its share of local burdens and responsibilities. In the old
disability days, when England, to her shame, refused the full rights
of citizenship to some of the most orderly and law abiding strangers
within her gates, the Jews of Portsmouth had perforce to live a life
apart and confine their energies within the four corners of their
dwellings; but with the grant of full political liberty, they at once
displayed all the qualities that make for good citizenship, and have
ever since taken an active part in the government and development
of the town. Among the local pioneers of progress the names of
several Jews are to be found, and Portsmouth gladly bears testimony

to the loyalty, the zeal, and the camaraderie of the entire community.[61]

Emanuel Emanuel was singled out for particular praise: 'his success was marvellous, and the town does well to remember with deep gratitude how many of the great improvements of the last half of the century are the outcome of his reforming zeal'. Emanuel was not the first Jew in Portsmouth to stand for civic office. In 1837, David Levy was approached but refused to stand as a town councillor, knowing that he would not be able to take the religious test. Emanuel decided to take the risk, 'He naturally refused to take the oath of office, which would have bound him on "the true faith of a Christian", and this rendered him liable to a penalty of £500 for every vote he gave, but happily no one was to be found in Portsmouth mean enough or uncharitable enough to inform against him.'[62]

William Gates argued that 'To the fact that Portsmouth has always been found on the side of civil and religious liberty must be attributed the early entry of the Jews into municipal life'.[63] It must be suggested that Gates reversed the order of causality and was somewhat overgenerous in his praise: it was not just by force of example through remarkable individuals such as Emanuel Emanuel or the Moss sisters that opinions changed, but because there was a favourable atmosphere in certain sections of Portsmouth society within which they and other middle-class Jews could prosper and gain respect. Emanuel Emanuel in particular aligned himself with what Gates called the 'progressive spirit', but might more meanly be linked to a tightly defined group of reforming entrepreneurs who had an economic as well as a political interest in transforming the town, especially in developing Southsea as a respectable, and indeed high class, seaside resort.[64]

Indeed, a counter-narrative to the Whiggish account provided by Gates of Emanuel Emanuel's rise, and mid-Victorian Portsmouth's acceptance of its Jewish minority, must be suggested. Rather than silence about his origins in 1841, Emanuel was forced to resign when a local radical drew attention to his Jewish origins, only subsequently being elected in 1844. Such opposition was not simply anti-semitic, although the language used against Emanuel at different stages of his career is striking for the power of the local hostile discourse which appears to have been conjured up with little difficulty. The *Hampshire Telegraph*, for example, later partly responsible for his idolisation within the town, complained in 1849 that he was an 'officious little Jew' when trying to have Southsea Common renamed 'Clarence Park' (Emanuel was close to the unpopular aristocrat, Lord Frederick Fitzclarence, the Lieutenant Governor).[65]

During the 1840s, Emanuel Emanuel led the campaign to abolish the ancient Portsmouth Free Mart Fair, an institution that increasingly upset 'respectable' society through its populistic culture of cosmopolitan showpeople, rowdiness, prostitution, drunkenness and petty crime. One of the major criticisms levelled at the Fair was that it enabled rich and poor to mingle freely in lowly pursuits, which 'brought with it the terrific demoralization of Portsmouth'. The lurid descriptions of activities during the Free Mart Fair from its opponents were not, indeed, dissimilar from those levelled at the poor Jewish pedlars of Portsea Hard some 40 years earlier and repeated thereafter. It is thus significant that Emanuel Emanuel, fast emerging as the secular leader of Portsmouth Jewry, became the leader of the anti-Fair movement, gaining the support of respectable lower middle class shop owners who feared competition from the Fair but also attracting the animosity of others in the town: 'To many Portmuthians, particularly those of the younger generation, the abolition of Free Mart Fair meant the loss of a valuable social amenity.'[66] The Fair, thanks largely to Emanuel's efforts, was shut down in 1847. In 1848 attempts to revive it were resisted by the police. Minor violence occurred, including an attack on Emanuel's house.[67]

Inspired by his success over the Free Mart Fair, Emanuel Emanuel became the leading force in municipal reform, including gas and water supplies, drainage, widening of streets, bringing the railway to the town, and creating its piers. In 1857 his efforts were rewarded with a civic banquet in his honour: 'As a citizen our friend has been the unflinching advocate of social, of commercial, and of industrial progress; and has been enthusiastic in advocating and promoting the great questions of the day – public health, public morals, and public education.' In 1866 he became Mayor of Portsmouth and his death in 1888 was marked by a huge public funeral.[68]

Yet as late as 1874 his career was marked by controversy – he was part of a group of businessmen determined to make Southsea Pier exclusively for 'Ladies and Gentlemen' and not the ordinary riff-raff of the town. In 1874, the Pier Company, of which Emanuel was a director and 'probably the most influential', decided 'to put a stop to the promiscuous mingling of the classes around its premises and erected a barrier between the Pier and the [surrounding area]'. The attempt led to the so-called 'Battle of Southsea' which for the Pier Company was far from a total victory. Crowds of up to 5000 gathered to open up access which eventually was partially granted. The radical opposition that had dogged his activities returned with a vengeance.[69] In a popular ballad, 'The Glorious Battle at Southsea', Emanuel was accused with the other directors of 'slyly scheming' and 'lin[ing] their greedy pockets'. The 'little Jew' was portrayed as a physical coward against the might of the ordinary men and women of Portsmouth. The ballad concluded 'May a pig's foot stick in the little Jew's gills/May the Directors suffer humanity's ills'.[70]

In its obituary of Emanuel Emanuel, the *Jewish Chronicle*, having outlined his impressive civic career, commented that it was upon the 'earnest, steadfast, sincerely pious Jew that we should chiefly dwell. From his earliest days he endeavoured with all his heart to make the name of Jew honoured. This was really his life's work.'[71] There is no doubt of Emanuel's commitment to the Jewish cause locally – he was a prominent contributor and leading force in its synagogue – and nationally – as the town's representative on the London Board of Jewish Deputies. Beyond such public identification with the Jewish cause, however, his courting of controversy throughout his political and business career in Portsmouth reveals a self-confidence in his Jewishness.

According to William Gates writing in 1900, when Emanuel died 'Portsmouth gave him the obsequies due to a perfect citizen. On the Parade at Southsea there is a strikingly handsome drinking fountain which was erected to his memory.' Another perspective is offered by the historian of the 'Battle of Southsea': 'Emanuel Emanuel was disliked locally on a number of grounds. For one thing, he was Jewish, which aroused the latent antisemitism of many locals.'[72] Emanuel Emanuel took the path of many Victorian Jews and allied himself with a middle-class ideology in which municipal improvement went alongside profit making and the desire for a clear separation, moral and physical, of the classes. He did so in a highly visible and strident manner, taking on controversial and potentially damaging battles. For many, rather than making the 'name of the Jew honoured' his activities provided the opportunity of releasing quite violent anti-semitism that had long been present in the town. Ultimately, he proved to be often on the winning side as Portsmouth was re-created largely according to the vision he and other emerging bourgeoisie shared. An account of the town published in 1880, for example, referring to the Free Mart Fair, could write, without much fear of eliciting controversy, that 'The Portsmouth folks old enough to bring this Fair to their recollection, now feel astonished that the scenes of noise, turmoil, dirt and demoralization should have been allowed for fourteen days to interrupt the traffic and to stop the commerce of the chief thoroughfare.' It was, the author added, 'a thing of the past, it pleased those who from the force of circumstance were unable to rise to higher aspirations, it served its time, it answered its purpose, but it is now dead and gone, and when old memories are conjured up respecting it, let us deal gently with it.'[73]

There is an irony that Emanuel emerged, more than self-assured, from a port Jewish community that had been accused of low morality, lawlessness and transience only to launch a sustained attack on such tendencies within Portsmouth as a whole. The craving for respectability that typified the leaders of Portsmouth Jewry in the early 1800s was turned into a much grander scheme by its most prominent nineteenth century son. Emanuel's success, however, was not totally complete, and Southsea, as a popular resort, did not escape the 'vulgarity' that he and his fellow directors had hoped it would avoid. Indeed, the final irony in relation to Emanuel Emanuel and his ambitions for the resort was that it provided the location for the thriving of what he would no doubt have seen as the dubious world of music hall and vaudeville. Here Portsmouth's most famous Jewish son emerged, the actor Peter Sellers. Sellers was almost delivered during a performance of the bawdy production 'Have a Dip!' and as a two-year-old was already appearing on stage. His mother, a direct descendant of the boxer Daniel Mendoza, was part of an acting and musical company consisting of a Cossack violinist, a black drummer and 'a refugee from Moscow who owned an authentic balalaika'.[74] Such cosmopolitanism and low culture on the brink of lawlessness was exactly the imagery that respectable Portsmouth Jewry had tried to distance itself from.

It is possible that the self-confident class and religious identity, bordering on arrogance, typified by Emanuel Emanuel, encouraged a greater confidence towards poorer Jews settling in Portsmouth towards the end of the nineteenth century. Certainly a range of bodies were set up to provide for the immigrant arrivals which contrasts markedly with the situation in Southampton.

From the 1880s onwards, one of the major tasks of the Southampton Hebrew Congregation was to ensure that while Jewish strangers in the town were provided with funds, they would not as a result want to stay in the port permanently. What the Rabbi, using the language of contemporary charity, referred to 'as the relief of the casual poor, which being a seaport, we get comers from the four corners of the earth',[75] was a constant irritation but also a fear of the community, especially when the issue of white slavery emerged. In 1896, the Gentlemen's Committee of the Jewish Association for the Protection of Women and Children sent delegates to visit ships leaving from Southampton bound for Buenos Aires to find out if there were any Jewish women at risk of falling into prostitution. Their 'worst fears' were confirmed and much time was subsequently spent checking the port for both alleged traffickers and Jewish prostitutes making sure that neither settled or were operating in Southampton.[76] The community had an ambivalent response to these

Jewish migrants – it was deeply concerned about its good reputation as model citizens by their presence, but a good proportion of its Rabbi's pathetic salary was made up of watching the ships for the possibilities of unaccompanied young women slipping into immoral ways. The respectable Jewish shopowners of Southampton could, if they were not careful, be identified with one of the classic vices of sailortown – prostitution, vice and criminality. It was a vibrant and cosmopolitan if somewhat sordid world thriving in the port districts of Southampton until well after the Second World War, which has been re-created evocatively by the writer Jonathan Meades:

> The Juniper Berry...down by the old town walls at So'ton [was] a queer's pub, *even during the day*; bum to bum with tars and tarts of *every sex*; knives outside in the shadows of the old town walls, tars falling where lascars have fallen before them; a strut down to the Hythe Ferry [across Southampton Water] is a walk through hell, or heaven – it's all french in French Street and you can guess the kind of pipe they blow in Bugle Street.[77]

Not surprisingly, every effort was made by the local Jewish community to remove any women suspected of being involved in prostitution or at risk of procurement or indeed any immigrants or poor Jews who might become a 'problem'. Generosity towards Jewish travellers through the town, although undoubted, was strictly short term.[78]

Both of the established and settled communities emerge in the nineteenth century as on the surface anglicised and integrated. This was certainly less true of the east European Jews of Portsmouth at the turn of the century. It was also totally irrelevant to the transmigrant Jews of Southampton who the elite tried to keep out of sight through the use of immigrant hostels in the town and who had previously often travelled on locked carriages in trains from London and elsewhere helping to boost the profits of the companies involved in this lucrative trade.[79] At a more general level, it is possible that a greater freedom operated at all levels for the provincial port Jew communities of Britain – the Seel Street Synagogue in Liverpool, for example, was possibly the first in which English was used for sermons.[80] Was this the freedom of port cosmopolitanism or the fear of appearing different in isolated and often violent localities in which Jews were occupying less than savoury roles and thus erecting barriers against foreign transmigrants? The somewhat greater size of Portsmouth Jewry undoubtedly allowed more freedom, even the possibility of being publicly brash as with Emanuel Emanuel, and an atmosphere in which many different forms of Jewish identity, secular and religious, could and did flourish throughout the nineteenth and early twentieth century: Emanuel's daughter, for example, Lady Magnus, became prominent as a writer and historian, following the apologetic model pioneered by the Moss sisters.[81]

Portsmouth Synagogue suffered three violent schisms in the 1790s, 1850s and 1890s. These have been interpreted as being in response to events in London but were perhaps more concerned with conflicting notions of local Jewish identity in a port setting and reflect, because of their very public nature, a degree of self-assuredness.[82] Southampton had suffered its own schism in the early 1850s,[83] but, by the end of the century, the tiny size of the settled Jewish community in Southampton, alongside the large-scale and alien presence of Jewish transmigrants, led to a defensiveness bordering at times on paranoia. The settled Jews of Southampton's collective identity could, it might be argued, be defined by their desperate desire not to appear as a port Jewish community. Where Emanuel Emanuel turned this concern outward, the Jews of Southampton were concerned to be model citizens of a town that they hoped would prosper with a patriotic but almost invisible Jewish community.[84]

To conclude: much of what I have outlined specifically has a provisional element in terms of the makeup, identity and responses to the port Jew communities of Southampton and Portsmouth. Nevertheless, at a general level it suggests that the port Jew concept can be extended in chronology, geography and approach. First, the new port Jewish communities of the eighteenth and nineteenth century, certainly in the case of Britain, were founded by Ashkenazi Jews of often very humble pedling backgrounds – this would include not just south coast communities such as Penzance, Plymouth, Chatham, Sheerness and Portsmouth but also Liverpool, Manchester and Glasgow. The identities they created were perhaps as confident as their Sephardi predecessors although arguably somewhat cruder in their execution, as with the example in Portsmouth of Emanuel Emanuel if less so in the case of his contemporaries in the same town, the Moss sisters, and later within Hampshire, Claude Montefiore and Lady Magnus. Their general lack of status in terms of intellectual, cultural and religious 'achievements', however, does not mean they are any less worthy of study.

Second, these were, alongside the local and national patriotisms manifested by the Jews, cosmopolitan in nature and were part of a truly global diaspora culture. Jews from Portsmouth, for example, at the close of the Napoleonic wars, emigrated to the new world, and 'where they pitched their tents there they built synagogues that are models of the one at Portsea. At St.Thomas, at New York, and at Barbados, such buildings are to be found, telling at once of the unchanging faith of the builders and the pleasant associations they must have carried away with them from Portsmouth.' Southampton's rabbi at the turn of the century settled in San Antonio in Texas. Even those who stayed briefly in Southampton kept their memories of the town. A sense of place is crucial in the construction of identity, and Portsmouth and Southampton, as ports with port Jewries, had a special part to play in such complex diasporic processes. Even Peter Sellers, the jet-setting international film star who had spent most of his youth in 'vaudevillian vagrancy', was drawn back to the place of his birth where he had spent only the first two years of his life. The restless, eternal wanderer, who never quite escaped a sense that, according to his biographer, he remained 'a little Jewish backstreet lad', when returning to 20, Southsea Terrace remarked, 'I knew where my cot was, the shape of the ceilings. It was uncanny, really uncanny'.[85]

Third, this essay has, through the example of Southampton, pointed to the importance of transmigrancy, a neglected but vital part of the world Jewish experience in the nineteenth and twentieth centuries. Defined narrowly as a settled community on its own, Southampton was small and not particularly distinctive. In relation to its integral focal point as a transmigrancy centre, it becomes a place where the local and the global merge and are made indistinguishable. Indeed, transmigrancy on a crude level because of its economic importance but more subtly because of its multi-layering of Jewish identity, has been integral to the nature of large and small port Jew communities whether they be in London, Manchester, Liverpool, London, Hull, Grimsby or Southampton. The scale of transmigrancy queries our fetishising of the permanent as well as problematising what it means to be a settler when thousands around you are on the move – in the case of Southampton for the period from the 1890s to the 1930s representing a ratio of one settled Jew to 40 in transit. Whether in denial of their presence or not, the transmigrants affected the identity of those rooted to the town, Jewish and non-Jewish. From the perspective of current British history and Jewish studies Southampton Jewry has hardly ever merited a mention. It is significant, however, that from the perspective of international migration studies, Southampton becomes a key player. As a publication from Ellis Island puts it: 'Piraeus, Trieste, Naples, Marseilles, Rotterdam, Southampton, Hamburg – all the great port cities of Europe played host to generation after generation of southern and eastern Europeans leaving the old world for the new.'[86]

Among this Ellis Island list, of course, are some of the classic port Jew cities of history. We can thus see how, by utilising a grassroots approach that looks at the port Jew idea from the bottom up and allows for the fluidity that epitomises the modern Jewish experience, Southampton and Portsmouth seem less oddly placed in the company of Salonika, London, Amsterdam, Odessa and Trieste.[87] Port Jews thus confirm Doreen Massey's observation on the importance of places and their pasts, that 'the local is always a product...of "global" forces'. Indeed, the concept of port Jews, while always reflecting particular contexts of geography and chronology to produce specific types, must also be regarded as being timeless and generic.[88]

NOTES

1. Lois C. Dubin, *The Port Jews of Habsburg Trieste: Absolutist Politics amd Enlightenment Culture* (Stanford: Stanford University Press, 1999), p.6.
2. David Sorkin, 'The Port Jew: Notes Toward a Social Type', *Journal of Jewish Studies*, 50.1 (spring 1999), p.87.
3. Ibid.., pp.89–97, esp. p.97.
4. Lucien Wolf, 'The First Stage of Emancipation', *Jewish Chronicle*, 7 and 14 August 1903 reprinted in *Essays in Jewish History by Lucien Wolf* ed. by Cecil Roth (London: Jewish Historical Society of England, 1934), pp.123–4. Wolf was probably mistaken in his belief in the very early origins of Portsmouth Jewry.
5. Extending the chronology forwards does not imply that its usefulness as a concept could not also be taken back to antiquity and the Middle Ages.
6. For the recent discovery of the Anglo-Jewish experience, admittedly from an elite perspective, see David Ruderman, *Jewish Enlightenment in an English Key: Anglo-Jewry's Construction of Modern Jewish Thought* (Princeton: Princeton University Press, 2000).
7. David Cannadine, 'Cousinhood', *London Review of Books*, 27 July 1989.
8. Norman Davies, *The Isles: A History* (Macmillan: London, 1999). Similarly, Davies has placed European history in a global context. See his *Europe: A History* (New York: Oxford University Press, 1996).
9. This has led to a defensiveness on behalf of its practitioners. See, for example, the inaugural lecture of Alan Everitt when taking the chair of Local History at the University of Leicester, published as *New Avenues in English Local History* (Leicester: Leicester University Press, 1970). For a similar process at work in another discipline, see A. Sayer, 'Behind the Locality Debate: Deconstructing Geography's Dualisms', *Environment and Planning A*, 23 (1991), pp.306–7.
10. Valerie Marett, *Immigrants Settling in the City* (Leicester: Leicester University Press, 1989) and Lorna Chessum, *From Immigrants to Ethnic Minority* (Aldershot: Ashgate, 2000) for studies, of Asians and Afro-Caribbeans respectively, of settlement and race relations in Leicester. See also Panikos Panayi, 'The Impact of Immigrant Food Upon England', in *Migrationsforschung und Interkulturelle Studien* ed. by Jochen Oltmer (Osnabruck: Universitatsverlag Rasch, 2002), pp.194–201. Government figures predicted a white minority in Leicester by the end of the first decade in the twenty-first century.
11. Sorkin (see note 2), pp.88, 89, 91–2, 95.
12. For studies of Portsmouth Jewry in order of publication see Rev. I.S. Meisels, 'The Jewish Congregation of Portsmouth (1766-1842)', *Transactions of the Jewish Historical Society of England* 6 (1908-10), pp.111–27; Cecil Roth, 'The Portsmouth Community

and its Historical Background', *Transactions of the Jewish Historical Society of England* 13 (1932-35), pp.157-87; Rabbi Eugene Newman, 'Some New Facts about the Portsmouth Jewish Community', *Transactions of the Jewish Historical Society of England* 17 (1951-52), pp.251-68 and Aubrey Weinberg, *Portsmouth Jewry*, Portsmouth Papers 41 (1985). There is also much relevant material in Geoffrey Green, *The Royal Navy & Anglo-Jewry 1740-1820* (Geoffrey Green: London, 1989).

13. Figures from the religious census of 1851 analysed by Vivian Lipman, 'A Survey of Anglo-Jewry in 1851', *Transactions of the Jewish Historical Society of England* 17 (1951-52), pp.179, 188.

14. Cecile and Marion Moss, *The Romance of Jewish History* (1840), *Tales of Jewish History* (1843) (Miller & Field, 1843); Lady Magnus, *Outlines of Jewish History* (1886).

15. R.A. Peel, *The Portsmouth Grammar School and Aria College* (Portsmouth: Portsmouth Grammar School, 1999); William Gates, *Illustrated History of Portsmouth* (Portsmouth: Carpenter and Co., 1900), p.366.

16. Michael Galchinsky, *The Origin of the Modern Jewish Woman Writer: Romance and Reform in Victorian England* (Detroit: Wayne State University Press, 1996), p.133.

17. Lipman (see note 13), pp.179, 188.

18. David Katz, *The Jews in the History of England 1485-1850* (Oxford: Oxford University Press, 1994), p.6.

19. Geoffrey Alderman, *Modern British Jewry* (Oxford: Clarendon Press, 1992), p.53. For the only sustained (that is over one sentence) account of Southampton Jewry see Cecil Roth, *The Rise of Provincial Jewry* (London: The Jewish Monthly, 1950), p.100.

20. Daniel Langton, 'An Englishman of the Jewish Persuasion: Claude Montefiore, Christianity, and Liberal Jewish Thought' (PhD thesis, University of Southampton, 1998).

21. Roth, 'The Portsmouth Community' (see note 12) and *The Jews in the Defence of Britain: Thirteenth to Nineteenth Centuries* (London: Jewish Historical Society of England, 1940), pp.5, 13. The latter was his Presidential address to the JHSE given at a time of national military crisis and when the loyalty of British Jews, especially the refugees from Nazism, was under question; Wolf, 'A Peep into the Portsmouth Pinches', *Jewish Chronicle*, 15 August 1890.

22. Green (see note 12), p.182.

23. See, for example, Nadav Kashtan (ed.), *Seafaring and the Jews* (London: Frank Cass, 2001), which while not focussing on ports themselves does cover the whole period from antiquity to the twentieth century.

24. Bill Williams, *The Making of Manchester Jewry 1740-1875* (Manchester: Manchester University Press, 1975), pp.vii-iii.

25. Doreen Massey and Pat Jess, 'Introduction' in *A Place in the World?* ed. by Massey and Jess (Oxford: Oxford University Press, 1995), p.4.

26. Doreen Massey, 'Places and Their Pasts', *History Workshop Journal* 39 (spring 1995), p.183.

27. Doreen Massey, 'Double Articulation: A Place in the World', in *Displacements: Cultural Identities in Question* ed. by A. Bammer, (Bloomington, IN: Indiana University Press, 1994), p.120.

28. Hans Meyer, *City and Port: Urban Planning as a Cultural Venture in London, Barcelona, New York and Rotterdam* (Utrecht: International Books, 1999).

29. W.H. Hudson, *Hampshire Days* (London: Chapman & Hall, 1903).

30. In 1980 by Oxford University Press and most remarkably his writings on Hampshire types, revealing the influence of race science, reproduced in *Hampshire of One Hundred Years Ago* ed. by Barry Stapleton, (Stroud, Gloucestershire: Alan Sutton, 1993), pp.36-43.

31. Morley Roberts, *W.H. Hudson: A Portrait* (London: Eveleigh, Nash and Greyson, 1924), pp.214-5. See also Paul Rich, *Prospero's Return: Historical Essays on Race, Culture and British Society* (London: Hansib, 1994), pp.13-15.

32. Hudson, *Hampshire Days* (see note 29), pp.222–3.
33. H.V. Morton, *In Search of England* (London: Methuen & Co, 1933, orig. 1927), pp.viii, 14, 32. On his influence more generally see C.R. Perry, 'In Search of H.V. Morton: Travel Writing and Cultural Values in the First Age of British Democracy', *Twentieth Century British History* vol.10 no.4 (1999), pp.431–56.
34. Brian Vesey-Fitzgerald, *Hampshire Scene* (London: Methuen & Co, 1940), pp.vii, 2, 130.
35. Mathew Baker, *Jem Bunt* (1846), quoted by Green (see note 12), p.118.
36. Henry Slight, *The History of Portsmouth and Stranger's Guide Book* (Portsmouth: John Miller, 1844), p.2.
37. Howard Spring, *Heaven Lies About Us: A Fragment of Infancy* (London: Constable, 1939), pp.43–4.
38. Ross Cameron, 'The Most Colourful Extravaganza in the World: Images of Tiger Bay, 1845–1970', *Patterns of Prejudice* 31.2, pp.59–90; Glenn Jordan, 'Tiger Bay, *Picture Post*, and the Politics of Representation', in *'Down the Bay': Picture Post, Humanist Photography and Images of 1950s Cardiff* ed. by Jordan, (Cardiff: Butetown History & Arts Centre, 2001), pp.9–21.
39. See the *Southampton Times* in 1919 for the violence in Southampton. For the violence in other cities see Jacqueline Jenkinson, 'The 1919 Race Riots in Britain: A Survey', in *Under the Imperial Carpet: Essays in Black History 1780–1950* ed. by Rainer Lotz and Ian Pegg, (Crawley, Surrey: Rabbit Press, 1986), pp.182–207.
40. Telford Varley, *Hampshire* (London: Adam and Charles Black, 1909), p.256.
41. Modern Southampton has not been well served by historians. See, however, Bernard Knowles, *Southampton: The English Gateway* (London: Hutchinson & Co, 1951); *Collected Essays on Southampton* ed. by J.B. Morgan and Philip Peberdy (Southampton: The County Borough of Southampton, 1958) and A. Temple Patterson, *Southampton: A Biography* (London: Macmillan, 1970).
42. Editorial: 'Free Trade for Southampton', *Southampton Times*, 29 April 1905.
43. See Tony Kushner and Katharine Knox, *Refugees in an Age of Genocide: Global, National and Local Perspectives during the Twentieth Century* (London: Frank Cass, 1999), chs 1 and 3.
44. 'Freemantle Liberals Talk about Aliens', *Southampton Times*, 22 April 1905.
45. Kushner and Knox (see note 43), pp.45–6, 149–50.
46. Ian Mikardo, *Back-Bencher* (London: Weidenfeld & Nicolson, 1988) for a vivid autobiographical description of this Jewish influx from the East End. See also Weinberg (note 12*)*, pp.15–17.
47. Report on the Southampton Hebrew Congregation, 31 January 1895, to the Chovrei Zion, in Central Zionist archives, Jerusalem, A2/78. More generally see Kushner and Knox (see note 43), pp.36–7.
48. Figures from the United States Diplomatic Records, Despatches from US Consuls in Southampton, 1790–1906 (T239), 19.55 (9 August 1904).
49. See Kushner and Knox (see note 43), chapter 3.
50. Green (see note 12), p.16. For an indication of the rules, regulations and fines imposed in order to control the behaviour of the community, see the minutes of the synagogue reproduced in Meisels, 'The Jewish Congregation of Portsmouth', pp.111–27, esp. p.112.
51. 'The Jews in Ohio', *The Occident and American Jewish Advocate*, February 1844. I am very grateful to Nils Roemer for drawing my attention to this article by one of its founding members, a Plymouth-origin Jew, Joseph Jonas.
52. For Marryat see David Hannay's introduction to *Peter Simple* (London: Macmillan, 1895, orig. 1834), pp.vii–xv and pp.10–11 and chapter 11 for descriptions of Jews in the book itself.
53. Green (see note 12), p.34 and chapters 3 and 7.

A TALE OF TWO PORT JEWISH COMMUNITIES 109

54. Bryan Cheyette, 'Introduction' in *Contemporary Jewish Writing in Britain and Ireland: An Anthology* ed. by Cheyette (Lincoln, Nebraska: University of Nebraska Press, 1998), pp.xiv–xvi. See also Michael Galchinsky, *The Origin of the Modern Jewish Woman Writer*, chapter 3 which is devoted to the Moss sisters; Linda Gertner Zatlin, *The Nineteenth-Century Anglo-Jewish Novel* (Boston: Twayne Publishers, 1981), pp.29–33, 72 and Nadia Valman, 'Jews and Gender in British Literature, 1815–1865' (PhD thesis, University of London, 1996). Cheyette, Valman and Zatlin see the Moss sisters as writing apologetically to a non-Jewish audience, whereas Galchinsky argues that they were freed from a male defensiveness and aiming at a Jewish audience.
55. Zatlin (see note 54), p.72.
56. Henry Slight, *Chronicles of Portsmouth* (London: Lupton Relfe, 1828), p.95. Among the subscribers were Ezekiel Emanuel and Jacob Jacobs.
57. Weinberg (note 12), p.15.
58. Ibid., p.15.
59. Green (see note 12), pp.28, 171–2.
60. Ibid., pp.170–1 and obituary of Emanuel Emanuel in *Jewish Chronicle*, 4 January 1889. I would like to thank Stuart Olesker for sharing his interest in Emanuel Emanuel with me.
61. Gates (see note 15) (Portsmouth: Carpenter & Co, 1900), chapter 7, esp.364.
62. Ibid., pp.366–7.
63. Ibid.
64. Gates (see note 15), p.366; J. Field, *The Battle of Southsea*, Portsmouth Papers 34 (1981), pp.7–8.
65. *Hampshire Telegraph*, 23 June 1849 quoted by Field (see note 64), pp.10–1.
66. John Webb, *Portsmouth Free Mart Fair: The Last Phase 1800–1847*, Portsmouth Papers 35 (1982), pp.8, 14, 18.
67. *Hampshire Telegraph*, 15 July 1858.
68. Obituary in *Jewish Chronicle*, 4 January 1889; Gates (see note 15), pp.366–7.
69. Field (see note 64), passim, esp. p.11.
70. Ibid., p.17 where the Ballod is reproduced in full.
71. *Jewish Chronicle*, 4 January 1889. See also *Hampshire Telegraph*, 5 January 1899.
72. Gates (see note 15), p.367; Field (see note 64), p.11.
73. W.H. Saunders, *Annals of Portsmouth* (London: Hamilton, Adams, 1880), pp.203, 206.
74. Alexander Walker, *Peter Sellers: The Authorized Biography* (London: Weidenfeld & Nicolson, 1981), p.11; Roger Lewis, *The Life and Death of Peter Sellers* (London: Random House, 1994), p.5.
75. Fyne to the Chovrei Zion, 31 January 1895, Central Zionist Archives, Jerusalem, A2/78.
76. Minutes of the Gentlemen's Committee, 31 May, 7 and 21 June 1896 in University of Southampton archive, MS 173/2/2/1.
77. Jonathan Meades, *Pompey* (London: Jonathan Cape, 1993), p.127.
78. See the Southampton Hebrew Congregation minutes for the 1890s and 1900s and Gentleman's Committee of the Jewish Association for the Protection of Women and Children, 21 June 1896, 15 October and 19 November 1899, 4 October 1900 in University of Southampton archives, MS 173/2/2/1 and 5.
79. One of the Rothschild daughters, Mrs Eliot Yorke, opened the Emigrants' Home which soon became Atlantic Hotel. See *Southampton Times*, 11 November 1893. Nicholas Evans is working on the transmigrant trade in Britain and in particular the Wilson Line of Hull. See a report of his contribution to the 21st international conference on Jewish Genealogy in the *Jewish Chronicle*, 13 July 2001.
80. See Alderman (note 19), p.22 and Williams (note 24), passim for Liverpool Jewry.
81. For Lady Magnus, see Ruth Sebag-Montefiore, *A Family Patchwork: Five Generations of an Anglo-Jewish Family* (London: Weidenfeld & Nicolson, 1987), pp.64–8. Roth, 'The

Portsmouth Community' (see note 12), p.157 described her as 'one of the most gifted women who ever graced the Anglo-Jewish community'.

82. Roth, 'The Portsmouth Community' (see note 12), p.167 but see Weinberg (note 12), pp.6–9 for a more convincing stress on local factors.
83. Lipman (see note 13), p.179.
84. See Kushner and Knox (see note 43), pp.36–42.
85. Gates (see note 15), pp.365–6 for Portsmouth. For Southampton records of the Hebrew congregation, correspondence, and *Eastleigh Weekly News*, 2 October 1931 for the formation of an 'Atlantic Park Club of New York'. Atlantic Park was a huge transmigrant camp which operated throughout the 1920s several miles from Southampton. See Kushner and Knox (note 43), chapter 3, for a full history of Atlantic Park; Walker (see note 74), p.158; Lewis (see note 74), pp.19, 33.
86. David Brownstone, Irene Franck and Douglass Brownstone, *Island of Hope, Island of Tears* (New York: Barnes & Noble, 2000 [orig.1979]), pp.105.
87. See the other contributions in this volume for studies of these port Jew communities.
88. Massey, 'Places and Their Pasts' (see note 26), p.183.

The Forgotten Port Jews of London:
Court Jews Who Were
Also Port Jews

DAVID CESARANI

In 1655, England went to war against Spain with the consequence that Spanish merchants and their property in the country were rendered liable to seizure. In March 1656 the property of Antonio Rodrigues Robles, a merchant of Portuguese origin who was superficially a New Christian, was impounded by the authorities in London on the grounds that he was an enemy alien. On 24 March 1656, six Iberian-born merchants, all former New Christians, petitioned Oliver Cromwell, the head of state, asserting that they were Portuguese 'of the Hebrew nation' and not Spanish. They sought to preempt measures against their conduct of trade and obtain permission to live and worship in London as Portuguese Jews.[1] In this démarche, the Portuguese Jews in London were driven to act by a threat to their mercantile interests. Emerging openly as Jews was, paradoxically, the best way to parry the danger. Religious identity and maritime enterprise were fused: their location in a port city was crucial in the first moves towards the resettlement of the Jews in England.[2]

This is, of course, a familiar story, and the centrality of economic interests to the readmission of the Jews, while not unambiguous or uncontested, is well established. It is all the more surprising, then, that relatively little attention has been paid to the specificity of London qua port city as the *locus mirabilis* for this extraordinary run of events. Jewish immigration, settlement, transmigration, and economic activity is wholly absent from the standard histories of the port of London and barely impinges on histories of London, either. This is hardly unexpected in such celebratory and chauvinistic works as Arthur Bryant's *Liquid History*, but even a superb social history such as Roy Porter's fails to connect the city and the port or to integrate Jews into the narrative of either. Porter tends to replicate the historiography which depicts Jews as marginal at best or a problematic presence at worst.[3]

Such works barely mention the readmission and resettlement of the Jews through the port of London in the mid-seventeenth century and pay only cursory heed to the accretion of Jewish immigrants and transmigrants in the late nineteenth century. The same cannot be said of British Jewish historiography which for decades was fixated on chronicling the readmission in minute detail. Yet there is much more to be said beyond the well-known facts that London was a major port, that trade was important to London and England, as well as being of supreme interest to Cromwell's government, and that the Spanish and Portuguese Jews were major players in international trade in precisely the regions and commodities that interested Cromwell. It is because the nexus linking Jewish history with London's maritime and mercantile history has been treated with such negligence that I have entitled this essay the 'forgotten' port Jews of London.

In this essay I want to suggest an agenda for revisiting English Jewish history in the light of Lois Dubin's conceptualisation of a 'port Jewry' and David Sorkin's construction of the 'port Jew' as a 'social type'. However, as Dubin and others have observed, Sorkin's approach closes off several important lines of inquiry that relate to the specificity of port cities. These singular characteristics, in turn, highlight peculiar features of London which by their very difference throw into relief the generic aspects of the 'port Jew' experience.

In 'The Port Jew: Notes Toward a Social Type', David Sorkin makes the focus of his inquiry the figure of the port Jew and the collectivity of Jews in port cities. He sets out thereby to illuminate historical processes 'embodied in individual and group experience'. His primary goal is to establish the experience of the port Jew as a route to modernity comparable with the better known and more heavily researched case of the court Jew. His other major concern is to reinstate the Sephardim in the narrative of modernisation which, until now, has been largely confined to the journey taken by the Ashkenazi court Jews of central Europe. By deploying the port Jew as an individual and collective type that exemplifies the characteristics of a modernising community, he challenges the notion that the Jewish road to modernity is singular to Ashkenazi court Jews or that the model represented by the Haskalah is the only one pertinent to understanding how the Jews were transformed in the course of the late seventeenth and eighteenth centuries.[4]

One drawback of this approach is that the a priori definition of the 'social type' as a harbinger of modernity tends to exclude individuals or groups that do not conform to the economic, demographic, social, or cultural and religious patterns by which Jews are held to have entered the modern world. So, as Lois Dubin points out, even though Sorkin's model is framed with the laudable aim of retrieving a lost chapter of the Sephardi story, his approach rules out Spanish and Portuguese Jews who settled in areas that did not experience modernisation along the lines of the Atlantic seaboard or indigenous Jewish populations in non-Atlantic zones which did. Hence, the Jews, Sephardi and Ashkenazi, in the ports of Tangiers, Istanbul, Smyrna, and Salonica are marginalised.

Furthermore, by placing the accent on individuals or groups who are evaluated according to the tenets of modernisation in central Europe, to see whether or not they conform to these criteria, there is a danger of missing the importance of a specific location. Sorkin shows that port cities were special places that fostered a particular kind of Jew and Jewish community. But the port city, as a generic urban formation, is more or less incidental to his analysis. Attention is focused primarily on those port cities that seemed to exert a transformative effect on the Jews, defined mainly in terms of modernisation. I would suggest that we need to begin with a definition of the port city or city port rather than the universal processes which it may or may not have engendered in its Jewish population. Having established a definition we can then take several locations that share these characteristics and examine the interaction between Jews and their environment so as to detect any common features.

David Sorkin defines the particular locus for his study as 'cities, polities, or colonies that were built upon and valued commerce'. If we turn to geography and historical geography we encounter more precise and nuanced definitions that open further vistas for exploring the Jews of city ports. A more elaborate definition is not only useful for a synchronic approach, but may also offer possibilities for diachronic analysis – that is, one useful not only for achieving a more textured understanding of port Jews in one place at any one time, but also for comprehending the evolution of Jewish communities in ports over time, and the dynamic of their relations with their milieux. The results may be surprising. The very factors that made Atlantic-oriented capitalistic port cities a welcoming environment for Jews, both in terms of their commercial character and the legal or constitutional conditions under which Jewish life was lived, could in certain circumstances prove negative. By contrast, port cities in empires that were politically or economically 'backward' could prove quite benign. By first looking at the nature of port cities, we can also move beyond their narrow role in the modernisation of Jewish society and explore their significance in Jewish life throughout the nineteenth and into the twentieth century.

Port Cities

Brian Hoyle and D.A. Pinder have observed that 'The city port, or port city, is one of the quintessential elements of the modern European space economy, symbolising the fusion of cultural diversity and historical experience that characterise this focal world politico-economic region.'⁵ Port cities are dynamic urban formations and they have evolved over the ages as their motor force, the nature and technology of maritime activity, has mutated. As economic relations changed, so have power relations within the city port.⁶

In the ancient world, the port and the city were closely juxtaposed. The waterfront was the focal point of activity, and the centre of the town was dominated by the merchant class. In the mediaeval city port great merchant palaces and civic buildings were erected adjacent or close to the harbour, enabling and symbolising the nexus of wealth and power between maritime trade and governance. In the early modern period, overseas trade grew in importance and the technology of maritime transport improved sufficiently to give men a sense of relative mastery over the oceans, incorporating the sea into the rational planning of their activities. The sea became a medium through which to project economic and military power. The city port went from being a centre of exchange at the junction between the locality and the region, ruled by a mercantile elite, to the nodal point of trade and naval influence. Now located at the interface between the local and the global, the national and the international, the city port became the portal through which empires extended their influence and exercised control over sea routes, economic arteries, natural resources, new populations, and territorial acquisitions.

The port was still essentially a site of exchange, and power relations reflected this. The individual merchant, merchant prince or guild of merchants was superseded by the joint-stock companies which became as much a force in local politics as they were in economic affairs. In nineteenth-century Europe, however, change accelerated. The city port was transformed from a simple market into a place for storage, processing, distribution and trans-shipment. Technological change, notably the coming of steam and the vastly increased size of ships, consigned many traditional port cities to obsolescence. Ports were increasingly separated from cities and enclosed for better management of commodities and workers. From the late nineteenth century onwards the city port was less a market and more a single point along a distribution chain at which were located industries for processing and enhancing raw materials. In this phase, power slipped definitively from the hands of the mercantile elite, and power relations in the port city became more diverse and complex, including trades unions as well as industrialists, shipping and trading interests.[7]

Each of these phases and each of these functions had very particular implications for the Jews, which I will discuss below. But before that I want to look a little more closely at the evolution of the city port in the light of recent work by the Dutch geographer Hans Meyer. By examining perceptions and images of the port, Meyer has added an important dimension to urban history, which also offers a critical insight into a turning point in Jewish history.

Hans Meyer depicts the city port as a phenomenon of modernity. But he also sees it evolving through several phases which he relates to the Kondratieff cycle of economic change. From the late eighteenth to the mid-nineteenth century the enclosed port functioned as the final destination for goods and commodities that were held in depots within the city and then marketed or processed. From the mid- to late-nineteenth century port cities shared in the era of infrastructural change based on the railways. They became transit points, occupying a transitional space between sea lanes and railway lines, now often located outside the city. In the first half of the twentieth century, city ports were reconfigured into centres of industrial production and trans-shipment: the port and the city steadily diverged.[8]

Meyer suggestively explores the social and political ramifications of these spatial and economic transformations. From earliest times to the mid-nineteenth century, the port was under the sway of a settled mercantile elite whose business was exchange within an extensively regulated and circumscribed orbit. During the era of European overseas expansion the port city was often planned and beautified so that in architectural and spatial terms it symbolised economic as well as political order and power. But in the modern era, a period dominated by laissez faire, it acquired an ambiguous character. The port was intrinsically modern and 'presupposes a willingness to remove oneself from an existing context, the willingness to relinquish a past and an ideology'. It became the domicile of the 'exile, the foreigner, and the immigrant'. The waterfront in the modern port was typified by a chaotic intermixing of workers, seaman, immigrants, wealthy passengers and poverty stricken transmigrants, warehouses, industry, entertainments and services. It was frequently said that 'a visit to a port city was a visit to the world'.[9]

This chaos was aggravated by phases of wild economic uncertainty, unplanned urban growth, and population explosion. From the Lower East Side of New York to the East End of London, from Tangier to Naples, the harbour side was increasingly perceived as a threatening place, the interface between safety and danger, and a 'hotbed of marginality'. Meyer comments that 'In the twentieth century, the perception of the modern port as a factor that could seriously undermine urban life became more and more dominant in most port cities, and formed not only a basis for a social policy aimed at those living in harbour districts, but also a foundation for urban plans attempting to isolate harbour areas or eliminate them from the urban context.'[10]

These shifting perceptions and functions of city ports are the matrix for the development and depiction of port Jews from the eighteenth to the twentieth centuries. In the rest of this essay I will take London as a case study to illustrate how a refined definition and conception of the port city can help us to draw out neglected themes in Jewish history and shed new light on the already familiar.

Port and Court

It is often remarked that, thanks to the expulsion of the Jews in 1290, the Spanish and Portuguese Jews who resettled London in the mid-seventeenth century benefited from the absence of any body of Medieval legislation regulating Jewish life. It is certainly true that there were few laws pertaining to Jewish behaviour (as against Jewish belief – about which there was no shortage).[11] But the focus on Jewry laws casts London in a misleading, falsely benevolent light. It may be more pertinent to observe that the Jews were fortunate to return to London at a time when the extensive legislation governing alien merchants in general had fallen into desuetude. For, in the middle ages, London was a port city in which merchants wielded considerable power, and through their control of local governance maintained stringent controls over foreign rivals. In his study of alien merchants in England in the middle ages, T.H. Lloyd observes that 'The welcome extended by early medieval Englishmen to alien merchants visiting their shores was decidedly mixed, but if there was a guiding principle it was probably that strangers should be encouraged to come here, although their activities should be strictly controlled once they arrived.'[12]

The mercantile elite exercised domination via the guilds and fraternities they controlled and through their intimate ties with the court and the crown. They set the terms of charters that regulated the conduct of trade and business in the city that, throughout this period, enfolded the port. Alien merchants were allowed freedom of movement for the purpose of conducting business, but they were otherwise confined to separate residential districts. German merchants lived in the Steelyard, a compound enclosed by a high wall to protect them from the City apprentices 'whose jealousy against the foreigner could be easily and terribly aroused'. Had foreign-born Jews been present in this period they too would have faced strict regulation and probably ghettoisation.[13] What is notable, then, about the reentry of the Jews is not so much the absence of a specific body of legislation pertaining to Jews, but the changed circumstances of foreign merchants in a leading port city – an improvement from which Jews benefited incidentally and indirectly.

Nevertheless, between 1655 and 1690 there were repeated attempts by English merchants to obstruct the resettlement of Jews in London and several moves to curtail their activity or throw them out altogether. The initiative of Menasseh ben Israel, who pleaded to Cromwell for the readmission and toleration of the Jews on religious and economic grounds, fared badly precisely because he played to the gallery of merchants in London. Commercial values and pragmatism cut both ways. Whereas Oliver Cromwell saw the value of establishing a community of Spanish and Portuguese merchants with trading connections in the West Indies, a region into which he intended to extend English naval power and economic influence, merchants in the City regarded the interlopers as potential competition. During the Whitehall Conference which Cromwell summoned in December 1655 to consider the matter, the readmission of the Jews was strenuously opposed for both theological and economic reasons. In fact, the resistance was so stout that Cromwell dissolved the assembly and proceeded by other means.[14]

Cromwell's death and the collapse of the Protectorate threatened the existence of London's fledgling Jewish community. In December 1660, months after the restoration, London merchants petitioned Charles II to expel the Jews or subject them to special taxes. They made further attacks on the Jewish community in January 1661, 1664 and 1674. This pressure caused the leading Jewish merchants to seek reassurance from the crown, and soon afterwards they instigated the humiliating and expensive practice of presenting the Lord Mayor with an annual tribute of gold or silver plate. Lucien Wolf remarked that 'A good many years passed before the City became quite reconciled to the heterodox strangers in Portsoken', the district in which most Jews clustered. In 1677 the Court of Alderman tried to prevent the immigration of 'destitute aliens pretending to be Jews' and in 1680 the Lord Mayor called for a review of the mediaeval anti-Jewish laws. In 1685, soon after the accession of James II, London merchants demanded that Jews should pay the mediaeval alien duties. James parried this demand, and a malicious attempt to enforce the recusancy laws against the Jews. Pressure from the merchant lobby finally succeeded in 1689. Despite the good relations between William III and the Jews in both London and the Netherlands – from whence he had come, with their assistance, to take the English throne – they were forced to pay the tax on aliens.[15]

The recurrent debate about the Jewish mercantile presence in London calls into question the assumption that mercantilism and a positive attitude towards commerce in port cities automatically fostered a benign attitude towards the Jews. David Katz may be overstating the case with his provocative assertion that 'It is quite clear that motives of economics or trade had little to do with the readmission of the Jews to England.'[16] Yet he is correct to point out that efforts by Jewish apologists and their allies to justify the reestablishment of a Jewish community in London in terms of its mercantile acumen was like wielding a double-edged sword. While it may have been in the larger interests of the government to have foreign Jews at hand to circumvent the Navigation Acts and wartime embargoes, to the London merchants who were never over-friendly to foreign merchants this spelled competition.

The very attributes which Jews brought to port cities and which historians have treated as positive factors in their reception could also provide a source of irritation and cause tension. Stephen Fortune has shown that in the West Indies there was constant friction between Creole plantation owners and Jews who took a major share of the import and export trade on Barbados and Jamaica from the 1640s through the 1740s. To Cromwell, Charles II and William III the Jews were a useful tool of trade and a reserve of financial support. But they were forced to defend Jews against local interests in the West Indies as well as English merchants in Bristol and London.[17]

Gedalia Yogev explains the intense specialisation of Jewish merchants in London in the eighteenth century as being partly a consequence of their exclusion from the great trading companies. Jews were dangerously concentrated in the trade in diamonds, corals, gold and silver, and certain agricultural products emanating from the East Indies because they were barred from the freedom of the City. They were excluded from the East India Company and lacked any influence in the tightly drawn circle of merchants, MPs, and those who ruled the City. Indeed, Yogev argues that Jewish merchants were so alert to the hostility they faced that they voluntarily restricted the scope of their activity. When they built upon the existing diasporic and trading networks of Portuguese Jews this was not simply a rational exploitation of opportunity or a response to expectations that they would make use of their natural advantages. It was a forced response to difficult and adverse social and economic conditions: they were making the best of a bad job.[18]

The equivocal experience of London's port Jews between 1650 and 1750 suggests that there is some need to qualify the assignment of overwhelmingly positive attributes to the city port. Commercial values and pragmatism could work *against* the Jewish presence. Josef Konvitz in his study of planned port cities in the enlightenment indicates another reason for questioning the beneficence of the port city as a milieu. Konvitz locates the development and planning of port cities in the sixteenth–seventeenth centuries within the context of man's sense of mastery over the seas and utopian aspirations. City planners such as Simon Stevin (1546–1620) sought to embody reason in the layout and morphology of the city. When mercantilist governments resolved to expand existing ports or to build entirely new ones as a means to project naval and economic influence, they imported such utopian elements into the preferred designs.

In the 1660s, those most mercantilist of rulers Louis XIV and Colbert decided to construct four port cities which would symbolise and project the power of the state, serve as arsenals and bases for naval operations; support colonial expeditions; foster maritime trade; and attract manufacturing industries. They selected Rochefort, Sete, Lorient and Brest for development on these lines and planned the cities in minute detail. Each city boasted a rational and privileged tax regime. However, the cities were to perform social and cultural tasks, too. 'Directly involving itself in the task, the government tried hard to create a new urban culture in its own image, to make work in the arsenals and life in the new port cities uniquely French experiences. It used administrative authority and the Church to mould the inhabitants into an obedient and ordered community.' Foreigners and non-Catholics were viewed with suspicion. Dutch and Irish, Catholic as well as Protestant, were expelled once their tasks were fulfilled.[19]

Contrary to the thesis advanced by Salo Baron, which so heavily informs our approach to port Jews, the commerce and trade orientated, rational and centralising mercantilist, absolutist state was not automatically favourable towards the Jews. No Jews were invited or attracted to the planned port cities of seventeenth-century France, and given the highly regulated and assimilatory regimen which governed them, this is hardly surprising. It may have been a blessing in disguise that planning did not proceed very far in seventeenth-century London after the Great Fire destroyed most of the constricted mediaeval waterfront. The City merchants were not yet ready to part with the port and it was revived where it had been: under their noses. Even when the port was moved downstream to enclosed docks in the 1800s, the merchants were careful to ensure that all their privileges and powers over trade and commerce moved with it.[20]

Unlike in Amsterdam, the evolution of the joint stock company did not give London Jews greater access or influence in matters of trade and commerce. The great companies were mainly founded before the return of the Jews and excluded them rigorously once they arrived. As David Katz notes, Jews remained a marginal economic and political element in the life of London. Their economic base was narrow and precarious. Arguably, they survived and prospered not because London was a port but because it was the capital city of the country and centre of an emerging overseas empire. London is unique among the port cities in which Jews settled in the sixteenth–seventeenth centuries because it was home to the court as well as functioning as a centre of international maritime trade. In the Middle Ages the proximity of the mercantile elite and the court created difficulties for foreign merchants, but by the mid-seventeenth century the interests of the crown and the city had begun to diverge. While certain privileged merchants for a time profited from the system of trade monopolies under James I and Charles I, the monarchy's increasingly rapacious treatment of customs and dues eventually alienated the City. Jews ultimately benefited from this divergence since they enjoyed the protection of the sovereign who, by the time of the readmission, was accustomed to acting against the interests of the merchants. In this sense, London's Jews were uniquely *both* court Jews *and* port Jews.

Cromwell was inclined to protect Jews because Ibero-Jewish merchants like Antonio Fernandez Carvajal, Manuel Dormido and Simon de Carceres supplied his government with useful intelligence about Spanish trade in the West Indies and elsewhere, Spanish naval dispositions and diplomatic activity.[21] Charles II had seen for himself the utility of the Jews while he had sojourned in the Netherlands during his exile. His marriage to Catherine of Breganza brought with it an influx of Portuguese-Jewish merchants, like Duarte da Silva and Fernando Mendes da Costa, who serviced the new court.[22] The synthesis of court Jews and port Jews reached its apogee under William III. He hired the Amsterdam-based firm of Portuguese Jewish contractors Machado and Pereira to provision his expedition to England and, later, his invasion of Ireland. Lopes Suasso contributed heavily to his bid for the English crown and was later invited by William to settle with his family in England. Solomon de Medina, knighted in 1700, succeeded Machado and Pereira to became William's most important army contractor and banker.[23]

During the eighteenth century the development of London Jewry was framed by the City, the court and the port. A small group of merchants evolved into bankers and stockbrokers in the City. Some, like Sampson Gideon, Abraham Mocatta and Joseph Salvador, extended major loans to the government or handled the crucial flow of bullion into and out of the exchequer. The close ties between London and Amsterdam Jewry were an important element in their successful conduct of the bullion trade.

Others, including John Mendes da Costa, Abraham Prado, David Mendes da Costa and Aaron Hart were commissionary officers to British forces operating in Europe during the Seven Years War, in America, and Canada. All the same, while Jews took an important part in British overseas trade their role was somewhat marginal due to their continued exclusion from the major trading companies. They made fortunes as independent merchants, but by risky operations in the interstices between the joint stock companies and warring empires.[24]

As Todd Endelman has observed, these hybrid port/court Jews were soon highly integrated into Georgian society and excelled in acculturation. To that extent they were similar to the court Jews on the continent, but their modernisation was undogmatic, unselfconscious and uninformed by philosophical ideas.[25] Even so, a recent work by David Ruderman has drawn attention to the fearless engagement in the intellectual currents of the day by certain members of the Jewish social elite, such as Isaac d'Israeli. These Jewish, mainly Sephardi, polemicists dashed off pamphlets and wrote books explaining and defending Judaism, and argued for the integrity of the Hebrew bible against the exegetical and interpretative ravages perpetrated on it by Christian scholars. They were frequently critical of rabbinic Judaism, too, a characteristic trait of the 'port Jew' Sephardim. They were, in other words, classical harbingers of Jewish modernity, but 'in an English key'.[26]

The Migrating Image of 'Port Jews'

From the mid-seventeenth to the late nineteenth century, London's Jews were primarily engaged in the business of exchange. Whether as shopkeepers or brokers they became respectable and valued members in business circles and the mercantile community. During the campaign for the relief of civil disabilities, the City was a stronghold of support for the Jewish cause. Yet by the 1860s the port of London had been transformed, and exchange had ceased to be its primary function. With the transformation of the port, the image of the merchant and the romance of exchange palled. The port was now a place of trans-shipment, processing and manufacture. It was crowded, filthy and dangerous. In the last phase in the development of port cities with which this essay is concerned, Jews moved from being merchants who engaged in exchange to being commodities that were shipped from one place to another. From the 1880s, London was both a point of entry for mass Jewish immigration from Eastern Europe and a stopping-off place for Jews en route to North or South America and South Africa. These Jews played no part in the mercantile community and their fate was determined elsewhere. Whereas in the age of exchange London's merchants had political power to determine the ingress and egress of goods and people, in the mass age the government regulated immigration within a democratic political framework. Now the masses, not merchants, decided the fate of other masses.

The mass immigration of Jews to Britain between 1880 and 1914 has been exhaustively chronicled and analysed,[27] but one aspect has been omitted: the interconnection between the image of the port city and the image of the port Jew. As Hans Meyer has suggested, there is a link between ports and prejudice. In the twentieth century ports became associated with squalor, social chaos, criminality, miscegenation, irresponsible unrestricted commerce, rootlessness, and all those who were alien. It is no coincidence that when T.S. Eliot selected the images for the deracination, corruption, decay and degeneracy that he associated with modernity he selected Jews and ports: in fact, port Jews. In 'Gerontion' (1920) Eliot laments:

My house is a decayed house,
And the Jew squats on the window sill, the owner,
Spawned in some estaminet of Antwerp,
Blistered in Brussels, patched and peeled in London.

The revolting Mr Bleistein in 'Burbank with a Baedecker; Bleistein with a Cigar' (1920) is a 'Chicago Semite Viennese'. Eliot describes him as follows:

A lustreless protrusive eye
Stares from the protozoic slime
At a perspective of Canaletto.
The smoky candle end of time

Declines. On the Rialto once.
The rats are underneath the piles.
The Jew is underneath the lot.
Money in furs...[28]

The port as gateway to empire and enterprise that welcomed Jews has now been transformed into a gaping sewer. Again, it is no coincidence that these poems were composed and published at a time when stringent immigration controls were being enforced against the Jews and many were deported.[29] The dockside had become an arena for contested assessments of 'the Jew' and a site of renewed struggle over the Jewish presence.

Eliot's poetry testifies to the tremendous dynamic in the role, function and cultural meanings of the city port throughout history. More research is needed to uncover and understand this dynamism and the precise ligaments that articulate the history of city port with Jewish history and culture. We have identified a social type that can be linked to a particular locus during a particular era, but the social type may not be universal to all port cities and, in any case, ports change. They were not necessarily rational, benign, or welcoming to Jews. They had a negative as well as a positive impact on Jewish history.

In a study of Jamaican port towns, B.W. Higman comments that 'The ports were by nature Janus-faced, barriers as well as portals to profits and progress'. Port cities do not exist in a vacuum but have complex relations with their hinterland in terms of political, commercial and cultural ties. Group relations and power relations within them are no less complex and dynamic.[30] Some Jews may have reacted to these circumstances by seizing the main chance; others, it seems, became 'reluctant cosmopolitans'.[31] The port Jews of London may have fallen somewhere between these two, but for now any conclusion must be tentative because we are only just beginning to understand this forgotten dimension of Anglo-Jewish history.

ACKNOWLEDGEMENTS

I am grateful to Professor Tony Kushner for his comments on an earlier draft of this paper.

NOTES

1. This story has been told many times, with significant variations. For the most recent and authoritative account, see David S. Katz, *The Jews in the History of England* (Oxford: Oxford University Press, 1994), pp.114–17 and 133–4.
2. See for example, Edgar Samuel, 'The Readmission of the Jews to England in 1656, in the Context of English Economic Policy', *Jewish Historical Studies*, vol.31 (1988–1990), 153–170. Cf. Katz (see note 1), pp.108–9.
3. On the ports of London see, J. Pudney, *London's Docks* (London: Thames & Hudson, 1975); on the Port of London (PLA), see J. Broodbank, *The History of the Port of London*, 2 vols (London: Daniel O'Connor, 1921); Arthur Bryant, *Liquid History* (London: privately printed, 1960); F.J.A. Broeze, 'Paradigm of Britain: The Port of London in the 19th and 20th Centuries', in L.M. Akveld and J.R. Bruijn (eds.) *Shipping Companies and Authorities in the 19th and 20th centuries* (The Hague: Nederlande Vereniging wer, 1989), pp.63–80; Roy Porter, *London: A Social History* (London: Zeegeschiedenis, 1994). For a stimulating attempt to integrate London's history with the history of trade, immigration, and transmigration, see Nick Merriman (ed.) *The Peopling of London* (London: Museum of London, 1994).
4. David Sorkin, 'The Port Jew: Notes Towards a Social Type', *Journal of Jewish Studies*, 50:1 (1999), 87–97.
5. B.S. Hoyle and D.A. Pinder, *European Port Cities in Transition* (London: Belhaven Press, 1992), p.1.
6. Ibid., pp.2–3. See also Catherine Nash, 'Historical Geographies of Modernity' in Brian

Graham and Catherine Nash (eds.), *Modern Historical Geographies* (London: Longman, 2000), pp.13–40, for a general interpretative framework and specific references to the case of Bristol.

7. Ibid., pp.6–8. See also, Josef Konvitz, *Cities and the Sea: Port City Planning in Early Modern Europe* (Baltimore: Johns Hopkins University Press, 1978) on port city planning during the Enlightenment.
8. Hans Meyer, *Port and City* (Rotterdam: International Books, 1999), pp.17–23.
9. Ibid., pp.30–2.
10. Ibid., p.35. See also Nash (note 6), pp.33–5.
11. See H.S.Q. Henriques, *The Jews and the English Law* (Oxford: Oxford University Press, 1908).
12. T.H. Lloyd, *Alien Merchants in England in the High Middle Ages* (Sussex: Harvester, 1982), p.9 and 10–14.
13. Sylvia Thrupp, *The Merchant Class of Mediaeval London [1300–1500]* (Ann Arbor: University of Michigan Press, [1948] 1977 edn), pp.6–7, 14, 53–60, 219–22.
14. Katz (see note 1), pp.114–34.
15. See Lucien Wolf, 'The First Stage of Emancipation', in Cecil Roth (ed.), *Essays in Jewish History* (London: Jewish Historical Society of England, 1934), pp.117–28; Katz (see note 1), pp.146–56.
16. Katz (see note 1), p.109. The experience of Jews in Bordeaux was similar: Frances Malino, *The Sephardic Jews of Bordeaux: Assimilation and Emancipation in Revolutionary and Napoleonic France* (Tuscaloosa: University of Alabama Press, 1978), pp.3–6.
17. Stephen Alexander Fortune, *Merchants and Jews: The Struggle for British West Indian Commerce, 1650–1750* (Gainesville: University of Florida Press, 1984).
18. Gedalia Yogev, *Diamonds and Corals: Anglo-Dutch Jews and Eighteenth Century Trade* (Leicester: University of Leicester Press, 1978), esp. pp.15–19.
19. See Konvitz (note 7) in general and pp.124–6 in particular. But compare Lois C. Dubin, *The Port Jews of Habsburg Trieste: Absolutist Politics and Enlightenment Culture* (Stanford: Stanford University Press , 1999), pp.198–225.
20. Konvitz (see note 7), pp.159–74.
21. Lucien Wolf, 'Cromwell's Jewish Intelligencers', in Roth (ed.) (see note 15), pp.93–114; Fortune (see note 17) pp.38–9.
22. Edgar R Samuel, 'The First Fifty Years' in V.D. Lipman (ed.), *Three Centuries of Anglo-Jewish History* (London: Jewish Historical Society of England, 1961), pp.31–5.
23. Ibid., pp.38–9.
24. Harold Pollins, *Economic History of the Jews in England* (East Brunswick, NJ: Littman Library/ Associated University Press, 1984), pp.48–8.
25. Todd Endelman, *The Jews of Georgian England* (Philadelphia: Jewish Publication Society of America, 1982).
26. David Ruderman, *Jewish Enlightenment in an English Key* (Princeton, NJ: Princeton University Press, 2000).
27. Lloyd Gartner, *The Jewish Immigrant in England* (London: Vallentine Mitchell [1961] 2001 edn; David Feldman, *Englishmen and Jews* (London:Yale University Press, 1994).
28. T.S. Eliot, *Collected Poems, 1909–1962* (London: Faber, 1974), pp.39, 42–3.
29. David Cesarani, 'Anti-Alienism in England After the First World War', *Immigrants and Minorities*, 6.1 (March 1987), 5–29.
30. B.W. Higman, 'Jamaican Port Towns in the Early 19th Century', in Franklin Wright and Peggy Liss (eds.), *Atlantic Port Cities. Economy, Culture, and Society in the Atlantic World 1650–1850* (Knoxville: University of Tennessee Press, 1991), p.141.
31. Daniel M. Swetschinski, *Reluctant Cosmopolitans: The Portuguese Jews of 17th Century Amsterdam* (London: Littman Library, 2000) and Miriam Bodian, *Hebrews of the Portuguese Nation: Conversos and Community in Early Modern Amsterdam* (Bloomington: Indiana University Press, 1997).

Port Jewry of Salonika: Between Neo-colonialism and Nation-state

MARK LEVENE

The concept of Port Jews as postulated by David Sorkin and Lois Dubin provides us with an important corrective to historiographic wisdoms which locate the Jewish encounter with modernity as essentially a product of middle European and hence largely Ashkenazi interactions with the wider world.[1] By focusing instead on a handful of western Sephardi merchant communities, notably Bordeaux, Amsterdam and Trieste in the seventeenth and early eighteenth centuries – in some cases, a generation or more before the phenomenon of either the Court Jew or the *maskil* became significant – the Sorkin-Dubin thesis offers an alternative paradigm in which the economic take-off of the west is implicitly the transitional key. The forging of a distinctively western Sephardi encounter with modernity is thus predicated on a series of symbiotic relationships with commercially-orientated polities geared towards the opening of the new Atlantic economy and/or its transformative linkage with much older Mediterranean trading networks.

The argument is compelling, perhaps not least because it seems to chime in so clearly with our own ostensible Zeitgeist. Not only could the Port Jewish 'success story' be taken as one of a victory of economic pragmatism over religious bigotry, but it also has the added advantage of proffering a model for Jewish integration into a broader societal space without the diminution of Jewish political and cultural autonomy which we associate with a later, emancipatory trajectory. The creation of a social and political environment in which communal groups can be definably and self-sustainingly themselves, while still being able to operate freely within an inclusive network of commercial and cultural exchange, appears to be one of the benefits of globalisation. And as a sub-set of a middleman minority peculiarly predisposed and suited to make the most of such opportunities, could one not posit Sephardi port Jewries as a harbinger of exactly this sort of inclusive but plural, open yet multicultural milieu otherwise denied by the implicit or explicit straightjacketing, exclusion, or worse, of the intervening two centuries so largely shaped or dominated by the nation-state?

With this in view the purpose of this contribution is twofold. First, it seeks to consider whether the Port Jew concept can be applied to Salonika Jewry at a critical juncture in its existence between 1878 and 1912. By moving the goalposts, so to speak, eastwards, to another key Sephardi community, while continuing to apply the basic Port Jew terms of reference, might we not have grounds for reinforcing the model? All the more so if it could be shown that such a framework is pertinent to a communal development otherwise chronologically divorced from Sorkin and Dubin's focus. With Salonika Jewry itself the driving force behind a 1912 bid to turn the town into a free port, entirely dedicated to international trade and commerce, might one not argue, indeed, that the port Jew ideal reached its culmination at this point in time and place?

However, if this sounds like grounds for celebration, the second and more important intention here is to problematise the issue. Certainly, the fin-de-siècle emergence – or more accurately re-emergence – of Salonika as a city dominated by its cosmopolitan and outward-looking Jewry may provide a significant historical pointer to the development of the interconnected, post-national 'global village'. But it could equally underscore the conundrum of being a middleman minority in polities and societies attempting to grapple with forces of rapid, externally imposed economic change.

Here one might equally argue that it is exactly the complexity of what is truly modern which sets fin-de-siècle Salonika apart from its early modern Sephardi predecessors. The effulgent luminosity of the community's life came in a brief window between the twilight years of its existence under the Ottoman empire from 1878 and its *force majeure* supercession by a Greek nation-state in 1912–13. A generation on and the community would come to a definitive terminus, responsibility resting in this case entirely with the Nazis. Yet the survival of the Salonika community in the intervening years between 1913 and 1943, while all around them other non-Greek Salonicans – Bulgarians, Turks, *dönme* – were being expelled or massacred, can in some sense only add to the conundrum.[2] Was the community's survival in any way the result of its trading, middleman status? In which case, why were other Ottoman Armenian and Greek communities, with at least some similar attributes to the Jews, the victims of expulsion, ethnic cleansing and genocide in that part of the residual Ottoman empire which was turning itself into another – Turkish – nation-state? Adana, a key port city with a mixed population was the scene of a major Armenian massacre in 1909, in the wake of the Young Turk revolution of the previous year.[3] Smyrna

(Izmir), historically a major port rival of Salonika's was completely expunged of both its Armenians and Greeks with enormous violence, in 1922.[4] As for Salonika itself, the following year witnessed, albeit on a smaller scale to events in western Anatolia, the 'repatriation' [sic] to Turkey of the entire 12,000–13,000 dönme community.[5]

These specifically urban disasters were, of course, only the elements of an entirely ruined ethnically heterogeneous landscape throughout the Balkans and Anatolia which were the most visible to a western public, and in which practically every conceivable 'minority' community suffered major displacement or killing in the late or post-Ottoman years of nation-state formation.[6] Salonika Jewry, in fact, also suffered a series of major disasters, not least when it was swamped by 100,000 Anatolian Greek refugees in the wake of the infamous Treaty of Lausanne 'Exchange' of 1923, thereby eliminating the community's long-term demographic primacy.[7] If thus, the paradoxical survival of Salonika Jewry without forcible displacement represents one facet of its post-1912 existence, this has to be set against a precipitous decline in its fortunes which mirrors the more general implosion of post-Ottoman 'minority' communities. The question which thus poses itself is this: to what extent was this tension between survival on the one hand, and communal retreat in the face of nation-state homogenisation on the other, grounded in the same circumstances – or preconditions – which also provided the wherewithal for the community's pre-1912 advantage? If it can be shown that there is some causal linkage, then celebration of the port Jew phenomenon as a harbinger of globalisation – at least in Salonika's case – would not be simply premature but, arguably, entirely misplaced. But to explore this dichotomy further we need first to consider the appropriateness of the port Jew ascription to post-1878 Salonika.

Salonika Jewry in the Ascendant?

The singular, indeed quite exceptional position of the Salonika Jewish community under the Ottomans is well known. Nowhere else in the empire was there a compact Jewish mass translating itself into a communal demographic preponderance. At its height, in the immediate pre-1912 era, close to or possibly more than half of its inhabitants were Jewish – estimates range from 60,000 to as many as 90,000 out of a total population of anywhere between 120,000 and 200,000.[8] This numerical primary was replicated in broad commercial and cultural terms, and perhaps more strikingly, in the degree to which at all levels of the town's occupational structure Jews were represented. From bankers and industrialists at one end of the spectrum, through to a genuinely proletarian base at the other,

Salonika was an authentic Jewish economic entity in a way no other city in the world could compare. It was also thanks to the political advantages of general Ottoman Jewish millet status largely unscarred by the religious–secular divides of comparative Ashkenazi milieux. In spite of obvious class divisions and conflicts, one commentator has attested that Salonika Jewry was not only a remarkably cohesive community but in critical respects a genuinely civil society.[9] In this sense alone, the port Jew type of the Sorkin-Dubin model, based as it is on essentially wealthy entrepreneurial elites[10] is extended, not to say transcended in the case of Salonika.

Most commentators however agree that the flourishing status of Salonika circa 1900 represents a significant turn around from a situation of acute decline from some 40 or 50 years earlier. Even as late as 1875 common observations were of a community suffering from serious social, demographic and educational decay.[11] This makes what happened in the space of a generation from the late-1870s or early-1880s all the more remarkable. In a period of little more than 20 years Salonika underwent a veritable economic take-off of the modern kind. Indices of this shift are evident in the creation of a brick factory, another for tiles, a further one for nails, a distillery, several breweries, a handful of soap factories, two cotton spinning mills employing no less than 800 workers and a large cigarette-rolling plant employing a further 400 workers. This on its own doubled production between 1888 and 1892 in a factory which by Balkan standards was a giant enterprise.[12] Capital for these ongoing developments, including mechanisation, was provided particularly by the Banque du Salonique founded in 1888. In this as in nearly all of the major new enterprises Jewish entrepreneurs, especially the Allatini family, played critical roles.[13] But the impact of the economic upturn which the new enterprises in part fuelled also enhanced wider employment prospects for a much larger section of the Jewish and non-Jewish population.

It has been estimated that taking into account the port workers and those in smaller ateliers, there were 20,000 Salonika workers towards the end of our period. A sizeable proportion of these were Jewish including the port stevedores and porters who had for generations operated as an ethnically closed shop. But this did not prevent attempts after 1908 to create an organised workers movement – the Federacion Socialista Laboradera – across the port's ethnic divides, very much on the initiative of Jewish socialists led by Avraham Benaroya.[14] The vibrancy of the town's wider political and cultural life also carried with it a major, one might argue primary, Jewish input. The burgeoning of a polyglot press did not preclude the primacy of those published in Ladino, while what operated as a lingua franca in the commercial life of the port also found its way into theatrical productions, the new theatres again being further indication of the city's ongoing transformation.[15] A more overtly Jewish middle-class participation in the wider social scene is clearly evident too in the formation of a number of masonic lodges which were to play a supporting role in the Young Turks' rise to power,[16] and in proposals made in 1907 for the creation of a university of Salonika.[17]

If these developments should suffice to indicate the voluntary integration of Jews at all levels of Salonika life – and in so doing confirm the community's candidature for port Jew status according to an implicit aspect of the Sorkin-Dubin model – they do not derogate from another aspect, namely the sustainability of a specifically communal Jewish life. With no serious inroads into the community's autonomy emanating from the state before 1909, and this in spite of the various mid-century Tanzimat rescripts promoting the concept of a general Ottoman citizenship, Salonika Jewry was free to continue and develop its communal organs more or less as it chose. True, in response to an imperial decree of 1856 which required a general reorganisation of millet administration, decision making in the community became increasingly dependent on its lay rather than its rabbinic leadership. But this tendency actually conforms well to the secular-orientated modernisation of the Port Jew model. Again, in the key area of this development, namely schooling, the children of better-off Jewish Salonikans – both boys and girls – were largely educated outside direct communal control in private French or Italian colleges. However the same was not so for the vast majority of poorer Jewish youth who found their route to educational and vocational improvement through the seven communal schools that were mostly founded after 1870, albeit supported, staffed and closely supervised by the elite French organisation, the Alliance Israélite Universelle.[18] An Association of Alliance Alumni was one of a number of specifically Jewish Salonican cultural groups, literary clubs or sporting organisations which emerged and flourished in this period.[19] Many of these organisations also participated heavily in charitable work, providing an all-important corollary to the traditional but increasingly hard-pressed support systems for the poor, the sick and the marginal as administered by the communal council.[20]

The reminder that economic deprivation and immiseration were still very much a part of the Salonika Jewish scene – a problem which arguably was actually worsening in our period, however – begs an important question. If as the wretchedly complacent saying goes, 'the poor will be always with us', could one not by the same token argue the same for the term port Jewry? After all, there had been a continuous Sephardi-dominated Jewish presence in the town for almost 400 years prior the 1870s. The physical geography of the place had not changed, either in itself as 'the only noteworthy Mediterranean port for Balkan trade'[21] or in relationship to its immediate hinterland. True, the size of its internal market in this region embracing not only Macedonia but also Albania, Epirus and Thrace had grown by the 1900s to an estimated four million people[22] and this market, as we shall see, was at this stage becoming much better connected with the port than it had ever been previously. But Jewish port-related activity and consequent prosperity had hardly begun at this point.

On the contrary, the heyday of the town's commercial life was in the 1500s, that is, at the very inception of the Ottoman–Sephardi nexus, though one might add maintaining a momentum as such for considerably longer than the period under our spotlight. Critical commercial criteria we associate with the Sorkin-Dubin model, including Jewish involvement in shipping, brokerage and finance were all present. So too were specifically town-based enterprises based in this case on utilising the chief agricultural product of the surrounding area – wool – for textile manufacture and export.[23] Moreover, the specifically Sephardi advantage of extended-family connections with other mercantile port communities throughout the Mediterranean and beyond ensured Salonika's interconnectedness in the realm of international trade. One could go further and argue that as Salonika's ascendancy much preceded that of the western Sephardi foci of Sorkin-Dubin interest, a case could be made for shifting the focus of the whole Port Jew hypothesis away from the seventeenth century Atlantic periphery to a much more central and obvious location in the sixteenth century Eastern Mediterranean.[24]

This argument, however, would fall down on a very simple element again implicit (though not always explicit) in the Port Jew model. The sixteenth century Salonika Jewish success story is a function of the rise of the Ottomans as a self-sustaining world empire. That of the port Jew 'type' however is a by-product of an incipient world economy, that is, one essentially either monopolised or at the very least determined by the west. The two systems – as Immanuel Wallerstein and others have argued – are incompatible.[25] The rise of the latter to global hegemony ensured the retreat and ultimate collapse of the former's essentially regional frame of reference. To be sure, the process was not only very prolonged but by no means regular or consistent. But all the way from its early falterings in the early seventeenth century through into the period of complete rupture in the early nineteenth, the weakening fortunes of the empire's political economy were closely replicated in that of Salonika's.

Indeed, from the moment when it became clear that its early seventeenth-century textile mainstay could no longer compete with imported English products,[26] through to the loss of its one assured state market in the form of clothing for the Janissary corps – when the Sultan turned his guns on them – in 1826,[27] Salonika's abiding story, as epitomised by its textile industry, is one of long-term economic reversal and implosion. With its foreign trade increasingly captured by Greek competitors, many of whom latterly were able to make good their fiscal advantage through Russian capitulatory protection,[28] and with that trade increasingly turning even in the field of basic grain commodity from one of export to import,[29] Salonikan Jewish dependency on both the patronage and protectionist economics of the Ottoman system were proving to be little short of disastrous. With its revenues diminished the community's ability to hold its own as a centre of Jewish learning and publishing, which had been a key feature of its sixteenth century glory, equally faltered. Neither the arrival of the Tanzimat reforms, nor the implicit acknowledgement which went with them of an Ottoman readjustment to the political economic imperatives of the emerging western-controlled world economy saw a fundamental change in the community's prospects. Salonika Jews, for the most part, did not rush to take advantage of the opportunities to act as agents for European firms, as did many Greeks and Armenians.[30] Even the clogging up of its harbour with British and French ships during the Crimean war of 1854–56 does not seem to have especially triggered a more persistent upturn in Salonika's trade as one might expect.[31] Indeed, even taking into account the upturn which did materialise from the 1880s the volume of exports from the port remained a fraction of the imports primarily coming from European or European-controlled sources.[32]

All of this would seem to make the underlying causes of Salonika's undoubted post-1880 revitalisation all the more intriguing. Interestingly, a signpost to this change does link us back to the main thrust of the Port Jew thesis. A small 'privileged' sub-grouping within Salonika Jewry had been making economic headway since the eighteenth century. But strictly speaking its status was anomalous. These Francos (lit. 'westerners'), were incomers whose family and trading connections were primarily with the 'open' Italian ports of Livorno and Trieste. As foreigners they were entitled to the relevant consular protection as well as exemption from taxes normally owing to both the Ottoman state and the Jewish community.[33] In this way, too, as well as being directly linked by kinship to the Port Jew phenomenon, one might argue that they were true avant la lettre representatives of maximalist 'free trade' principles, extraterritoriality as provided by a western-imposed capitulations system both enabling them and acting as a galvanus to the development of their unfettered entrepreneurial interests. Equally significantly, the product which they particularly wished to develop in the Salonika region was one with which many port Jews were already intimately associated in their trans-Atlantic dealings: tobacco.[34] Franco families like the Allatini and Recanati, in seeking to encourage çiftlik estate owners in climatically suitable parts of Macedonia and Thrace, especially in the Serres region, towards the more extensive cultivation of this new cash-crop thereby not only sought to confirm their monopoly in its sale, primarily in the first instance to the Italian market[35] but also to create thereby a capital accumulation with which to develop and diversify their business ventures.

It is no coincidence that it was these same Franco families who were instrumental in the gathering pace of industrial development both before and during our key take-off period.[36] But is also no coincidence that the 'extraterritorial' framework within which Francos had been operating up to this juncture received what amounted to a general political sanction after 1878.

The Benefits of Neo-Colonialism

The 1878 Congress of Berlin is mostly remembered in Jewish annals, on the one hand for the clauses requiring the new post-Ottoman Balkan states to adopt civil and political rights, thereby legally assimilating the Jews of those states to the western emancipatory model, and on the other for the refusal of Romania to comply with them.[37] In truth, however, these were only relatively minor items on a Great Power agenda to create and enforce an entirely new political and economic order throughout the Near East, and in which the Ottoman construct henceforth was to serve as a neo-colonial facade for the preservation and extension of those same Great Power interests. Or, to put it another way, rather than liquidating the imperium and attempting to carve up its territorial assets between themselves, 'It was easier and more profitable to dominate the empire's market through privileges and concessions from a single centralised Ottoman administration.'[38]

From the position of a great world empire, the Ottoman state thus was reduced to one where in all key areas of its economic and political self-determination its actions were subject to the say-so of its foreign creditors, backed up in turn by their respective chancelleries. At the political level, for instance, the new order was exemplified in 1903 by the formation in Salonika's immediate Macedonian hinterland of a gendarmerie under Great Power licence whose underlying purpose was not so much to improve law and order in the region as to create a balance of power between competing Russian and Austrian interests.[39] Much more importantly for our focus, outside economic control was effectively streamlined from 1881 with the creation of an International Public Debt

Administration for Ottoman finances. This not only maintained an oversight of the empire's entire fiscal machinery, effectively curtailing the Porte's independent action, at least at the intra-state level, but also took over a significant portion of its revenues. Ostensibly this was in order to ensure that its foreign creditors received the interest on the £200 million of loans dating back to the Crimean war period and upon which Ottoman default in 1875–76 had precipitated the crisis of state which had led to Great Power 'resolution' in the first place.[40] In practice, the Administration's farming out of these revenues to foreign leaseholders offered to them seriously lucrative returns.

The most important monopoly or regie now ceded in this way – asset-stripped might be the more appropriate modern terminology – was in the purchase, manufacture and resale of tobacco.[41] The regie was won by a consortium comprising the largely Anglo-French Ottoman Bank, the Rothschild-controlled Creditanstalt of Vienna and the Bleichröder bank of Berlin.[42] Key authorities on the role of European investment banks in these developments – not just to do with the regie but that of the rescue and shoring up of Ottoman finances more generally – have tended not to consider or dwell upon the fact that so many of them were Jewish-controlled or dominated houses.[43] Again, with lack of additional evidence to argue the case, one can only surmise what this sub-text may have meant for Franco entrepreneurs with their already pre-existing stake in the tobacco industry as they sought additional capital for both it and related development. What we can say with some certainty is twofold. First, Salonika tobacco exports – assisted by a drastic reduction in duties and with rapidly increasing global demand for an item whose export value had risen to ten times that of wheat[44] – may have vastly increased, while still retaining the old Habsurg Trieste connection. One third of the port's tobacco exports in this period went to Austria-Hungary.[45] Second, it was again increasingly to Central European sources that local entrepreneurs looked for seed money, the Allatinis' great enterprise, the Banque du Salonique, for instance, being founded as a cooperative venture primarily with the Austrian Landerbank but with Hungarian and French sources also contributing to its initial capital of 10 million francs.[46]

Of course, this case was very much the exception. While European investment capital post-1878 began to flow into an empire now supposedly secured and guaranteed by Great Power imprimatur, very little of this was for the direct benefit of indigenous private enterprise. The vast majority was for infrastructural projects, in other words with the Ottoman state itself as purchaser, an estimated two-thirds going into railways and a further ten per cent into ports and port facilities.[47] Yet these inflows were themselves instrumental in Salonika's reorientation as 'a leading nodal point of the incorporation of the empire into the capitalist world economy.'[48] Railway communications, linking Salonika with Constantinople and other local towns had already been underway prior to 1878 under the auspices of Baron de Hirsch's 'Oriental' railway concessions. After this date, however, the extension of railway networks from Berlin, Vienna and Paris into the Balkans and beyond quickened while remaining dependent on routing down the Vardar valley to Salonika itself or, conversely, via the Vardar and Vistritsa for the opening up of Salonika's more inaccessible hinterland. A new harbour facility created in 1889 likewise confirmed that rapid access and egress for foreign commerce was literally the route determining the port's future progress and prosperity.[49]

Yet in these all-important developments, too, there was a Jewish sub-text. Baron Maurice de Hirsch, the maverick financier who from the late-1860s had practically single-handedly pioneered international investment in the direction of Balkan railway building, thereafter, not unlike some earlier day Geoge Soros, proceeded to act as a one-man redistributor of Ottoman wealth in favour of the Alliance schools in the empire.[50] In so doing, he helped to dramatically facilitate a process by which the great bulk of Salonika Jewry not only became modernised but – not least through the acquisition of French language – westernised. Which in turn, of course, greatly enhanced many of their employment prospects with foreign companies wishing to do business with, or set up shop in, the port. When, moreover, Hirsch decided to sell his Oriental holdings in 1886, a key player in their transfer to the German government-backed Deutsche Bank was none other than Bismarck's personal banker, Gerson Bleichröder, again otherwise best known in Jewish annals for his behind-the-scenes efforts to achieve Romanian Jewish emancipation at the Berlin Congress.[51] Bleichröder, as it so happened, as well as having his own relatively modest stake in Hirsch's Oriental railway network also had a much larger and entirely more significant one in the tobacco regie.[52]

The fact that Hirsch and Bleichröder were key intermediaries, not to say power brokers in the emerging relationship between Ottomans, banking houses and European chancelleries does not, of course, of itself explain either the creation or evolution of a late nineteenth century Salonika port Jewry. What perhaps it does point towards is the degree to which the community was a beneficiary of economic and political developments whose origins lay not in a derelict Ottoman empire but in European powerhouses. The fact that some of these were Ashkenazi investment banks to whom Franco entrepreneurs came, in some sense as supplicants, certainly would undermine the autonomous logic of the basic eighteenth-century Sephardi model. But then the port Jewry being delineated here is one which in some critical sense had been cast adrift from its moorings. To whom, after all, did post-1878 Salonika Jewry owe its allegiance? To the Ottoman empire? To the Great Powers? Or was it, perhaps, to both?

Salonika Jewry as a Comprador Entity?

What we have thus far attempted to propose is that the revitalisation of Salonika was at bottom a function of its serviceability to western commercial interests in an era where – at least as far as the Ottoman empire was concerned – these had become hegemonic. Like a number of comparable Ottoman ports, notably Smyrna, Beirut and Alexandria,[53] the motor of Salonika's transformation lay in its ability to turn itself into a safe and efficient warehouse for the distribution of incoming western goods, on the one hand, and for the shipping out of Macedonian primary products on the other. But this clearly also entailed a two-way process. If Salonika chose not to play the western card, those interests would surely have taken themselves elsewhere, perhaps most obviously to the port's historic rival and competitor, Greek-dominated Smyrna. An enlightened Turkish governance certainly was critical in consciously modernising the city, the culmination of which in the 1890s was with the introduction of a gas lighting system and electrically propelled tramways.[54] But if this gave to incoming European business people a sense that they were more 'at home', what about the natives' welcome?

There was nothing unusual of course about the Jews acting as middlemen. This was, after all, at the very heart of their diasporic condition. In the context of the Ottoman empire, moreover, they were hardly alone – many Greeks and Armenians fulfilling identical roles. The latter too were also notably enthusiastic in their absorption of western culture, as Charles Issawi pointedly notes, 'with almost no reservations'.[55] And of course for Jewish Salonikans this was indeed no more, nor less, than what their western port Jew 'predecessors' had achieved or aspired to. The problem was that to act as both commercial collaborators and cultural disseminators of the western interest in the context of a new neo-colonial order carried with it implications which clearly did not arise in eighteenth-century Trieste or Bordeaux. It particularly brought with it the charge of compradorship.

The term compradorship in itself is harmless enough. A comprador according to a standard dictionary definition is 'a native agent of a foreign enterprise'.[56] But in an age of polarised national and class politics it has come to denote exactly that sort of selfish pursuit of profit not only at the expense of larger society but more pointedly in a way which denies that larger society the opportunity to acquire or tap wealth which might otherwise have enabled it to undertake its own genuinely independent process of modernisation. In the 1960s and 1970s the identification of western economic hegemony as the root of third world under-development, in both dependency and world-system theories, further underscored the role of a comprador bourgeoisie as parasitic and hence entirely unforgivable.[57] Given, moreover, that specific 'outsider' ethnic groups have been particularly associated with the nomenclature, the results in terms of radicalised class or national politics have been little short of catastrophic. Simply consider the ejection of the Gujerati community from Uganda and Kenya, most infamously in the former case under Idi Amin, or the repeated attacks on Chinese communities in much of south east Asia, or indeed, in the most extreme example of theorisation being translated into genocidal practice, in the form of the Khmer Rouge regime assault against both Chinese and Vietnamese minorities between 1975 and 1979.[58]

What all this might highlight, however, is the degree to which the term and/or its implications are fair or appropriate. Not surprisingly, perhaps, historians of late-Ottoman Greek and Armenian communities have been particularly resistant to the whole notion, refuting the argument that either of them monopolised particular sectors of commerce or trade while further pointing out – quite correctly – that the majority of Greeks and Armenians were not business people at all but farmers and craftsmen.[59] But this counter-claim is again hardly surprising when so much of the contemporary historiography's characterisation of these minorities focuses exactly on their commercial connectedness with western interests, and with the way that a foreign-imposed capitulatory system in favouring them also impeded a full state fiscal extraction or, as its potential corollary, a state-led capital formation normally associated with nation-building.[60] Implicit in the Ottoman compradorship theorisation thus appears to be a form of legitimisation for these communities' elimination, the pursuit of which between 1915 and 1923 took place not simply in economic terms but in the Armenian case through mass physical extermination, and in the Greek case by mass ethnic cleansing.[61]

The paradox is that Ottoman Jewry either has been generally exempted from this negative treatment or at least has suffered it less severely. A reality which happens to coincide with the general lack of state-led physical violence against it offered by either Young Turks or Kemalist successors.[62] Yet this is doubly paradoxical, not least because the comprador appellation, while it may not suit Ottoman Jewry – nor Armenians and Greeks as a whole – arguably it is most appropriate to the position of Salonika port Jewry in our period.

Of course, such a statement must come with a number of caveats, though ironically it has never prevented Jewish leftist or Zionist critiques engaging in their own negative assessments of an essentially 'parasitic' middleman Jewish diaspora in toto.[63] Regarding Jewry as a collective monolith also has been a stock-in-trade of the anti-semite, a misapprehension particularly well answered by the very social and occupational diversity of our Salonika subject. The very fact, moreover, that at the culmination of our period, in the wake of the Young Turk takeover, this same community was riven by strikes, demonstrations and more overt political dissensions surely puts paid to any notion of some seamless, one-dimensional unity.[64]

Yet in an important sense this is both to jump the gun – 1908 does mark a critical watershed – and overlook what Salonika Jews, whether mill worker or banker, white collar clerk or professional, actually did have in common. Much of this, of course, was deeply grounded in their corporate status under Ottoman Muslim law. To be sure, all were zimmi – tolerated non-Muslims – which in the light of post-emancipatory western equality before the law often has been taken as evidence of an entirely subordinate, second-class position in society.[65] This certainly may have been so. But while being zimmi did not prevent freedom of religion, domicile, or trade – in fact it guaranteed these entitlements – it also exempted members of Jewish and Christian millets from key civic requirements and responsibilities, most obviously military service, which would otherwise have more fully absorbed them into the demands of the – albeit pre-modern – Ottoman state. However, if this was the traditional relationship between community and polity, the point about our period is that this did not fundamentally change. As Aron Rodrigue succinctly puts it: 'In spite of Tanzimat and of the principled desire of the pre-1908 Porte to Ottomanise and hence nationalise its subjects, Jews, together with other non-Muslims, continued to be disassociated from and non-integrated into a poorly developed public sphere.'[66]

What, however, had changed after 1878, as we have already seen, was the overarching framework within which this apparently political statis was perpetuated. A framework which particularly enabled Salonika Jewry – because of its demographic weight, economic potential and geographical position – to be both nominally loyal to the empire while essentially free to pursue its own path to economic and cultural modernisation in the service of a western neo-colonial order. This was a peculiar situation, even one might say a highly privileged situation – conforming in this sense with the Port Jew model – but ultimately also one which emphasised an entirely distinct form of dependency. The survival of a specifically semi-detached Salonika port Jewry, indeed, was predicated, on the one hand, on the perpetuation of an essentially weak benignly neglectful Ottoman polity – yet hopefully one which was not so weak that it would fall apart[67] – and on the other hand by the contiguous patronage of genuinely powerful European states who were, at the same time, not prepared to rock the political status quo.

In this sense, while it may not be appropriate to speak of a comprador class, it might not be inappropriate to speak of a Salonikan Jewish comprador entity. Whatever they ultimately aspired to, the poor as much as the rich, even the socialist as much as the capitalist, were dependent for economic survival on the essential contours of this particular Ottoman-Great Power arrangement. Equally noteworthy, the Alliance with its not inconsiderable leverage on the community's development also favoured it. Like all the western Jewish organisations with an interest in the 'uniform outward march of the Jews all over the world'[68] the primary purpose of Alliance intervention in the modernisation of their fellow Jews in the east was avowedly to prepare the ground for their civil and political emancipation.[69] An agenda which one might expect, according to its own assimilationist criteria, leading to efforts within its Ottoman schools to inculcate the values and language of the dominant society. True, pre-1908 'Ottoman' society did not equate with Turkish language per se.[70] Even so, the complete lack of any effort in this direction by contrast with the very conscious Alliance efforts to create both a francophone and culturally francophile constituency implicitly assumed the perpetuation – and not just in Salonika – of a semi-detached Ottoman Jewry operating in the western interest.

The great problem with this formula was that it was built on some notion of permanence. The reality was quite different.

Nationalism Intervenes

Then as now roseate assumptions about the creation of a western-shaped world economy leave out one essential by-product: nationalism. Just as the west had imported its economic interests into the Ottoman empire so it penetrated critical sections of its population with ideas. And nationalism was one imported idea which, on the one hand, took on an increasing centrality in nineteenth century Ottoman – and anti-Ottoman – discourse while on the other fatally exposing the fragility of Salonika Jewry's own best interests. In classically contradictory mode, the Great Powers, having let the genie out of the bottle, attempted to contain it at the Berlin Congress by preventing the Balkan states, to which they had at the same time given international sanction, from undertaking a further wholesale carve-up of what remained of the Ottoman empire in Europe. The new territorial boundaries were, of course, also designed to maintain a balance of power between the Great Powers themselves and, as such, Jewish Salonika had reason to be grateful that much of its Macedonian hinterland was not otherwise absorbed into a Russian-backed greater Bulgaria.[71]

By the same token it could be argued that the dominance of the Great Powers in the region was the very motor driving the elites of its diverse ethnic communities towards ever more irreconcilable forms of sacro egoismo.[72] Salonika, by contrast, as an authentic microcosm of the Ottoman multi-ethnic construct, in which different communities had always managed to co-exist, represented a tangible bulwark against such zero-sum tendencies. Yet with the creation of nation-states in its near-proximity, the different ethnic appellations for the city: the Turkish Selanik, the Greek Thessaloniki, or the Bulgarian Soloun took on an entirely new meaning. Set against their implication that the city could only belong – even by implication be inhabited – by one national body, the post-1908 efforts of Benaroya's socialist movement to create a genuine federation of its workers drawn from different ethnic communities began to look distinctly ragged not to say redundant.[73]

The very provisionality of Salonika's post-1878 existence, moreover, was made utterly manifest in 1912 when the Ottomans abandoned the city in the face of Greek and Bulgarian armies in the first Balkan war. When the Greeks subsequently ejected the Bulgarians the following year in a second multi-player Balkan conflict, it both confirmed their undivided control over the city, and so abruptly terminated more than 400 years of its continuous Jewish relationship with the Ottoman empire.[74]

But while absorption into the Hellenic state also took away the props which had enabled the Salonika community to pursue its quasi-independent destiny, one should be wary of seeing the Greeks as the specific bête noire of the piece. Whether it had been the Bulgarians, the Greeks, or for that matter the Serbs – another local contender for control of the port[75] – fundamentally the same limitations on port Jewish freedom would have applied. Trade and commerce either would have been reorientated or subsumed within a programme of national economic development, while Jews as members of an ethnic group who did not obviously fit the national criteria would either have been removed or required – possibly under duress – to conform to whatever cultural, educational or linguistic requirements were now demanded. Certainly, if the Jews had been asked their opinion on the matter they would have preferred Bulgarian control as the lesser of the evils, and not least because with Sofia's economy increasingly gearing up for the export of agricultural products to European markets the port would have provided not only the obvious point of exit but one still linked to a large hinterland.[76] Greek control offered no such consolations. Indeed, with the ports of Piraeus and Volos already well developed the one thing for which the Greek state did not want Salonika was its economic value. Certainly, Athens had plans for the development of the port as a naval facility but this was implicitly about blocking off its new Macedonian and Thracian borders, not about creating porous, tariff-free ones. With the vast majority of its historic hinterland now beyond those borders, the long-term prospects for a Salonika primarily dependent on its entrepot function were bleak.

Yet at this seminal moment in the winter of 1912–13, when the Turks were removed but neither the Greeks nor Bulgarians were firmly in control, the Jewish communal council did not single out the Greeks as the problem, or make supplications for Bulgarian control, or even ask for the return of the Turks. On the contrary, what did they proclaim? 'Salonique n'est ni grec, ni bulgare, ni turc: il est juif.'[77]

We will return to the community's substantive proposal for the internationalisation of the port in a moment. What we briefly need to consider here is the significance of this singular statement not just vis-à-vis the Greeks and Bulgarians but more pointedly with regard to the Turks. For it has become almost a cardinal item of faith in much recent Turkish historiography that Salonika Jewry were not simply fully and enthusiastically behind the Committee of Union and Progress (CUP), the new national movement commonly referred to as the Young Turks[78] which took power in Constantinople in August 1908, but were somehow integral to its development.[79]

Salonika, of course, was at the very centre of, as well as the launching pad for, the CUP revolution against the regime of the Sultan Abdul Hamid II.[80] And given Jewish predominance in the town it might be considered natural to find a linkage between revolutionary party and community. The problem is that these links are actually rather tenuous. There were, it is true, a handful of Salonikan Jews – the name of Immanuel Carasso (or as Turkified Karasu) is particularly cited – who took on high office under the CUP as well as rather more who were involved as technocrats and officials in some of the early ministries.[81] There is also one name which we can unequivocally associate with the more overtly national politics of the movement. Moise Cohen was a Salonikan who adopted the Turkish name of Tekinalp and who became arguably the key theoretician of an anti-comprador Turkish national economy.[82] It is true, too, that there was quite open support for the revolution on the streets of Salonika at its outset – though this was hardly isolated to its Jews; for a few honeymoon months, everybody seems to have been enthused by it.[83] Certainly, radical and hence more meaningful support from the Federacion seems to have lasted somewhat longer. But the important point is that it did not last.[84] Nor when CUP-Federacion understanding broke down did members of the latter go over into the ranks of the former. There was no Ottoman equivalence of the situation in post-1917 Russia where socialist Jewish cadres became a significant part of the activist and administrative backbone of the Bolshevik regime.

But the reasons why the thesis favouring a CUP–Salonika Jewish affinity fails conversely highlight the specifically port Jewish interests of the community. One problem, for instance, which the thesis fails to address, is why it was that Salonika Jewry was so politically quiescent under the Hamidian regime. Abdul Hamid II's rule is generally portrayed as one which was despotically authoritarian, violently oppressive and, in its pan-Islamic leanings, explicitly hostile to the aspirations of its non-Muslim millets. There is no doubt that the regime's relations with Armenians and Greeks – the communities most comparable to the Jews – were atrocious. Armenians both in Constantinople and throughout their Eastern Anatolian heartlands suffered repeated state-sponsored massacres between 1894 and 1896,[85] while the Hellenic state's efforts to – unsuccessfully – wrest Crete from Ottoman control in the war of 1897 naturally inflamed tensions between Porte and Greek communities throughout the empire.[86] One such recipient of these tensions was Macedonia, the Greek consulate in Salonika indeed becoming heavily involved in the financing, organising and direction of pro-Greek guerrilla operations in the area.[87] The effect was to help catalyse a competitive spiral of assaults by all interested contenders, with Salonika itself, particularly after 1903, a regular venue for terrorism and inter-ethnic violence.[88]

Yet in spite of all these convulsions Salonika Jews were neither protagonists in these events, nor viewed as such by the state. On the contrary, Abdul Hamid characterised his Jewish subjects as 'obedient, faithful, devoted', while the Alliance repaid the compliment in 1893 – a year of markedly deteriorating Ottoman–Armenian relations – with a report offering the view that he was 'a generous sovereign and a protector of his Israelite subjects'.[89] Jewish travellers from neighbouring countries like Bulgaria, supposedly a constitutional monarchy, also vigorously corroborated the sense of greater freedom which they felt under Hamidian protection;[90] indeed, one of the reasons that the Salonika community became so large in our period is because it was the most obvious haven for Jewish refugees fleeing Greek or Bulgarian persecution.[91] The prime Hamidian years of the 1890s, one modern commentator concludes, were also 'the best years of Ottoman Jewry in modern times'.[92]

The accent thus is very firmly on Jewish loyalty to the pre-1908 status quo. The community, particularly those more politically aware elements within it, may not have liked the Hamidian regime as such. And some, through the Masonic lodges, worked actively with the nascent oppositional CUP for his removal.[93] But this should not suppose that Jewish interests and what certainly became Young Turk interests after 1908 were in any fundamental sense congruent. A limited framework of Ottoman rule gave to the Jews all the scope they needed. They were not for a disruptive rupture but for a continuity, though preferably under a more obviously liberal and progressive regime. Indeed, if one were to speculate about an elective affinity at all, the place to look would be not so much with the CUP per se but with Salonika's substantial *dönme*, a community which had become part of the town's 'enlightened' administrative establishment yet one which appears to have retained close social and cultural links with its Jewish neighbours.[94] One might even wish to compare this relationship with that between western port Jewish communities and outwardly Christian-practising marranos. The point however is this: with this sort of political support system available to buttress their developing economic ones, there was no objective reason for Salonika Jews to become Turkish nationalists, or aspire to some megale idea, or even cut down to size, to the equivalent of the Armenian revolutionary aspiration for autonomous vilayets. The notion of a Jewish national settlement in Palestine there may have been, but efforts to accomplish it in the Hamidian era came from Ashkenazi Jews based in Berlin. Salonika Jewry's active interest in Zionism before 1908 was minimal.[95]

Yet what is equally clear is that after 1908 unstinting Salonika Jewish loyalty to the Ottoman state begins to be increasingly challenged by those other strategies famously identified by Albert Hirschmann – exit and voice.[96] Clearly, it did not happen all at once. Loyalty combined with a tangible Ottoman patriotism, for instance, is self-evident in the Salonika port workers' enforcement of the boycott of Austrian goods, in retaliation for the Habsburg annexation of Bosnia-Herzegovina, soon after the CUP takeover. Even though objectively, of course, this militated against the port's commercial interests.[97] More venally, elements of the Salonika's commercial elite appear to have supported the CUP's further boycott of all Greek traders, including indigenous ones – perhaps recognising in this an opportunity to particularly make gains at Smyrna's expense – when Crete attempted to declare union with the Hellenic state a year later.[98]

Yet it was exactly this sort of state-directed attack on the equality of all the peoples in the empire which would have set the Salonikan alarm bells ringing. Intimidation or persecution of Greeks could just as easily become an attack on any other ethnic or religious group. Indeed, from late 1909, a tranche of coercive legislation did follow. Some of this, in the form of anti-association and strike laws, appeared to be specifically directed against well-organised political associations such as the Federacion. Closed down and with Benayora himself eventually arrested and exiled, the basis for a mass Salonika Jewish mobilisation in support of a regime faced with the sort of counter-revolutionary threat which nearly toppled it in spring 1909 had been entirely negated.[99] But such measures were also extended to restrict organisations based on nationality or denomination, and thus could appear to be much more pointed derogations of millet autonomy. That this was in fact the case crystallised very rapidly with CUP proposals to oversee communal schools and extend military conscription regardless of traditional non-Muslim exemptions.[100]

What had undoubtedly begun as an unadulterated Salonika Jewish support for the CUP was thus wrecked on two accounts. The first, entailing the regime's volte face on open, liberal, constitutional government – which all oppositional political groupings had assumed to be part of its integral restorative programme – was serious enough. But ultimately it was not nearly as serious as the way the party's increasingly Turkifying and centralising agenda clashed with and overrode the community's own best interests. Certainly, Salonika port Jewry had had reason to welcome a political movement which seemed resolute and determined in maintaining the integrity of an empire in the face of what had appeared, in 1908, as an imminent Great Power-sponsored carve-up.[101] But if this implied turning everybody in the process into Turks, it completely undermined the basis upon which the community understood the terms of its modus operandi within the late-Ottoman construct. By 1911, moreover, with an Italian invasion of Tripolitania, there was little evidence that the CUP could even save the construct.

What all this might have meant for long-term CUP–Salonika Jewish relations had they had an opportunity to develop, remains speculative. We know that by 1912, in confirmation of the exit strategy, many of the rich Jews were getting out, or more specifically were sending abroad their sons who were eligible for conscription.[102] There is also some evidence that in terms of 'voice', Jewish oppositional groupings, including the Federacion, were making approaches to Itilaf (the Entente Liberal Party), the Young Turk breakaway grouping which wanted to promote an Ottoman form of federal decentralisation. This aspiration, plus its commitment to laissez-faire economics, not to say emphasis on 'personal initiative', made it the obvious forum for Salonikan Jews disenchanted with the CUP.[103] But whether it was anxiety about making common cause with Armenians and Greeks who were prominent within it – given Salonika Jewry's ongoing poor relations with these communities[104] – or

more historically embedded fears of open disloyalty against the
government which acted as an inertial drag, there is no definitive
evidence of an emerging communal understanding. Besides, with Itilaf in
power as the Greeks marched into Salonika – thereby underscoring its
actual military–political febrility – the community decided to make a
dramatic move in its own right.

Salonika Jewry and the Great Powers: A Final Paradox

The decision by the Salonika Jewish Council to seek Great Power
intervention in favour of the port's internationalisation certainly may be
indicative of a minority community acting in extremis. But alternatively
might we not see this as a logical culmination of its port Jewish interests?
The denial of the opportunity to achieve a full potentiality in this
direction was, after all, not simply the fault of Greece. It was implicit in
the nature of competing latecomer nationalisms tout court. And in this
sense the definitiveness of the 1912 terminus was already prefigured in the
emerging dirigiste thrust of CUP politics. Taking that thrust to its logical
conclusion would ultimately have put paid to the cosy, two-masters
arrangement which Salonika had enjoyed since 1878, replacing it instead
with a single undiluted, capitulations-free, national sovereignty. Which, of
course, is exactly what did happen in the Anatolian residue of the empire
under Kemal Atatürk.

What then is equally significant about the community's winter
1912–13 démarche is that this was an attempt to remove Salonika from the
field of politically-inspired, inter-ethnic conflict by seeking a protective
umbrella which could firmly and unequivocally fix it outside the national
framework altogether. To achieve this goal the community unashamedly
offered the port as a conduit for the Great Power's own exploitative
purpose. The Jews would run the port along with 600 square kilometres
of the surrounding hinterland, but its key beneficiaries would be those
powers specifically cited – Britain, France, Germany and Austria. To
make it even more obvious what was intended, the models proffered for
its development were the already existing free ports of Tangiers in
Morocco and Dairen in Manchuria; in other words, examples par
excellence of open-door commerce in the neo-colonial interest and at the
territorial and economic expense of the surrounding de jure state.[105]

Which leaves us with one final paradox. Given that this in itself
represented a blatant repudiation of the national interest, why did the
Greeks, having taken firm control of the town, not send its Jews packing?
After genocidal-style killings and ethnic cleansings committed by all
parties in the Balkan wars,[106] we can be assured that there was no

sentimentality acting as a brake on this likely trajectory. On the contrary, not only had Jews been the subject of ethnic cleansings from Greece (and Bulgaria) on previous occasions, but the intensity of traditional economic and religious animosities against them was now fuelled by the bitter nature of the Darwinian struggle to Hellenise the Salonika region.[107] The answer to our conundrum interestingly may lie with the one ingredient in this particular narrative which is clearly at odds with the seventeenth and eighteenth century port Jewish experience and which places it instead firmly in the modern world of acute, overwrought judeophobia. It also gives it a final twist.

The very fact that the Salonika internationalisation proposal, as received by all the major western and Central European Jewish organisations including the Zionists, subsequently found its way into the bureaux of the Great Power chancelleries suggests a degree of Jewish kudos and power on the world stage which, by fin-de-siècle, few even in those very same quarters were prepared to deny. Objectively speaking one can, of course, see in the possibility of Franco entrepreneurs having access to Bleichröders and Rothschilds who in turn were sometimes able to play the role of inter-governmental political brokers, a transmission belt which seemed to bring even the 'Oriental' periphery close to the metropolitan corridors of power. Geographically and economically marginalised the Sephardi elite may have become, but through the good offices of their Ashkenazi 'co-religionists' they could still operate within the European mainstream. Clearly, at some level, the notion that European Jewry on the cusp of the contemporary era was entirely powerless is a fallacious one.

Yet what is thoroughly extraordinary is how these Jewish connections were portrayed and interpreted. Elsewhere, I have laboured to show how non-Jewish perceptions of Jews rather than the reality of Jewish life in the early part of the twentieth century is key to understanding the high political behaviour of the European powers towards what actually remained a highly dispersed and disparate diaspora.[108] Of course, looked at through some global overview there were Jews who were both prominent in finance and in radical, even revolutionary politics. But the supposed 'Jewish' connections between these two extremes were developed, embroidered and ultimately fantasised into something entirely more potent and toxic by none other than leading European statesmen, diplomats and foreign office civil servants.

We know that this was the case, at least with regard to events in Salonika, through the extant diplomatic records of the supposedly most liberal of the Great Powers, Britain and France. Sir Gerald Lowther, Britain's ambassador to the Porte after 1908, for instance, insisted in his dispatches back home that behind the Salonika army coup which had brought the CUP to power was actually a secret conspiracy of freemasons, *dönme* and socialists. The connecting thread linking all these nefarious elements was of course none other than the Jews themselves, and as for the CUP, it was, Lowther asserted, really the 'Jew CUP'.[109] But it did not stop there. Lowther's inference that behind these dealings was the interests of one specific Great Power – Germany – was not treated back at the British Foreign Office as the idiosyncratic confabulations of one particularly addled brain. On the contrary, the fact that some Salonikan freemasons were Jewish, and that German Zionists operating in the Near East were also – naturally – Jewish led to a general Foreign Office conviction that Jews qua Jews were not just arch-conspirators and Levantine manipulators in their own right, but actually in league with the Machiavellian machinations of the Wilhelmstrasse.[110]

This emerging wisdom was entirely shared by the Quai d'Orsay. The key outside Jewish body working in Salonika was none other than the intensely patriotic French Alliance. Yet this seems to have cut little ice with French diplomats in hot pursuit of the activities in the area of German Zionists and of the non-Zionist Hilfsverein der Deutschen Juden, again apparently wilfully ignoring that these were entirely rival organisations.[111] The great irony of the internationalisation proposal is that Salonika Jewry certainly did send their proposal to all these foreign Jewish organisations as well as leading British, Austrian and Italian ones, in the hope that they would collectively intercede with the Great Powers as they had done in 1878. And in the further hope that those same Great Powers would respond in kind, by acting in concert – just as they had done at Berlin – to redeem the situation.

The immense tragedy for Salonika Jewry is that by 1912 there was no European concert. It had been entirely wrecked on the byzantine machinations of those selfsame Great Powers, who now, it appeared, were projecting their failings back onto one little community which genuinely desired to be international. And in this there was a tremendous irony. In order to pull its chestnuts out of the Balkan national fire, the Salonika community was seeking the assistance of the very parties who had stoked the fire in the first place and were now moving inexorably to fan it into a global conflagration. Yet in this situation lies not only our final paradox but with it a saving grace.

The two chancelleries which evinced most interest in the internationalisation scheme were Rome and Vienna. Both Italy and Austria, of course, did have some very important long-term connections with the Salonika community not least through the tobacco trade. And Vienna, certainly, sought to amplify these connections further in the winter of 1912–13, by having its Salonika consulate facilitate the sale of a large number of Austrian passports specifically to members of the Jewish community.[112] But the Austrian effort here had little to do with either altruism or historic ties. Rather, it was actually one last desperate throw at keeping alive its own very specific version of the Drang Nach Osten through which it hoped to dominate the Balkan region but which, in the face of the actions of the Balkan allies, it now feared would be scuppered for all time. With direct or indirect control of Salonika seminal to its strategy, the Ballhausplatz thus even entered into some informal discussions with the Zionist Organisation to discuss how the free port scheme might be floated at any possible ensuing peace conference. But equally hastily, it dropped the idea when it became evident that the other Great Powers would not for a moment countenance Austrian sponsorship.[113]

If this put paid to the scheme once and for all, it also highlighted the fact that none of the Great Powers understood internationalisation to equate with political neutralisation. As such, with both Austria and Italy in 1912 on that same side of the Great Power fracture as Germany, the occasion of the Austrian pourparler was just the sort of event likely to appeal to the conspiracy theorists in Whitehall and the Quai d'Orsay as 'proof' of their contention that Jews in general, and in this case, Salonika Jewry in particular, were aligned to the 'enemy' Triple Alliance. But if this really was the case, and the Salonika community through its broader 'international' connections had such powerful friends abroad, could an incoming Greek administration afford to alienate it, let alone physically assault it?

The contrast which is instructive here is with the Ottoman Armenians. 1912 also proved to be a fateful year for them, providing an apparent opportunity to break free from CUP tutelage by aligning themselves with a Russian proposal for the resurrection of an otherwise defunct scheme for the international supervision of the Ottoman Armenian vilayets.[114] Just as Vienna's interest in Salonika Jews was an attempt to wrest advantage from the Balkan war crisis, so was Russia's support of the Armenians a cynical ploy to take a further bite out of what was left of the Ottoman empire. The key difference, of course, was that when the whole thing finally exploded into the Great War of 1914, and the CUP dragged that empire into the war on the side of Germany and Austria, the Armenians became fatally exposed as alleged Russian, and more generally Entente stooges. The result, as we know, was genocide. It is at this point, however, that the apparent symmetry with the Salonikan Jewish position deviates markedly. The community may have been assumed to be pro-German and equally pro-Turk by a Greek state which eventually joined the Allies and indeed by the Allied countries themselves.[115] But this did not translate into state-sponsored violence against it.

Could it be, then, that the myth of Jewish power, even a Jewish power arraigned on the enemy side, while it would provide the galvanus for 'a final solution' a global war later, in the context of the Balkan wars and their aftermath actually protected Salonika Jewry from displacement and destruction? What is striking, after all, is the degree to which Greek Prime Minister Venizelos after 1912 literally pussyfooted around issues which would have been bound to arouse foreign Jewish as much as indigenous Jewish ire – military conscription, the maintenance of communal autonomy, even throwing in, albeit cosmetically, promises for compensation and support after the devastating fire which destroyed practically the entire Jewish quarter in 1917.[116] There was a downside, of course, in that Salonika Jewry henceforth could never shake off the charge that they were really the agents of the Germans, or the Turks, or the Bulgarians.[117] Yet, even under increasing pressure from the Greek refugee incomers, the Hellenic state never seems to have contemplated directly expelling the Jews as it had done other ethnic communities.

Survival of course is one thing; well-being, prosperity and inter-communal harmony another. While throughout the inter-war period there still was a Jewish community in Salonika to squabble and fragment along communal lines, a basis indeed for a new nationalist-orientated historiography to chart the rising fortunes of the Zionist camp,[118] even still a substantial community for the Nazis to exterminate in 1943, it was all a long way from the halcyon days of an authentic port Jewry.

But where from our contemporary perspective does that leave us? On one level, perhaps with a communal experience which attempted to go against the grain of nation-building and state-formation to find its own free unfettered place in the capitalist sun. The sociologist Robin Cohen has proposed in a recent book that diasporas are disproportionately advantaged to exploit and be adaptive to conditions associated with globalisation and to take further advantage of the economic and cultural opportunities on offer.[119] If port Jews could indeed be argued to be at the cutting edge of one particularly notable diaspora, then by the same token Salonika's free port bid of 1912 may have been a bold if albeit premature image of what diasporas in the future might become.

Yet for those of us who have serious doubts about the whole thrust of globalisation, such celebration seems to rather too blatantly leave out of the equation those not invited to the party. If the Salonika port's upswing and takeoff after 1878 was certainly in significant part a tangible product of dynamic entrepreneurial Jews, the fact that they were only able to achieve this as agents of western penetration not to say political, social, economic and cultural dislocation, must also demand that we pay attention to those who, at the very least, perceived themselves to be left behind in the process, or marginalised, or exploited. In the twenty-first century it may not be a reactive nationalism per se which will be the single expression of such grievance but so long as prosperity, economic openness and commercial opportunity follow the contours of hegemonic interests at the expense of others the position of latter-day Salonikas is likely to remain fragile and exposed.

NOTES

1. David Sorkin, 'The Port Jew: Notes toward a Social Type', *Journal of Jewish Studies* 50.1 (spring 1999), 87–97; Lois Dubin, *The Port Jews of Habsburg Trieste: Absolutist Politics and Enlightenment Culture* (Stanford: Stanford University Press, 1999).
2. George F. Kennan, *The Other Balkan Wars, A 1913 Carnegie Endowment Inquiry in Retrospect with a New Introduction and Reflections on the Present Conflict* (Washington, DC: Carnegie Endowment for International Peace, 1993; original edn, 1914), pp.187–95.
3. See Vakahn N. Dadrian, 'The Circumstances surrounding the 1909 Adana Holocaust', *Armenian Review*, 41.4 (1988), 1–16.
4. Marjorie Housepian, *Smyrna 1922: The Destruction of a City* (London: Faber & Faber, 1972).
5. Ben Zvi Izhak, *The Exiled and the Redeemed* (Philadelphia: Jewish Publication Society of America, 1957), p.134.
6. See for example Justin McCarthy, *Death and Exile: The Ethnic Cleansing of Ottoman Muslims, 1821–1922* (Princeton, NJ: Darwin Press, 1995); Mark Levene, 'Creating a Modern "Zone of Genocide": The Impact of Nation and State Formation on Eastern Anatolia 1878–1923', *Holocaust and Genocide Studies*, 12.3 (winter 1998), 393–433.
7. See Dmitri Pentzopoulos, *The Balkan Exchange of Minorities and its Impact upon Greece* (Paris: Mouton, 1962)
8. Paul Dumont, 'The Social Structure of the Jewish Community of Salonika at the End of the Nineteenth Century,' *South-Eastern Europe*, 5.2 (1979), p.34, for the lower figures. The higher ones come from the Jewish New Year Book 1912 , as cited in the *Jewish Chronicle*, 8 November 1912.
9. Andrew Apostolou, '"The Exception of Salonika": Bystanders and Collaborators in Northern Greece', *Holocaust and Genocide Studies* 14.2 (fall 2000), p.170.
10. Sorkin (see note 1), p.89.
11. See Walter F. Weikler, *Ottomans, Turks and the Jewish Polity, A History of the Jews of Turkey* (Lanham, New York, London: Jerusalem Center for Public Affairs and University Press of America, 1992), p.177.
12. See Halil Inalcik and Donald Quataert (eds.), *An Economic and Social History of the Ottoman Empire 1300–1914* (Cambridge: Cambridge University Press, 1994), p.902.
13. Dumont (see note 8), p.56, estimates that of 50 large enterprises in Salonika 38 were Jewish owned. See also John R. Lampe and Marvin R. Jackson, *Balkan Economic History, 1550–1950: From Imperial Borderlands to Developing Nations* (Bloomington: Indiana University Press, 1982), p.308.
14. Paul Dumont, 'Une Organisation Socialiste Ottomane: La Federation Ouvriere du Salonique, 1908–1912', *Etudes Balkaniques* 1 (1975), p.78.
15. See Maria Vassilikou, 'Politics of the Jewish Community of Salonika in the Inter-War Years: Party Ideologies and Party Competition,' unpublished Ph.D thesis (University College, London, 1999) pp.31–5.
16. Paul Dumont, 'La franc-maconnierie d'obedience Francaise a Salonique au debut du XXieme siecle', *Turcica* 16 (1984), 65–94.
17. Dumont, 'Une Organisation Socialiste Ottomane' (see note 14), p.78.

18. Vassilikou (see note 15), pp.28–9.
19. Weikler (see note 11), pp.226–7 for more details.
20. Vassilikou (see note 15), pp.22–3.
21. Mark Mazower, 'Salonika between East and West 1860–1912,' *Dialogos* 1 (1994), p.106.
22. Ibid.
23. See I.-S. Emmanuel, *Histoire de l' industrie des tissus des Israélites de Salonique* (Paris: Libraire Lipshutz, 1935). More generally Joseph Nehama, *Histoire des Israélites de Salonique*, vol.3, *L'Age d'or du Sefardisme Salonicien, 1536–1593* (Paris and Salonika: Librairie Durlacher, Librairie Molho, 1936).
24. For something along the lines of this theme see Gerard Nahon, *Metropoles et Peripheries Sefarades d'Occident, Kairouan, Amsterdam, Bayonne, Bordeaux, Jerusalem* (Paris: Le Cerf, 1993).
25. Immanuel Wallerstein, Hale Decdeli and Resat Kasaba, 'The Incorporation of the Ottoman Empire into the World Economy,' in Hurí Islamoğlu-İnan (ed.), *The Ottoman Empire and the World-Economy* (Cambridge: Cambridge University Press, 1987).
26. Nehama (see note 23) vol. 5 (Salonika: Emmanuel Sfakianakas, 1959), p.86.
27. Nehama (Salonika: Communauté Israélite de Thesallonique, 1978) vol. 6–7, p.295.
28. Lampe and Jackson (see note 13), p.40.
29. Inalcik and Quataert (see note 12), p.831; Wallerstein *et al.* (see note 25), p.92.
30. Charles Issawi, 'Transformation of the Economic Position of the Millets in the 19th century' in Benjamin Braude and Bernard Lewis (eds.), *Christians and Jews in the Ottoman Empire: The Functioning of a Plural Society* (New York and London: Holmes & Meier, 1982), vol.1, pp.261–84.
31. See Weikler (note 11), pp.177–8.
32. In the period from 1840 to 1914 Salonika imports grew by a factor of 36, exports by a factor of ten. Charles Issawi, *The Economic History of Turkey, 1800–1914* (Chicago and London: University of Chicago Press, 1980), p.103.
33. Dumont, 'Social Structure' (see note 8), p.56.
34. See for instance, Jonathan Israel, 'The Changing Role of the Dutch Sephardim in International Trade, 1595–1715', *Dutch Jewish History* 1 (Jerusalem, 1984) pp.31–51.
35. Lampe and Jackson (see note 13), p.40; Weikler (see note 11), p.81. Nearly a third of the Macedonian tobacco export went to Italy in this period, the Allatini family monopolising the Trieste trade in the product.
36. Vassilikou (see note 15), p.32.
37. See James Parkes, *Emergence of the Jewish Problem 1878–1939* (London: Oxford University Press, 1946), pp.98–103. More generally Carol Iancu, *Les Juifs de Roumanie, 1866–1919: De l'exclusion a l'emancipation*, (Aix-en-Provence, 1978).
38. Inalcik and Quataert (see note 12), pp.761–2.
39. For more on the infamous Murzsteg Agreement see Misha Glenny, *The Balkans 1804–1999, Nationalism, War and the Great Powers* (London: Granta, 1999), pp.207–8.
40. Chistopher Clay, *Gold for the Sultan, Western Bankers and Ottoman Finance 1856–1881: A Contribution to Ottoman and International Financial History* (London: I.B. Tauris, 2000) for the entire background.
41. Ibid., pp.492–502, for the origins of the regie.
42. Issawi (see note 32), pp.249–50.
43. One might cite the Rothschilds, the Pereire brothers of Crédit Mobilier and the Oppenheims as among most prominent. Full details of their involvement and that of other key Jewish banking houses can be found throughout Clay (see note 40) but minus reference to their 'Jewishness'.
44. Inalcik and Quataert (see note 12), p.827; Lampe and Jackson (see note 13), p.282.
45. Donald Quataert, *Social Disintegration and Popular Resistance in the Ottoman Empire, 1881–1908* (New York: New York University Press, 1988), p.123.
46. Lampe and Jackson (see note 13), pp.264, 308.
47. Inalcik and Quataert (see note 12), p.774.
48. Aron Rodrigue, 'From Millet to Minority: Turkish Jewry', in Pierre Birnbaum and Ira

Katznelson (eds.), *Paths of Emancipation: Jews, States and Citizenship* (Princeton, NJ: Princeton University Press, 1995), p.251.

49. See Dumont, 'Social Structure' (see note 8), p.33; Lampe and Jackson (see note 13), p 208–9.
50. Fritz Stern, *Gold and Iron: Bismarck, Bleichröder and the Building of the German Empire*, (London: George Allen & Unwin, 1977), p.420; Aron Rodrigue, *French Jews, Turkish Jews: The Alliance Israélite Universelle and the Politics of Jewish Schooling in Turkey, 1860–1925*, (Bloomington and Indianapolis: Indiana University Press, 1990), pp.55–7. For more on Hirsch see also Clay (see note 40), pp.197–202; Kurt Grunenwald, *Turkenhirsch, A Study of Baron Maurice de Hirsch, Entrepreneur and Philanthropist* (Jerusalem: Transaction, 1966).
51. Stern (see note 50), ch.14, 'Romania, the Triumph of Expediency'.
52. Ibid., pp.420–1.
53. Issawi (see note 30), p.271.
54. Dumont, 'Social Structure' (see note 8), p.33.
55. Issawi (see note 30), p.278.
56. *Collins English Dictionary* (London and Glasgow: Collins, 2nd ed., 1986), p.324.
57. See for instance, Samir Amin, *Unequal Development: An Essay on Social Formations of Peripheral Capitalism* (Hassocks: Harvester Press, 1976), pp.296–98, 314–15.
58. Generally see Walter P. Zenner, 'Middlemen Minorities and Genocide' in Isidor Wallimann and Michael Dobkowski (eds.), *Genocide and the Modern Age* (Westport, CT: Greenwood Press, 1987), pp.253–82; more specifically for the Khmer Rouge assaults on Chinese and Vietnamese, Ben Kiernan, 'The Cambodian Genocide: Issues and Responses,' in George D. Andrepoulos (ed.), *Genocide: Conceptual and Historical Dimensions* (Philadelphia: University of Pennsylvania Press, 1994), pp.198–99.
59. See Stephen H. Astourian, 'Foreword,' in Hilmar Kaiser, *Imperialism, Racism, And Development Theories: The Construction of a Dominant Paradigm on Ottoman Armenians* (Ann Arbor, MI: Gomidas Institute, 1997), pp.viii–ix and 1–2.
60. Ibid. throughout for more on this theme.
61. For some of the connections between the two acts, see Norman M. Naimark, *Fires of Hatred: Ethnic Cleansing in Twentieth Century Europe* (Cambridge, MA and London: Harvard University Press, 2001), ch.1, 'The Armenians and Greeks of Anatolia'.
62. This is not to dispute a limited range of expulsions and killings committed against the Palestine yishuv between 1914 and 1917. See Isaiah Friedman, *Germany, Turkey and Zionism 1897–1918* (London: Oxford University Press, 1977), pp.347–73..
63. See, for example, Abram Leon, *The Jewish Question: A Marxist Interpretation* (New York: Pathfinder Press, 1970).
64. See Issawi (note 32), pp.51–2, Dumont, 'Une Organisation Socialiste Ottomane' (see note 14), p.81 for some of these conflicts.
65. Bat Ye'or, *The Dhimmi, Jews and Christians under Islam* (Rutherford, NJ and London: Fairleigh Dickinson University Press and Associated University Presses, 1985).
66. Rodrigue (see note 50), p.34. For more on this theme see Kemal H. Karpat, 'Millets and Nationality: The Roots of the Incongruity of Nation and State in the Post-Ottoman State', in Benjamin Braude and Bernard Lewis (eds.) (see note 30), pp.141–70.
67. This is my own formulation but after writing this I see that Feroz Ahmad has said something almost identical for the Ottoman non-Muslims in general. See Feroz Ahmad, 'The Late Ottoman Empire', in Marian Kent (ed.), *The Great Powers and the End of the Ottoman Empire* (London: Frank Cass, 1995), p.22.
68. Lucien Wolf, leader in the *Jewish World*, 28 March 1881.
69. See Andre Chouraqui, *Cent ans d'histoire, L'Alliance Israélite Universelle et la renaissance juive contemporaine* (Paris: Presse Universitaires de France, 1965) for the classic enconium to the organisation's programme.
70. See, however, David Kushner, *The Rise of Turkish Nationalism 1876–1908* (London: Frank Cass, 1977) for the quickening pace of Turkish language reform and educational follow-through pre-1908; especially pp.76–98.
71. See Glenny (note 39), p.133, for the San Stefano treaty, overruled at Berlin.
72. Paul R. Mendes-Flohr (ed.), *A Land of Two Peoples: Martin Buber on Jews and Arabs* (New

York: Oxford University Press, 1983), p.16, takes the term to mean 'that the egotistic pursuit of the interest of one's own group, even if it involves the disregard and abuse of another group, is "sacred" and hence morally self-sufficient'.

73. Dumont, 'Une Organisation Socialiste Ottomane' (see note 14), pp.80–82, for Benaroya's efforts. Jews were not necessarily alone in their efforts to maintain a multi-ethnic city. The Internal Macedonian Revolutionary Organisation (IMRO) remained committed to the idea of an autonomous and multi-ethnic Macedonia as a whole, despite vicious conflict with its Bulgarian patrons, while smaller minority groups like the Koutzo-Vlachs were equally exposed to the dominance of any single group, as were the Jews. On IMRO see Glenny (note 39), pp.185–7.

74. Rena Molho, 'The Jewish Community of Salonika and Its Incorporation into the Greek State 1912–1919', *Middle Eastern Studies* 24 (1988), pp.391–403. Also Mark Levene, 'Between Greeks and Bulgars: Salonika Jewry and the Balkan Wars 1912–1913', in *Between Trieste, Saloniki and Odessa: Perspectives on Jewish History in Southeastern Europe, 1492–1918* ed. by Dan Diner, Markus Kirchhoff and Desanka Schwara (Leipzig: Leipziger Universitatsverlag, forthcoming).

75. See M.I.A. Todorovitch, *Salonique et la question balkanique, Paris 1913*, cited in Rena Molho, 'Salonique après 1912. Les propagandes étrangères et la communauté juive', *Revue Historique* 287 (1992), 136–38.

76. In the brief interlude when the town was jointly occupied by Bulgarian and Greek troops, Salonika Jewry as well as international Jewish organisations were courted by both states. See *Jewish Chronicle* reports, 3 and 31 January 1913.

77. See N.M. Gelber, 'An Attempt to Internationalise Salonika', *Jewish Social Studies* 17 (1955), 118–9 for the full text of the second community memorandum, 3 January 1913.

78. See for instance, Feroz Ahmad, 'Unionist Relations with Greek, Armenian and Jewish Communities of the Ottoman Empire 1908–1914', in Braude and Lewis (eds.) (see note 30), pp.403, 425; Stanford J. Shaw, *The Jews of the Ottoman Empire and the Turkish Republic*, (Basingstoke and London: Macmillan, 1991), p.218.

79. See notably Kemal Karpat, 'The Memories of N. Batzuria: The Young Turks and Nationalism', *International Journal of Middle East Studies* 6.3 (July 1975) p.280; Robert Olson, 'The Young Turks and the Jews: A Historiographical Revision', *Turcica* 18 (1986) 219–35.

80. Further evidence of disproportionately high CUP connections with Salonika, including that of all three members of the CUP triumverate, Talaat, Enver and Cemal, can be gleaned from the Biographical Index in Feroz Ahmad, *The Young Turks: The CUP in Turkish Politics: 1908–1914* (Oxford: Oxford University Press, 1969), pp.166–81.

81. See Shaw (note 78), pp.218, 250–1. But of Karasu, notes Ahmad (see note 80), p.173: 'Influential but not as influential as people thought'. Interestingly after having amassed a huge fortune as a government food controller during the 1914–18 war, Ahmad also notes that Karasu opted for Italian citizenship and settled in Trieste!

82. Jabob M. Landau, *Tekinalp: Turkish Patriot, 1883–1961* (Leiden: Institute historique et archeologique neerlandais de Stamboul, 1984).

83. Leon Sciaky, *Farewell to Salonica: Portrait of an Era* (London, W.H. Allen, 1946), ch.14, 'Homecoming', for a vivid evocation of post-revolution Salonika.

84. Dumont, 'Une Organisation Socialiste Ottomane' (see note 14), pp.84–5.

85. Johannes Lepsius, *Armenia and Europe: An Indictment* (London: Hodder & Stoughton, 1897) for the best contemporary account.

86. Glenny (see note 39), pp.194–5.

87. See Douglas Dakin, *The Greek Struggle in Macedonia, 1897–1913* (Thessaloniki: Institute for Balkan Studies, 1993), pp.198–209; Gerasimos Augustinos, *Consciousness and History, National Critics of Greek Society 1893–1914* (New York: Columbia University Press, 1997), ch.6, 'Nationalist Dilemma, The Greeks in the Ottoman Empire'.

88. George W. Gawrych, 'The Culture and Politics of Violence in Turkish Society 1903–13', *Middle Eastern Studies*, 22.3 (1985), pp.308–9; Sciaky (see note 83), ch.8 'A Covenant with Death' particularly for the violence in Salonika itself.

89. Paul Dumont, 'Jewish Communities in Turkey during the last decades of the 19th century

in the Light of Archives of the Alliance Israélite Universelle', in Braude and Lewis (eds.) (see note 30), p.221.

90. See Avigdor Levy, *The Sephardim in the Ottoman Empire* (Princeton, NJ: Darwin Press 1992), p.123.
91. Shaw (see note 78), pp.190–91, 205, proposes that a Jewish population increase from 28,000 in 1876 to a supposed 90,000 in 1908 was substantially due to refugee inflows. David Florentin in his December 1912 memorandum on the position of Salonika Jewry does not refer to this cause in his much smaller Jewish population total of 60,000 but does suggest that out of 14,500 families, 6,000 were destitute and dependent on hand-outs. See Gelber (note 77), p.117.
92. Levy (see note 90), p.121.
93. See for instance Sciaky (note 83), pp.145–8.
94. See Izhak (note 5), ch.2, 'The Sabbateans of Salonica'.
95. See Esther Benbassa, 'Zionism in the Ottoman Empire at the End of the 19th and the Beginning of the 20th Century', *Studies in Zionism* 11.2 (1990), p.131, note 25.
96. Albert Hirschmann, *Exit, Voice and Loyalty* (Cambridge, MA: Harvard University Press, 1970).
97. Quataert (see note 45), p.145.
98. Ahmad 'Unionist Relations' (see note 78) p.407; Sciaky (see note 83), p.180.
99. Dumont (see note 14), p.84.
100. Sciaky (see note 83), p.178–82 for a sense of the growing disenchantment with CUP rule.
101. Glenny (see note 39), p.215.
102. *Encyclopaedia Judaica* (Jerusalem: Keter Publishing House, 1971), vol.14, 'Salonika', p.703. See also Sciaky (note 83), ch.16, 'The Old Order Passeth'.
103. Dumont, 'Une Organisation Socialiste Ottomane' (see note 14), p.85; M. Şükrü Hanioglu, *Preparations for a Revolution: The Young Turks, 1902–1908* (New York: Oxford University Press, 2001), p.250; Ahmad, 'Unionist Relations' (see note 78), p.409. Interestingly, also see Ahmad, *Young Turks* (note 80), p.161, where he describes the grouping as one of Europeanisers but not 'modernisers'.
104. Ernest E. Ramsaur Jr., *The Young Turks: Prelude to the Revolution of 1908* (Princeton, NJ: Princeton University Press, 1957), p.129, charges that the Armenian parties actually dominated Itilaf.
105. Gelber (see note 77), pp.118–19. The fine details of the scheme included the proposal that Swiss and Belgian experts should have oversight of its administrative organisation and of its law and order.
106. See Kennan (note 2), throughout.
107. See Maria Vassilikou, 'Greeks and Jews in Salonika and Odessa', this volume.
108. Mark Levene, *War, Jews and the New Europe: The Diplomacy of Lucien Wolf, 1914–1919* (Oxford: Littman Library of Jewish Civilisation and Oxford University Press, 1992)
109. Lowther to Hardinge 29 May 1910, dispatch quoted in entirety in Elie Kedourie, 'Young Turks, Freemasons and Jews', *Middle Eastern Studies* 7(1971), pp.89–104.
110. Ibid., p.93,where Kedourie perfectly appropriately quotes another key British maker of the modern Middle East, G.F. Clayton, intelligence director at the Cairo office. August 1916: ' There are English Jews, French Jews, American Jews, German Jews, Austrian Jews and Salonica Jews – but all are JEWS, and moreover practically all are anti-Russian. You hear peace talk and generally somewhere behind is the Jew. You hear pro-Turk talk and desires for a separate peace with Turkey – again the Jew (the mainspring of the CUP).'
111. Rodrigue (see note 50), pp.152–4.
112. Molho (see note 74), p.395 notes Austria sold 450 passports to Salonika Jews in this short period. Austria's willingness to flood the passport market was also confirmed by Esther Benbassa in conversation with me at the 'Historicising Balkan and Related Jewries' Conference, Leipzig, November 2000.
113. Austria already had its own scheme for Salonika internationalisation. See Gelber (note 77), p.106; more generally Ernst Christian Helmreich, *The Diplomacy of the Balkan Wars, 1912–1913* (Cambridge MA: Harvard University Press, 1938), pp.165–9, 303–5.

114. See Roderic H. Davison, 'The Armenian Crisis 1912–1914', *American Historical Review*, 53.3 (1948), pp.481–505; Manoug Somakian, *Empires in Conflict: Armenia and the Great Powers, 1895–1920* (London and New York, 1995), pp.46–9.
115. See Donald Bloxham, 'Cumulative Radicalisation and Mass Murder: The Beginning of the Armenian Genocide Reconsidered' (*Past and Present*, forthcoming) for the British exemption from the wartime Alien Restriction Order for Ottoman Armenians and other Christians on the grounds that they were 'friendly'. No such exemptions existed for Salonikan Jews, many of whom were interned as 'enemy aliens'. See Manchester Jewish Museum, Louis Bernadout deposit, no.1713. For the obverse side of the coin, namely in this case economic criteria for treating Jews – and *dönme* – as German and CUP 'allies' and Armenians and Greeks as Anglo-French backed 'enemies' see the revealing discussion of the German contemporary writer Alphons Sussnitzki in Kaiser (see note 59), p.31–2.
116. See Board of Deputies (archives, Woburn House, London) C11/ 2/ 12, Aide-mémoire of Anglo-Jewish Association meeting with Venizelos, 23 November 1917; also Wolf to Bigart, 26 November 1917.
117. See Alliance Israélite Universelle (AIU) Archives, Paris, file France II/ D10, M.P. Argyropoulos (ex-governor of Salonika), 'Le Probleme Juif à Salonique pendant les premières années de l'occupation hellenique,' n.d. c. 1919; Apostolou (see note 9), p.172; Vassilikou (see note 15), pp.98–9.
118. Vassilikou (see note 15) for a full examination of these communal developments.
119. Robin Cohen, *Global Diasporas: An Introduction* (London: UCL Press, 1997), pp.175–6.

Greeks and Jews in Salonika and Odessa: Inter-ethnic Relations in Cosmopolitan Port Cities

MARIA VASSILIKOU

Greco-Jewish relations in Odessa and Salonika during the nineteenth and early twentieth century constitute the most representative case for the analysis of inter-ethnic relations within the multi-ethnic surroundings of cosmopolitan port cities under imperial rule. Generally speaking, both Jews and Greeks had a strong inter-ethnic composition built upon a common language and guaranteed by religious affiliation and strong family relations. Both groups were members of a widely-spread diaspora which lived and traded in the same geographical context, that is, from the Black Sea and the Mediterranean as far as northwest Europe and Great Britain.

In the case of Salonika, Jews and Greeks capitalised upon their common characteristics as members of trade diasporas and profited from the Ottoman Empire's policy of allowing its non-Muslim subjects to engage in commerce. In Odessa, the intention of Catherine the Great to make out of the newly-founded port the depot *par excellence* of Russian trade resulted in a number of liberal measures which not only favoured the settlement of many Greeks and Jews but actively supported their involvement in the city's trading activities.[1] Parallel to that, the dominant economic role of Greek and Jewish merchants bound their fate to the various fluctuations inherent in the dynamic life-cycle of such waterfronts. Salonika's geographic location in the mouth of the river Vardar, the most favourable line of penetration into the interior of the Balkan hinterland, exposed its Greek and Jewish population to the stormy course of modern Balkan nationalism. Turning now to Odessa, Greeks and Jews experienced all the consequences which the Russian-Turkish wars throughout the nineteenth century brought upon the Russian Empire's most important maritime outpost. Finally, the factor of Greek anti-semitism and its metamorphoses in the course of modern Greek history suggests the explosive potential hidden in the course of Greco-Jewish relations in the two cities.

Having shared the same social space of a port city, Jews and Greeks looked for paths of existence which could guarantee their group survival and favour their upward social mobility. Their choices were far from homogenous, but rather were conditional upon their economic background, social position and ideological legacy. The immediate outcome of this inter-communal fragmentation took the form of social behaviour which cut across ethnic barriers without, however, erasing their ethnic distinctiveness.[2]

Notwithstanding the different forms of interaction between the two groups, the existing bibliography has viewed Greco-Jewish relations through the narrow lens of nationalist historiography, laying emphasis solely on aspects and moments of unified ethnic behaviour. The history of the Greeks in Odessa and Salonika has been narrowed down to that of the most successful Greek businessmen and their relations with the movement of nineteenth century Greek nationalism. Turning now to the Jews, scholars have highlighted their intellectual and political activities intimately connected with, on the one hand, European interventionism in the case of Ottoman Salonika and, on the other hand, Russian political culture in Tsarist Odessa. As far as Greco-Jewish relations are concerned, the bibliography on Salonika remains scanty. In the case of Odessa, English-speaking studies have been limited to the participation of the Greeks in the pogroms of 1821, 1849, 1859 and 1871 as well as to the displacement of Greek magnates by Jewish businessmen in the grain trade in the aftermath of the Crimean War. This limited historical treatment can be accounted for by the combination of linguistic barriers, the limited use of archival material and micro-political considerations which – if anything – exacerbate the writing of studies with an inter-ethnic content.

This contribution will delineate forms of Greco-Jewish interaction first in Salonika and then in Odessa, which stretched from ignorance, mutual tolerance and cooperation to hostility and bloody pogroms. It will show that due to the constant flow of information and personnel across the two groups, Greeks and Jews experienced comparable developments, thereby establishing the most 'integrative form' of Jewish–Gentile relations within the cosmopolitan atmosphere of nineteenth century port cities.

In Salonika, the multi-ethnic composition of its population is a commonplace in all written testimonies recorded throughout the city's long history. Historians and travellers from Flavius Josephus and O. Tafrali to Nikiforos Choumnos, Evlia Tselembi and Mary Adelaide Walker in the early 1800s emphasised the human melting-pot of this port city, consisting of Jews, Greeks, Armenians, Muslims, Bulgarians and Europeans.[3] The Greeks, the Armenians and, later, the Jews constituted, according to the Ottoman *millet* system, separate communities subjected to the regular payment of taxes. They were placed under the immediate authority of their religious leaders, whose role as intermediaries between their co-religionists and the Sublime Porte contributed to their prestigious social standing.[4] The members of these communities lived in rather isolated, self-sufficient worlds, often engaging in trade, a form of activity which Muslim law utterly disdained. Nevertheless, mutual contact was often the case, as the different groups struggling for survival co-mingled with each other in the domain of commercial and professional relationships and created relations on the basis of antagonistic or compatible interests.[5]

For all the notorious manipulation of sources concerning population statistics, one could safely argue that in 1870 Salonikan Jews were the largest ethnic community in the city with a population varying between 50,000 and 75,000. They were followed by the Muslims (22,000–25,000) and third were the Greeks with 18,000–20,000.[6]

In the course of the nineteenth century dramatic changes were brought about by the enhanced and omnipotent presence of the West in the Ottoman Empire which set the course of Greek and Jewish communal affairs in the years to come. The modernising reforms [known as *Tanzimat*] undertaken by the Ottomans, along with the emergence of Balkan nationalism and the subsequent creation of nation-states in areas of declining Ottoman rule, testified to the all-powerful projection of 'western might into the region'.[7] They sought to revive the decaying empire by building a centralised state based on the principles of rationalisation and organised along a central bureaucratic system able to contain dangerous centrifugal local forces.[8]

Institutional reforms apart, revolutionary changes occurring in the fields of transport and communication from the mid-nineteenth century gave a boost to the declining economic life of the city. The construction of a rich network of railways that connected Salonika to Constantinople and through Serbia and Bosnia to the major European cities contributed decisively to the rapid and efficient distribution of commercial goods. The city's shipping industry grew, as a result of the combined efforts of the Ottoman state and foreign enterprises. Parallel to that, the establishment of telegraphic networks in the 1880s improved trading relations, while improvements in the credit system boosted investment and commercial transactions. Finally, a number of public works undertaken from the late 1860s onwards by Sabri Pasha, the governor of the city, led to the intensified urbanisation and modernisation of Salonika. Of cardinal importance was the improvement of the port-facilities, which although it dragged on for many years, did help to cope with the increased commercial traffic. [9]

Jewish families of Italian origin, the so-called Francos, along with Greek merchants were the first to take advantage of the 'wind of change'.[10] The Allatini, who had branches in London, Marseilles and Vienna, excelled in international commerce and banking ventures and, together with the Modiano, traded in cereals and the production of flour. Their activities culminated in the establishment of the first large flour mill in Salonika in 1857. They also invested in the tobacco trade and together with their foreign partners established the *Banque de Salonique*.[11] The families of the Capandji, Jehiel and Bensussan set up a lingerie factory in 1911, while the Modiano and the Fernandez founded the famous Olympos distillery.[12] As for the Greeks, although they ranked second to the Jews, their presence in the Salonikan economy was of decisive importance. They played the role of intermediary between the producers in Salonika's hinterland (Naoussa, Vodenna and Verria) and commercial houses abroad. They dealt with the import and export of leather, fur, food commodities, wood and raw silk. Following the example of their Jewish fellow-merchants, the Greeks set up the Bank of Mitilini (1899–1907) and the Bank of Athens (1905), as well as the Credit Bank of the Orient (1906).[13] At the time, out of a total of more than 50 large enterprises in Salonika 38 were run by Jews, eight by *dönme* – the successors of the Sabbatean Jews – and another eight by Greek families.[14]

A brief look at the social composition of both communities reveals the same structure of an industrialised urban population, ranging from bourgeois to proletarian and lumpenproletarian. The Francos and the wealthy Greek families profited from the development of the city and amassed huge fortunes. Greek and Jewish white-collar workers were to be found in the trading and banking sectors, whereas Jewish and Greek lawyers, doctors and schoolteachers constituted the members of the Salonikan middle class.[15] Finally, the development of the industrial sector gave birth to the formation of a strong working class, including workers from both ethnic groups. Around 20,000 workers (17 per cent of the population) were involved in industry and 5,000 in transport. In 1909 under the leadership of a Bulgarian Jew, A. Benaroya, they organised in the *Federacion Socialista Laboradera*. However, unlike the full-hearted support it received from Jewish workers, their Greek comrades showed little interest in the class struggle and preferred to join their voices with those of the bourgeois Greeks in favour of Greece's nationalist aspirations.[16]

Although the long history of ethno-religiously separated life-styles was – if anything – exacerbated by contemporary national movements, cross-ethnic characteristics between Greeks and Jews of the same social standing were to be found in economic structures and cultural patterns. To be sure, the ethnic division of labour was evident in the city's spinning industry, which employed 800 workers all of Jewish origin. On the other hand, the tile industry of the Jewish Allatini employed around 200 workers, mainly Greeks and Bulgarians, thus avoiding a homogeneous and – for that reason – powerful labour force. The same was the case in the Jewish distillery Olympos, where the Greeks were operating the machines and the Bulgarians were engaged in the process of bottling. Finally, in the city's extensive tobacco industry, 335 Jews worked together with 60 Greeks and Bulgarians. 85 per cent of these workers were women and young girls aged 10–18.[17]

The very character of residential choices made by Greeks and Jews of the same social class confirms the extent to which socio-economic criteria were preponderant over ethnic affiliation. Despite the fact that within the *intra-muros* city Jews and Greeks lived in separate ethno-religious worlds, Jewish and Greek traders lodged in the same quarter, which lay to the west of the centre of the city, known as 'Malta', where European merchants had dwelled since Byzantine times.[18] Moreover, many wealthy Jewish bankers, Greek merchants and Turkish officials chose to live in the neighbourhood of Hamidie, the new quarter which emerged after 1885.[19] This trend was accentuated in the aftermath of the fire of 1890, which accelerated changes to the old urban pattern. New neighbourhoods were created where Jews and Greeks of the same social standing lived together.[20]

In Salonika, towards the end of the nineteenth century, the burgeoning Jewish and Greek middle class had come into close contact with European languages and Western tastes. It was considered by many a rather provincial characteristic to speak only Greek, *Ladino* (the vernacular spoken by Salonika's Sephardim) or Turkish. They made efforts to disseminate the teaching of French, Italian and German, thereby strengthening their position along the international commercial routes crossing Salonika. At the same time, many of the 6,000 rich Westerners dwelling in Salonika preferred to associate with the wealthy members of the Greek and Jewish communities. For their part, a great many Greeks and Jews were employed in the service of the Foreign Consulates of Great Britain, France, Italy, Russia, Romania, Austro-Hungary and Greece as translators or secretaries. By the eve of the First World War a Franco-mania dominated Salonika, evident in the wide circulation of a French-speaking press; Greeks were publishing *La Liberté* and the Jews *L'Opinion, Le Progrés,* and *Le Journal de Salonique.* Such life-styles, strikingly rich in colours, sounds and experiences, challenged established cultural structures and created for many Greeks and Jews burning dilemmas over their ethnic identity. In the years following Salonika's annexation to the Greek state in 1912, the political and intellectual Greek and Jewish élites would try to mitigate and slowly contain this multi-ethnic legacy by preaching in favour of ideological schemata which emphasised national integrity and social cohesion.

The enthusiastic adoption of a cosmopolitan life style was only one side of the modernisation coin. Institutional reforms which occurred in the Ottoman legal system supported the struggle of the Greek and the Jewish bourgeoisie for the consolidation of their power, evident in their efforts to forge a communal spirit. Indeed, the *Hatti Serif* of Gülhane in 1839 and the *Islahat Fermani* in 1856 gave secular leaders a major say in communal decision making, while the religious leaders remained the official representatives. In 1869 a new law was passed which accorded Ottoman citizenship to all subjects of the Sultan. However, although these developments dealt a legal blow to the *djimmi* status, group identity gained importance.[21] For one thing, Ottoman citizenship remained a dead letter, as the efforts of the Ottoman state to make Ottoman citizens out of its subjects were marginalised.[22] For another, the fact that the *millet* administration retained its authority gave succour to current national aspirations, thus carving out of the communal space the arena for the propagation of ethnic interests. It is against the background of such developments that Greek and Jewish bourgeois reformers, represented by doctors, lawyers and merchants of liberal views, used the active support of their political satellites, within Salonika as well as beyond, and strove to monopolise communal administration.

It was the field of education which best reflected the novel influences brought about by secularisation, nationalism and modernisation. New schools were built by Greeks, Bulgarians, Serbs, Romanians, Italians, French and English, each one fighting a bitter war for the diffusion of national and religious interests.[23] In the case of Salonikan Greeks, education was put in the service of national aspirations. Encouraged by the Greek Consulate, Greeks set up in Salonika, from 1828 until 1912, eight nursery schools, five public schools, a primary school, a lycée, two girls' schools, a night-school, three private schools, a technical school and two *scholarchia*. The latter prepared teachers, whose appointment in schools in the internationally disputed area of Macedonia was supposed to strengthen Greece's national claims in the region.

In contrast to the straightforward course of Greek education, the educational life of Salonikan Jews followed numerous winding paths. The guiding principle, however, was the need for modern education, with special emphasis on the teaching of foreign languages (French and Italian) and secular subjects (mathematics and geography), which could assist the commercial ties between Salonikan Jewry and the West. Thus, many of the Francos welcomed and buttressed the educational efforts of the first international Jewish organisation, Alliance Israélite Universelle, which set up its first school for boys in Salonika in 1870. The broad curriculum, the high standard of teaching methods, as well as the acclaimed quality of its staff, exerted a profound influence upon the rest of the Jewish communal and private schools.[24] In addition to the *Alliance* establishments, there was also the *Hilfsverein der Deutschen Juden*, a German-Jewish organisation founded in 1901 for the amelioration of the conditions of the Jews in eastern Europe and the Orient. This move, the German answer to the French-inspired programme of emancipation, was encouraged by the Kaiser himself who considered the Oriental Jews important allies for the implementation of his *Drang nach Osten* policy.[25] This is the background to the establishment of the first school in Salonika by the Austro-German railway company in 1887, aimed at training the staff. As late as 1926, 3,500 Jewish children were attending the two French schools *(Mission Laicque Française, College des Frères des écoles Chrétiennes Jean Baptiste de la Salle)* and the two Italian schools Royal College for Boys and Girls' Royal College.[26]

The active presence of the Greek and Jewish bourgeoisie in the sphere of communal education was coupled with their efforts to upgrade communal administration, without, however, excluding the possibilities for cross-ethnic support. With regard to the Greeks, there was the Board of Charitable Institutions, which was responsible for the regulation of communal life. Based on private contributions, a number of communal institutions were created, such as the Thagenio Hospital (1863), the Charisio Old-Peoples Home (1899) and the Papafio Orphanage (1903). From 1870 onwards the activities increased, and by the beginning of the twentieth century the community ran 22 charitable, educational, sport, musical, theatrical and professional associations, plus several publishing enterprises.[27] The Jewish community possessed the Bikur Holim (society offering mutual aid to the sick), the Hevra Kadisha (burial society), a mental hospital, the Matanoth Laevionim (1901), and the Charles Allatini orphanage (1908).[28] However, the lack of a Jewish hospital until 1908 forced many Jews to visit the Greek and Turkish hospitals, which could deal with their medical problems despite the absence of kosher food for the Jewish patients.[29]

Finally, testimonies of the period report that Greek and Jewish notables contributed to each other's benevolent societies and honoured each other on the occasion of marriages and funerals.[30] It is important to note that the high degree of inter-communal accord between Greeks and Jews is connected to the absence of Greek anti-semitic manifestations. What accounts for this phenomenon is the sheer numerical supremacy of the Jewish community as well as the confidence that anti-semitic expressions would find no tolerance, let alone support, among the ruling Muslim population.

The efforts made by the liberal Greek and Jewish 'newcomers' were often viewed with increased suspicion and hostility by the communal 'old guard'. The former asked for the resignation of conservative religious leaders and pressed for the acceptance of individuals who were in tune with their liberal views. Abraham Gattegno replaced Ascher Covo as Chief Rabbi, and Gregorios Callides took the position of the Metropolitan Callinicos. In the early 1880s this intra-communal conflict was further politicised by the moves of certain Greek 'democrats' who succeeded in 'breaking the grip of [certain aristocrats] on the communal administration'. No less adamant were members of the liberal Jewish bourgeoisie who pushed for the same kind of democratisation in communal elections.[31]

By that time, the combination between a flourishing Europeanised middle class, an extensive educational and intellectual network, and an effective network of maritime lines and railways gave birth to the founding of different Masonic lodges in Salonika. The first lodge was founded by Salonikan Jews in 1904 under the auspices of the *Grand Orient de France*. It contributed occasionally to the maintenance of charitable institutions, scholarly establishments and, last but not least, assisted the community in case of disasters such as fire, economic crisis, epidemics or flooding. Although its founding members were all Jewish notables (Isaac Vita Modiano, Isaac Rabeno de Botton, Jacob M. Mosseri, David Joseph Cohen and Paul Isaac Modiano), by 1908 four Greeks, two Armenians and about 15 Muslims had joined. Nevertheless, the Jewish element remained predominant.[32]

Turning to Odessa, many of the aforementioned features of Greco-Jewish interaction in Salonika seemed to govern Greco-Jewish relations in the port city *par excellence* of the Russian Empire. Indeed, the political tolerance of the Tsarist regime coupled with the vast economic opportunities offered by the city's favourable geographic position for international trade made it a centre of attraction for different ethnic groups. Along with Poles, Bulgarians, Italians, Germans, Ukrainians and Russians, Greeks had come from the Balkans and Jews from New Russia (where Jews had been given the right to live since 1791), Volhynia, Lithuania, Belorussia and Galicia. Although the first All-Russian Imperial Census took place as late as 1897, we know that in 1826 Odessa's population was 32,995 and that the Greek community consisted of 1,329 people, registered as Ottoman citizens.[33] The first indication concerning the size of Odessa Jewry dates back to the late 1820s, according to which 4,226 Jews resided in the city. In the years to come, the Jewish population kept increasing, reaching in 1897 a total of 138,935 individuals, approximately 35 per cent of the total population.[34]

The newly founded city was blessed by the privileged status of a free port (1817–1959) and the appointment of a Governor General (until 1874), who guaranteed a high degree of political autonomy as well as the possibility of direct contact with the Tsarist government in St. Petersburg. The decisive boost to Greek and Jewish mercantile activities in Odessa was the establishment from 1820 of multi-ethnic networks between the commercial port cities found along the Mediterranean coasts and Western Europe. This development challenged the long-established English and French supremacy and opened up perspectives for daring newcomers.

As a result, trading relations were decisively facilitated between Greek merchants in Odessa and their associates – often relatives or simply compatriots – in the grain-markets of Syros, Trieste, Marseille and London. Between 1833 and 1860 Odessa Greeks, despite their numerically weak presence, were by far the most important commercial community, holding together with the Italians the monopoly in the export of grain. The commercial houses of Rodokanaki, Ralli, Papoudov, Zarifi and Mavros were in charge of the 62 per cent of the external trade done by the Greeks and 26 per cent of the total.[35] The same devotion to commerce was shown by many Jews who had come from Brody and, once in Odessa, engaged actively in banking and thrived as merchants and agents. Other Jews made fortunes as middlemen and agents operating in the extensive grain market. Employing the same practices as the Greeks, they kept contact with their fellow Jews in St. Petersburg, Brody and Berditchew as well as with Jewish mercantile houses in major European cities, gaining for their enterprising spirit the personal favour and acclamation of Count Vorontsov.[36] By 1855 seven Jewish merchants were registered in the first guild, 28 in the second and 442 in the third.[37] From that moment onwards, many Jewish merchants would prove able to take up the slack created by the departure of large Greek firms who were unwilling to work with slimmer margins of profit, a development connected with the falling prices of grain soon after the Crimean War.[38]

In Odessa, contrary to Salonika, the ethnic division of commercial activities was not as sacred. The existential importance which Odessa's Greek and Jewish merchants attributed to their economic gains flattened ethno-religious differences and led to occasional Greco-Jewish commercial alliances.[39] In the early twentieth century the Greek Recanati family together with a Greek-Russian merchant from Odessa and Alexander Gelfand, a famous Russian Jew, led the 'Grain mafia' in Odessa.[40] We also know about joint ventures during the crisis years of the First World War, when the Greek Alexandriki and the Jewish Brailov joined forces dealing in grain and oil, or when the Greek Kriona, the owner of a leather factory, came together with the Jewish Rubinstein, the son of a famous Jewish merchant.[41]

Mercantile activities apart, Greco-Jewish relations were complemented by instances of Greco-Jewish cooperation at a political level. It is known that throughout the nineteenth century Jews and Greeks served in many offices, such as the Council of Urban Planning, the Town Council, the Customs Office and the Chamber of Commerce. A case in point is the participation of prominent Greek and Jewish merchants in the municipal reform of 1859. Following the invitation of Baron Pavel Mestmaker, the Greeks Konstantin F. Papudov and Theodor R. Rodocannachi worked together with Osip A. Rabinovich as well as with 14 other fellow citizens to set up a municipal local charter destined to stir up the interest of the wider strata of the population in political issues.[42] Moreover, Greek and Jewish notables made their way to the upper echelons of the Russian political establishment thereby creating and exploiting their relations with the different Governors General, upon whose might depended the local application of laws and the preservation of order. The role of the Greeks Dimitrios Inglezes and Grigorri Marazli as holders of various public posts, not least as mayors, and that of O. Brodksi from the Jewish community, are examples of this.[43]

Greeks and Jews in Odessa were also to be found hand in hand in almost all non-mercantile occupations and neighbourhoods. Many Greeks were bakers and greengrocers, while others were engaged in the processing of food and animal products.[44] Jews were prominent as tailors, shoemakers, sawyers, manufacturers of woollen cloth and stoves, glaziers and peddlers.[45] Making a *Weltanschauung* of the motto 'brothers in commerce and comrades in problems', Greeks and Jews of the same social class intermingled in various neighbourhoods. Wealthy Jewish and Greek merchants lived in the well-to-do quarters of Aleksandrovskii and Bul'varnyi, whereas less well-off members of the two communities coexisted in the poorer neighbourhoods of Petropavloskii and Mikhailovskii.[46] Many offspring of these wealthy Greeks and Jews shared the same classroom and listened to the same teachers in the Lycée Richelieu, which opened in 1817 and in 1865 became Russian University, though, as Vladimir Jabotinski noted, close social relations did not exist.[47]

An indication of the parallel social fragmentation among Greeks and Jews is provided by differences in religious practices. For one, the rich Greek merchants visited the Ypapanti Church, whereas other less well-off Greeks went to the Church of the Holy Trinity in the northern suburbs of the city.[48] As far as the Odessa Jews were concerned, the elite of the Galician traders rejected the Beit-Knesset Ha Gadol, which had been erected in the late eighteenth century, and founded the Brody synagogue – thereby trying to back up their claims for political and economic leadership with their own prayer house.[49]

Within Odessa's cosmopolitan *milieu* members of the Greek and Jewish bourgeoisie moved beyond the narrow cultural frames of their communities and embarked upon a European life-style. Although their daring choices were often viewed as a novel trend justified by sheer economic prosperity, demonstrations of excess and arrogance caused feelings of embarrassment and resentment among moderate and traditionally-oriented individuals. Well-off Greeks and Jews entertained themselves in the city's restaurants, clubs and the famous Opera House; they looked for information and education in the city's libraries and the museum; they spent their roubles in luxurious emporia and food stores. G. Marasli, probably the most prominent member of the Greek Diaspora in Odessa, went so far as to marry at a late age the Jewish actress M.F. Kitz, thereby disappointing many of his fellow Greeks, who had hoped to inherit his large fortune.[50] However, basic elements of ethnic or religious competition never vanished from the local scene. Even at the Opera, Greeks and Italians now and then joined together as 'Christian brothers' and supported one diva against their Jewish fellow-spectators who applauded another.

Having said that, it is imperative to find out the content and, if possible, assess the hostility- and violence-potential of this ethnic segregation. Indeed, as in Salonika, a not inconsiderable number of wealthy Jews and Greeks, aware of their ethno-religious particularity and the need for communal autarchy generously invested time and money in important communal projects. Thus, in November 1826 representatives of the Galician élite took advantage of the authorities' positive attitude towards Jewish education and set up a modern secular school where pupils – to the disappointment of many traditional Jews – were taught languages (Russian, German, French), arithmetic, mathematics, biology, geography and history along with Biblical Studies.[51] The liberal spirit of Russian officials coupled with the high reputation of the school's teachers and the promising type of education made the school a point of attraction for Jewish children living in the immediate surroundings of Odessa. In 1835 a school was founded for Jewish girls, who could thus receive instruction in Russian, German and French as well as in Russian history, geography, calligraphy and Hebrew prayers. The school was visited in 1852 by the Minister of Public Instruction, A.S. Norov, who enthusiastically commented upon the high level of education.[52] In 1855 the list of communal institutions was long enough to include four synagogues, 34 prayer houses as well as a Jewish hospital with 75 beds set up during the years of the Civic Chief of Odessa, A.I. Levshin.[53]

Similar efforts to support education, foster communal spirit, and upgrade mercantile activities were undertaken by successful Greek merchants in Odessa. For one, the general absence of schools in Odessa encouraged A. Vrettos as early as 1800 to set up the first school, where about 70 pupils were taught writing, Greek, Russian and Italian. Some years later, the house of the Priest Sourmeli functioned as a private Greek school entirely supported by the Greek colony. The decisive step was made in 1814, when 60 wealthy Greek businessmen, merchants, insurers, ship-owners and freighters pooled their resources and set up the Greco-Commercial School of Odessa, which started functioning in 1817. A large number of Greek schoolchildren, not only from Odessa but also from Greece and the Ottoman Empire, profited intellectually and professionally from the modern curriculum, which included Greek, philosophy, economic geography, book-keeping, Russian and Italian.[54] Five years later the Greek Girls' School was opened, financed this time by the Russian state. Efforts to support female education resulted in the establishment of the 'Greek Rodokanakio Girls' School' in 1874 and the Greek Professional Girls' School in 1908.[55] Distinctively ethnic cultural activities were complemented by the creation of a Greek theatre in 1814.[56] In 1827 a Greek printing house was set up. It was entrusted not only with the printing of manuals of the Greek language, translations and educational books[57] but also with publications on international maritime issues – such as the regulation of commercial transactions, the keeping of registers, the setting up of accurate inventories with regard to the quality, quantity and ownership of merchandise.[58] Greek communal interests were finally served by the establishment of three Greek insurance companies (Graikon Asfaliston, Nea Graikiki, Graikiki and Graikorosiki)[59] and two charity societies, 'The Greek Brotherhood' in 1864 and 'The Greek Benevolent Association of Odessa' in 1871.[60]

However, the various efforts aimed at fostering a Greek ethnic identity among Odessa Greeks by laying emphasis on the Orthodox religion, the Greek language and Greek national history were potential springboards for the creation of monolithic self-images, for which the Jew was the 'dangerous Other'. As elsewhere in Europe, Greeks shared the popular belief in the evil of the Jews as the people of deicide. In Greek folk songs the stereotypical attributes which had informed the image of the Jews in medieval Europe are ascribed to Jews: Jews are unclean, leprous, sorcerers, while Jewish women are witches and killers of children. The image of the Jew is portrayed in similar negative colours in *Karangiozi*, the Greek shadow theatre, where the Jewish character is presented with the disagreeable characteristics of the Turkish *Karangiozi*, namely that he is a miser, a coward, crafty and a vulture.[61]

Connected with this was the burning of Judas, a custom which appeared in different versions in different areas in Greece and which was forbidden in 1891, the year of the Zakynthos and the Kerkyra pogrom, by a decision signed by the Athens Metropolitan Germanos in his effort to protect Jewish citizens.[62] No less important was the notorious blood libel accusation; indeed from 1840 until 1930, more than 30 cases of accusation of the blood libel were recorded in the Greek and Jewish press.[63] In the folk tradition, the accusation of deicide was accentuated by 'the symbolic representation of the Holy Passion and the Crucifixions which took place during the Holy Week and received dimensions of a drama which the people were experiencing with original expressions of mourning'.[64] When religious passions ran high during Easter time in Odessa, Greeks and Jews, who literally rubbed shoulders in the very same quarters, often took part in brawls. This kind of 'ceremonial violence' had the potential to turn into anti-Jewish pogroms as was the case in 1821, 1849, 1859 and 1871.

The first riot was connected to the dramatic events following the outbreak of the Greek War of Independence against the Ottomans. In their efforts to crush the Greek rebellion, Muslim officials ordered the hanging of the Greek Patriarch of Constantinople, Gregory V, on Easter Sunday, 10 April 1821. His remains were thrown into the sea and were found six days later by the crew of a Greek ship anchored in the Gulf of Horn under the Russian flag. The ship then sailed to Odessa, where, in the meantime, many Greeks had fled to escape Ottoman reprisals. At the personal intervention of Tsar Alexander the corpse was laid in state for three days' public worship and buried with all solemnity on the 19 April.[65]

Rumours that Jews had been directly involved in the Patriarch's ferocious murder fell on ready ears. Indeed, Greeks had traditionally perceived the Jews as Turkish acolytes, in the sense that the latter had tended to regard national movements as threats to the Pax Ottomana and, consequently, to their own vested interests. Indeed, during the height of the Greek national uprising many Jews in mainland Greece paid with their own lives for their continued support of Ottoman rule.[66] In Odessa, the birthplace of the Greek revolutionary movement of Philiki Etairia, there were certain Greeks who held Odessa Jews 'guilty by association'.[67] Joining forces with Russian anti-semites they made their way to the Jewish neighbourhood attacking Jews and their property. The tragic account of this pogrom rose to 17 casualties and more than 60 wounded. Anti-Jewish riots re-occurred on 22 August 1849 and were explained by the alleged Jewish reluctance to pay due respect to a church procession from the Mikhailovskii monastery. During Easter 1859, Odessa Jews fell victim

once again to Greek religious fanaticism, which sparked the first pogrom
in Odessa to attract journalistic attention from outside the city. It was,
however, the pogrom of 1871 and its tragic consequences which sealed
forever the character of Greco-Jewish relations. Although Russian officials
and reports published in the Russian press accentuated in a differentiated
way the deeper reasons for the violent manifestations of anti-Jewish
feeling, they all agreed on the participation of the Greeks in the pogrom,
which lasted four days spreading terror and destruction among the city's
Jewish population.[68] The pogroms of 1881 and 1905 occurred within a
completely different socio-economic context, and during them Russian
anti-semites happened to attack Greek houses as well.[69]

Notwithstanding these instances of conflict, the overall picture of
Greco-Jewish coexistence in Salonika and Odessa was much more
complicated, as neither the Jews nor the Greeks constituted
homogeneous ethnic groups with unified interests and consistent patterns
of behaviour. Although ethnic boundaries persisted, cross-ethnic
relations between Greeks and Jews of the same social standing were
possible in different spheres of public and economic life. For one, their
minority status within multi-ethnic societies endowed them with
comparable dilemmas concerning their legal situation and ethnic identity.
Answers were found either in ethno-centric choices, cosmopolitan life-
styles and international socialism, or in a mixture combining elements of
all these trends. Moreover, their conspicuous role in mercantile activities
in both cities made of many Greeks and Jews a Weberian 'ideal type' of
cosmopolitan merchant with the same business ethos and psychology.
This kind of social role was intimately connected to the multi-ethnic
societies within which these merchants lived and prospered, as well as to
the functional connection of their port-*milieu* with international politics
and the world economy.

Having said that, I propose to revisit Greco-Jewish relations in
Salonika and Odessa, as well as in other multi-ethnic port cities, such as
Trieste, Istanbul, Smyrna and Alexandria, in the light of a bipolar scheme
of analysis. For one, there are those which point to stereotypical self-
images and images of the 'Other', resulting in the following opposing
couplet: 'Anti-Ottoman Greeks vs. Philo-Ottoman Jews' or 'Greek
Orthodox Christians vs. Jewish Jesus-killers' or even 'Merchants of
Greek origins vs. Merchants of Jewish origins'. By contrast, due
consideration has to be given to ethnic-couplets underlining the
compatibility of Greco-Jewish interests: 'Greeks and Jews as minorities
against the ruling Muslim or Russian population', or 'Greeks and Jews as
diaspora people away from or without homeland against the state-based
Muslim or Russian population', or 'Greeks and Jews as traders, urban

dwellers and harbingers of westernised form of existence vis-à-vis Muslim and Russian peasants', or finally 'Greeks and Jews as inheritors of an ancient glorious past against the younger Slavic or allegedly inferior Ottoman culture'.

NOTES

1. For a general discussion of trade diasporas, their cultural blends and merchant settlements, see P.D. Curtin, *Cross-cultural Trade in World History* (Cambridge: Cambridge University Press, 1984).
2. This problematic has been elaborated in a collection of essays found in F. Barth (ed.), *Ethnic Groups and Boundaries: The Social Organization of Culture Difference* (Oslo: Universitetsforlaget, 1969).
3. H. Petropoulos, 'Ach, Allegra...', in *Thessaloniki* (Athens: Ekati, 1994), p.28.
4. B. Lewis, *The Jews of Islam* (Princeton: Princeton University Press, 1984), pp.125–6.
5. N.K. Moutsopoulos, 'Mia Poli anamesa se Dio Aiones', in *Thessaloniki* (see note 3), p.33.
6. R. Molho has discussed extensively this problem in *Oi Evraioi tis Thessalonikis, 1856–1919: Mia Idiaiteri Koinotita* (Athens: Themelio, 2001), pp.30–52.
7. A. Rodrigue, 'The Sephardim in the Ottoman Empire', in Elie Kedourie (ed.), *Spain and the Jews: The Sephardi Experience 1492 and after* (London: Thames & Hudson, 1992), p.180.
8. A. Rodrigue, 'From *millet* to Minority: Turkish Jewry', in Pierre Birnbaum and Ira Katznelson (eds.), *Paths of Emancipation* (Princeton: Princeton University Press, 1995), p.241.
9. M. Mazower, 'Salonika between East and West 1860–1912', *Dialogos* 1 (1994), p.110.
10. The origins of the *Francos* date back to the end of the sixteenth century when persecuted Jews found refuge in Livorno. The influx of Jews as well as of other persecuted groups (Catholics from England, Moors from Spain, Spanish and Portuguese *Marranos*) went on throughout the sixteenth and seventeenth century rendering Livorno a prospering port able to compete with Salonika and Venice. During the eighteenth century, Livornian Jews settled in Salonika, where they enjoyed foreign protection, and assimilated Western culture. Because they held foreign citizenship, they did not have to pay taxes raised both by the community as well as by the Ottomans; moreover, they could enjoy the benefit of guarantees and 'privileges granted to foreigners by the capitulations regime: consular protection, fiscal facilities, and all kinds of immunities. The connections that they possessed with foreign communities (Trieste, Venice, Ancone, Genoa, etc.) ensured them a dominant position in the Salonika market'. P. Dumont, 'The Social Structure of the Jewish Community of Salonika at the End of the Nineteenth Century', *South-eastern Europe* 5.2 (1979), p.56.
11. This bank was set up in June 1888 with the cooperation between the brothers Allatini and the three banks *Comptoir d'Escompte de Paris, Banque Imperiale et Royale Privilegiée des Pays Autrichiens, Banque de Pays Hongrois*. The base was in Salonika but in 1909 was transferred to Constantinople. E.A. Chekimoglou, *Thessalonike Tourkokratia kai Mesopolemos* (Thessalonike: Ekfrase, University Studio Press, 1995), pp.226–7.
12. E. Benbassa and A. Rodrigue. *Juifs des Balkans: Espaces Judéo-ibériques XIVe–XXe siècles* (Paris: Editions La Découverte, 1993), p.162.
13. K. Georgiadou, 'Oi Ellines tis Thessalonikis', in *Thessaloniki* (see note 3), p.133.

14. Dumont (see note 10), p.56. The *domme*, or Sabbatean Jews, were a Muslim sect descended from Jewish followers of Shabbetai Zvi who converted to Islam in 1666.
15. The Jewish white-collar workers were known as the *medianeros*. They were primarily trade agents including a motley group of people and specialisations, ibid., p.58.
16. D. Quartert, 'Protoi Kapnoi apo ta Ergostasia', in *Thessaloniki* (see note 3), pp.205–10.
17. Ibid., p.206.
18. Mazower (see note 9), pp.111–12.
19. V. Kolonas, 'Oi Architektonikes Metatropes', in *Thessaloniki* (see note 3), pp.187–188.
20. A. Gerolumbou, 'Mia Kosmopolitiki Poleodomia', in *Thessaloniki* (see note 3), p.178.
21. Rodrigue (see note 8), p.181. The status of *djimmi* afforded protection and legal rights to certain minorities although they were held to be inferior to Muslims and suffered discrimination in some areas of life.
22. F. Ahmad, 'Unionist Relations with the Greek, Armenian, and Jewish Communities of the Ottoman Empire, 1908–1914', in B. Braude and B. Lewis (eds.), *Christians and Jews in the Ottoman Empire: The Functioning of a Plural Society,* vol. I (New York: Holmes & Meier, 1982), pp.408–14.
23. P. Agrafiotou-Zachopoulou, *Scholia tes Thessalonikes* (Thessalonike: Ianos, 1997), pp.132–3.
24. R. Molho, 'Education in the Jewish Community of Thessaloniki in the Beginning of the Twentieth Century', *Balkan Studies*, 34.2 (1993), pp.259–69.
25. M. Öke, 'Young Turks, Freemasons, Jews and the Question of Zionism in the Ottoman Empire (1908–1913)', *Studies in Zionism* 7.2 (1986), p.207. The policy of *Drang nach Osten* was the expansion of German economic and diplomatic influence in the East.
26. Agrafiotou-Zachopoulou (see note 23) pp.132–9.
27. Georgiadou (see note 13), pp.136–8.
28. Molho (see note 6), pp.93–107.
29. Ibid., p.97.
30. Mazower (see note 9), p.120.
31. Ibid., pp.111–12.
32. P. Dumont, 'Franc-maconnerie d'Obédience Francaise à Salonique au Début du XXe Siècle', *Turcica,* 16 (1984), pp.67–73.
33. V. Kardasis, *Ellines Omogenis sti Notia Rossia*, 1775–1861 (Athens: Alexandria, 1998), p.81.
34. P. Herlihy, 'The Ethnic Composition of the City of Odessa in the Nineteenth Century', *Harvard Ukrainian Studies* 1 (1977), pp.54, 65–70.
35. Kardasis (see note 33), pp.201–5.
36. J. Tarnopol, *Notices historiques et caractéristiques sur les Israélites d'Odessa précédés d'un aperçu général sur l'état du peuple Israélite en Russie et suivies de notes statistiques et explications* (Odessa: 1855), p.65.
37. Ibid., p.182.
38. P. Herlihy, *Odessa: A History 1794–1914* (Cambridge, MA: Harvard University Press, 2nd ed., 1991), pp.212–14.
39. Alexander Pushkin, an admirer of the ancient Greek culture and civilisation, was disappointed to find out that the modern Greeks he encountered in Odessa were a pale imitation of their glorious ancestors. In the early 1820s he wrote 'we have seen the new Leonidases in the streets of Odessa and Kishinev. We are personally acquainted with a number of them; we attest of their complete worthiness; they have not the slightest idea of military art, no concept of honour, no enthusiasm. As cited in R. Clogg, 'The Greek Mercantile Bourgeoisie: 'Progressive or Reactionary?', in R. Clogg (ed.), *Balkan Society in the Age of Greek Independence* (London: Macmillan, 1981) p.85. On the other

hand, Odessa Jews were similarly suspected and accused of unbridled craving for material goods. Jewish journalists pointed in their newspaper articles to the danger, which blind commitment to commercial activities entailed for Jewish life and Jewish identity. Even more telling is the way in which Odessa came down in Yiddish folklore as the place where the surrounding seven miles burned with the fires of hell. S. Zipperstein, *The Jews of Odessa: A Cultural History, 1794–1881* (Stanford, California: Stanford University Press, 1986), Introduction and p.37.

40. This Jewish family had emigrated from Livorno in Italy to Salonika in the eighteenth century.
41. I. Pepelassis Minoglou and H. Louri, 'Diaspora Entrepreneurial Networks in the Black Sea and Greece, 1870–1917', *Journal of European Economic History* 26.1 (1997), p.70.
42. Herlihy, *Odessa* (see note 38), p.151.
43. Th. C. Proussis, 'Demetrios S. Inglezes: Greek Merchant and City Leader of Odessa', *Slavic Review* 50.3 (1991), pp.672–9.
44. Herlihy, 'Ethnic composition' (see note 34), p.72 and Herlihy, *Odessa* (see note 38), p.124.
45. Tarnopol (see note 36), p.147.
46. According to Herlihy's evaluation of population-statistics, we know that in Aleksandrovskii 19.7% of the inhabitants were Greeks and 32.8% Jews, in Bul'varnyi, 27.1% were Greeks and 11% Jews, in Petropavloskii 10.1% Greeks and 23.7% Jews and, finally, in Mikhailovskii lived 9% Greeks and 22% Jews. P. Herlihy, 'The Greek Community in Odessa, 1861–1917', *Journal of Modern Greek Studies* 7 (1989), p.238.
47. Zipperstein (see note 39), p.110.
48. Kardasis (see note 33), p.95.
49. Zipperstein (see note 39), pp.57–58.
50. M. Karavia, *Odessos. H Lismonimeni Patrida*, (Athens: Agra, 1998), pp.58–59.
51. Zipperstein (see note 39), p.47.
52. Tarnopol (see note 36), p.130.
53. Ibid., p.112.
54. E. Sifnaiou, 'Ellines Epichirimaties sti N. Rosia', *Ta Istorika*, 32, Vol. 17 (2001), p.111.
55. For the overall educational activities of the Greek community in Odessa, K. G. Avgitidis, *Ta Ellinika Ekpaideutika Idrumata tis Odissou (1816–1936)* (Giannina: Dodoni, 2000).
56. A. Tampaki, 'To Elliniko Theatro stin Odisso (1814–1818)'. *O Eranistis*, 16 (1980), pp.229–238.
57. K. G. Avgitidis, H Ekdotiki Drastiriotita ton Omogenoon tis Odissoou (1829–1917) (Giannina: Dodoni, 2000).
58. Sifnaiou (see note 54), p.112.
59. Kardasis (see note 33), p.92.
60. J.A. Mazis, 'The Greek Benevolent Association of Odessa (1871–1917): Private Charity and Diaspora Leadership in Late Imperial Russia', unpublished Ph.D. Dissertation (University of Minnesota, 1998).
61. F. Ambatzopoulou, *O Allos en Diogmo. He Eikona tou Evraiou ste Logotechnia: Zetemata Hestorias kai Mythoplasias* (Athens: Themelio, 1998), p.197.
62. Ibid., p.200.
63. B. Pierron, *Juifs et Chrétiens de la Grèce Moderne: Histoire des Relations Intercommunautaires de 1821 à 1945* (Paris: Harmatan, 1996), pp.116–122.
64. Ambatzopoulou (see note 61), p.199.
65. *Historia tou Ellinikou Ethnous*, vol. XII (Athens: Ekdotiki Athinon, 1975), pp.130–34.
66. S.J. Shaw, 'Christian Antisemitism in the Ottoman Empire', *Bebbeten*, Cilt: LIV Sa 211 (Aralik, 1990), pp.1073–149.
67. One should be careful to take into consideration the fact that not all Odessa Greeks

were in favour of the Greek War of Independence, lest any disruption of the status quo in the Levant endanger their commercial activities. Interestingly enough, the three founding members of Philiki Etairia were middle-class merchants who had been adversely affected by the fall of prices in the grain trade in the aftermath of the Napoleonic Wars. Clogg (see note 39), p.104.

68. J.D. Klier, 'The Pogrom Paradigm in Russian History' in J.D. Klier and Sh. Lambroza (eds.), *Pogroms: Anti-Jewish Violence in Modern Russian History* (Cambridge: Cambridge University Press, 1991), pp.17–32.

69. Karavia (see note 50), p.85.

A Port, Not a Shtetl: Reflections on the Distinctiveness of Odessa

JOHN D. KLIER

In 1820, the Jews of Odessa were offered a splendid political opportunity. The Russian state had, in 1816, authorised Jewish communities throughout the empire to elect formal representatives, to be called the 'Deputies of the Jewish People', and to send them to St Petersburg. These Deputies were to serve as formal communal representatives to inform the state about the needs and concerns of the Jews. In the empire, the right to petition the ruler was a jealously guarded prerogative, denied to the vast majority of the population in the guise of the peasantry. Among those who did enjoy such rights were the hereditary nobility, the *dvorianstvo*. Given Odessa's subsequent reputation as a centre for Jewish political activism, the response of the local Jews may seem surprising. They not only failed to send their own delegates to participate in the election of deputies, but after the elections, they assiduously avoided making the agreed-upon contribution towards the expenses of the Deputies as they lobbied for Jewish interests in St. Petersburg. So scandalous was their apathy that the provincial Jewish assembly threatened to break relations with the Odessans, and not to offer them any assistance when they fell foul of the authorities.[1]

The key to understanding Odessa Jewish apathy in 1820 is the key to understanding Odessa throughout much of its history. It was the most 'un-Jewish' of Jewish cities from the traditional point of view, and the most 'Jewish' from the perspective of non-traditional Jewish life and attitudes. The Odessa Jewish experience serves as a reminder that not all East European Jews lived in *shtetlakh*, the small market towns often seen as the cradle of traditional Jewish life.[2] Jews were also town dwellers, as exemplified by Vilna, Warsaw or Kiev. Small wonder that Orthodox Jews claimed that the fires of Gehenna burned seven miles around Odessa, although this did not prevent Hasidic *tzaddikim* from making periodic visits to the town in order to collect offerings from their followers.[3] Indeed, many a traditional Jew came to gape at Odessa's wonders, with a mixture of awe and disgust.[4]

Yet Odessa was also distinct even among urban Jewish centres. Odessa Jews were indeed 'Jews of a Port', if not 'Port Jews'. And this port of theirs

was something new, not only for East European Jewry and for the Russian
Empire itself. The city itself was founded by Empress Catherine II in 1794
as a port to link the grain-producing markets of the Ukrainian interior with
the markets of western Europe, via the Black Sea. Patricia Herlihy has
delineated the city's numerous advantages – location, excellent planning,
imperial favour, a cosmopolitan openness, and mercantile imperatives –
which prompted explosive growth throughout the nineteenth century.
Odessa was an 'instant city', which 'had no infancy', and 'rose like a
mushroom after a heavy rain'.[5]

As befit its new urban setting, Odessa's Jewish community was also
brand new, founded only in 1798. It was the youngster among the long-
established Jewish communities in the lands of the former Polish-
Lithuanian Commonwealth, now under Russian rule, heretofore
dominated by ancient centres of Jewish learning, like Vilna, Minsk,
Volozhin and Mir, as well as the numerous tiny shtetlakh with their
Hasidic courts, such as Liady, Liubovichi and Chernobyl. Odessa was the
jewel of lands known as 'Novorossiia' – New Russia', the provinces of
Kherson, Taurida and Ekaterinoslav. And new they certainly were,
supplemented by the territorial booty Russia claimed after victory in the
Russo-Turkish War of 1768–74. Odessa stood on the coast of a hinterland
so empty that the Russian state was determined to fill it with settlers of
any kind. This included the Jews, formally banned from settlement in the
empire until the First Partition of Poland in 1772. Catherine II's powerful
Viceroy in the region, 'the Prince of Tauride', Gregory Potemkin, was
determined to recruit human capital, 'even Jews'. He evaded Russian law
by ordering border guards to simply ignore the religious confession of any
immigrant who appeared at Russia's frontiers expressing the wish to settle
in New Russia.[6]

Under such circumstances, the population of Odessa was destined to
be cosmopolitan from the start. The city's Greek-derived name was an
open invitation to Greek merchants to help colonise it, and they did with
enthusiasm. (Before the Greek national uprising of 1821, Greeks were
Ottoman subjects, and free to ply their trade through the Straits.) Greek
merchants were generally credited with first developing Odessa's
commercial prowess before losing their pre-eminence to the Jews.

To speak collectively of 'Odessa Jewry' belies the diversity of their
national origins. Odessa's pioneer Jewish community was a mixed bunch,
with settlers from the Ukrainian provinces of Volynia and Podolia, and
from Lithuania – all acquired in the Second (1793) and Third (1795)
Partitions of Poland. Gradually the town began to attract settlers from
further afield, notably those from Austrian Galicia who gave their name to
the 'Brody' synagogue. These Galician Jews created the legend that the
town was a Jewish backwater until saved by their energising presence. As

Steven Zipperstein argues, this is at the very least an exaggeration, a claim buttressed by the early appearance of all the accoutrements of Jewish communal life: a cemetery (1793) predated the formal founding of the community by a year; the first *pinkis* (minute book) of an Odessa Jewish *khevrah* (charitable brotherhood) dates to 1795; the formal Jewish community, the *kahal* (or *kehillah*) was founded in 1798, along with the opening of the 'Main Synagogue' on Evreiskaia ulitsa (Jewish Street).[7]

With this pedigree, why then the apathy of 1820? Odessa Jews, like any Jewish homesteaders, were quite capable of establishing cemeteries and founding synagogues, hiring ritual slaughterers and rabbis, and creating benevolent societies, the *Khevrot*. What Odessa Jews lacked was the tradition of political activism which had characterised the Jews of the Polish-Lithuanian Commonwealth. Galician Jews residing in the Hapsburg lands of partitioned Poland, 'Galicia', had been treated differently by the Austrian authorities from Russian Jews – Galicia's Jewish communal institutions were abolished in 1772, and a process of germanisation begun.[8] Galician Jewry brought to Odessa these traditions, along with Haskalah, the Jewish Enlightenment movement associated with Moses Mendelssohn of Berlin, but they were not accustomed to an active political life. In short, Odessa was a town without 'native' Jewish traditions, where new Jewish traditions had to be created. Given this absence of the past, Odessa functioned as a kind of 'anti-shtetl'. Thus, while Odessa was never a centre for traditional Jewish learning, it produced whole cadres of Jewish intellectuals who played a major role in almost every movement which characterised modern Jewry. These included the eastern variant of Haskalah, all the various shades of Zionism, Territorialism, Autonomism, and the whole gamut of Jewish socialist activity. Odessa was the birthplace of a modern Jewish press in Russian, Yiddish and Hebrew.[9]

Odessa also served as a cultural centre, where Jews became acculturated to the dominant culture – Jews in traditional garb were to be seen in the city's magnificent opera house. The city served as a stage – literally – for some of the first productions of the modern Yiddish theatre associated with Avram Gol'dfaden.[10] The city played a major role in the development of both modern Hebrew and modern Yiddish literature, associated with the names of Mendele and Sholem Aleichem. Later the city produced one of the masters of modern Russian prose, Isaac Babel, who commemorated his birthplace in his collection of 'Odessa Tales'.[11]

While the Jews comprised a major component of Odessa's population (up to one-third by mid-century), they were not the only cause of the explosive growth of 'The Russian Chicago'. The city attracted a motley population from across the empire and from abroad: merchants and entrepreneurs, peasants, port workers, casual and seasonal labourers (who posed a constant public order problem). Like the 'City of the Big

Shoulders' on Lake Michigan in the United States, Odessa was well sited to
serve as the major entrepôt for Russia's major foreign export – grain. (The
city even had American-style grain elevators.) The grain trade served as
Odessa's 'leading sector', encouraging the strengthening of internal and
export transportation links: the port and the sailing and steam ships which
used it, and the railroads.

This led to the emergence of a new kind of Jew from the economic
point of view. Jewish porters and stevedores served the docks, Jewish
teamsters and carters brought grain by ox-cart from the interior, and a
Jewish commercial bourgeoisie of clerks and agents grew up within
Odessa's commercial environment. A Jewish *haute bourgeoisie* appeared
as well, making fortunes from banking and the stock market and from
innovation such as the commercial production of sugar from sugar-beet.
As Odessa's Jews became increasingly acculturated, they produced visual
artists, musicians, actors, writers – as well as the Jewish underworld ruled
by Babel's fictional Jewish gangster 'Benya Krik', the protagonist of the
short story 'How It Was Done in Odessa'.[12]

The growing population required all the amenities associated with life
in a modern city. Odessa's increasingly bourgeois leadership sought to
provide them: potable water, paved streets, food supplies, banking
facilities, as well as beach resorts and an opera house! (Some wags quipped
that Odessa, of all Russia's cities, was fortunate to have been founded by an
enlightened French aristocrat, the Duc de Richelieu, who bequeathed the
town a set of cultural pretensions which it never lost. Critics, on the other
hand, saw the city as exemplifying the characteristics of the parvenu and
the nouveau riche.)

The importance of the Jews to the unique development of Odessa was
well-recognised by the imperial authorities, who treated the community,
and especially its acculturated members, with respect. Thus, Odessa's
Governor-General at mid-century, Count A.G. Stroganov, urged a
reluctant central government to permit publication of the first Russian-
Jewish newspaper, *Rassvet* (*The Dawn*).[13] The progressive Overseer of the
Odessa Educational District, N.I. Pirogov, created a national sensation
when he singled out Odessa's Jewish charity school, a *talmud-tora*, for
praise and held it up as an example for Christians.[14]

Our focus on the city itself should not cause us to lose sight of the fact
that Odessa was linked in a symbiotic relationship to its hinterland, the
black-soil agricultural region of the southern Ukraine. City and region
should be viewed as an organic whole. The grain flowed into Odessa, first
by ox-cart and dirt track, and then by railroad, to be moved onward by
ship. Those same ships brought foreign goods for import to the interior,
while the city provided a livelihood for craftsmen and small
manufacturers, as well as banks and brokering houses. The nature of the

city/hinterland relationship was important for Russian Jewry, and any changes in it had a negative impact upon them.

The Jews of Eastern Europe had never been enserfed or tied to a particular area. This latter statement may seem contradicted by the existence of the Pale of Settlement, the name given to a collection of laws which restricted the movement of Jews into the interior of the old Muscovite state, its Great Russian ethnic heartland. What is often overlooked is that the Pale was enormous in size (larger than modern France) and even larger when combined with the Kingdom of Poland (Kongresowka) – the ethnically Polish part of the Russian Empire which is often shown on maps as part of the Pale, but which in fact had separate laws and regulations governing the Jews. Taken together, the Pale and Kongresowka comprised some of the most dynamic economic areas of the Russian Empire, including major industrial and transport facilities. (The real cause of the widely-observed impoverishment of the Jewish population in the Russian Empire was its remarkable demographic growth, from approximately one million in 1800 to five million in 1900.)[15] With some exceptions, for most of the nineteenth century the Jews enjoyed untrammelled mobility within the areas of their legal residence. Since the enserfed peasants did not enjoy such ease of travel, the Jews played a vital role in the semi-feudal economy as middlemen. In the Ukraine, they were active in the grain trade: buying grain before or after the harvest, and moving it themselves to both local and distant markets. When the trade grew in scope, Jews often served as agents and brokers for grain export firms. Jews were intimately connected with internal transport, as teamsters and carters, and as dealers in horses and other livestock.

The emancipation of the serfs in 1861 – Russia's dramatic bid for modernisation – had a negative impact on the Jews. The landowners, stripped of their sources of free labour, had to pursue more rationally organised economy, and began to manage their estates more carefully, eliminating the need for Jewish agents. The peasants, although still tied technically to the peasant community (the *obshchina*), had much greater mobility and could move their own produce to the market, if they so chose. Most importantly, the construction of the Russia's railroad network – not slow to reach Odessa – took the livelihood of small grain traders and their ox-cart means of transportation. The significance of these economic changes was noted by sharp-eyed contemporaries, such as the Odessa journalist and legal historian I.G. Orshanskii, who observed in 1869:

> The impoverished situation of our co-religionists in Russia is a transitory phenomenon, a temporary one, and will be eliminated to the degree that Jewry adapts itself to new structure of life, forgetting old trades and occupations which are now obsolete, and learning new ones.[16]

It was long assumed in the secondary literature that it was anti-Jewish legislation, such as the notorious May Laws of 1882, or the pogroms, that were the source of Jewish poverty, and the chief spur to out-migration. In fact, 'market forces' rather than anti-Jewish legislation, had the greatest impact upon Jewish economic well-being. The gradual modernisation of the Empire, on which Orshanskii staked future Jewish economic well-being, was too long in coming.

Historians argue over the extent to which the late Tsarist Empire was in 'crisis', and even more the extent to which it was failing or succeeding in resolving the political, social and economic dilemmas raised by efforts at rapid modernisation. This same debate could be framed in terms of Russia's (and Odessa's) Jews. The out-migration of more than two million Jews from the empire before the outbreak of the war, the policy of state anti-semitism which many historians have seen as characteristic of the late Tsarist empire, the rise of political dissidence on the part of individual Jews (an interesting marker of incipient modernisation 'on the Jewish street'), all bespeak a 'crisis'. Scholars have yet to ascertain the extent to which this crisis was specifically 'Jewish' as opposed to being part of the general Russian crisis. Odessa Jewry can serve as a useful test case to explore this question. At the same time, Odessa's Jewish community also cries out for inclusion in any comparative study of the Port Jew phenomenon.

NOTES

1. John D. Klier, *Rossiia sobiraet svoikh evreev* (Jerusalem/Moscow, 2000), p.281.
2. See John D. Klier, 'What Exactly Was a Shtetl?' in G. Estraikh and M. Krutikov, *The Shtetl: Image and Reality* (Oxford, 2000), pp.23–35.
3. Viktoriia Khiterer, *Dokumenty sobrannye Evreiskoi Istoriko-Arkheograficheskoi Komissiei* (Jerusalem/Kiev, 1999), pp.273–89.
4. See the wonderfully ironic portrait of the visit to Odessa of the title character of Mendele Moykher-Sforim's *Fishke the Lame*, exerpted in M. Zukerman *et al.*, *Selected Works of Mendele Moykher-Sforim* (Malibu, CA, 1991), pp.292–8.
5. Patricia Herlihy, *Odessa: A History, 1794–1914* (Cambridge, MA, 1986), p.9.
6. John D. Klier, *Russia Gathers Her Jews: The Origins of the 'Jewish Question' in Russia, 1772–1825* (DeKalb, IL, 1986), p.37.
7. *Evreiskaia entsiklopediia*, vol.12 (St Petersburg, n.d.), pp.50–1.
8. Steven J. Zipperstein, *The Jews of Odessa: A Cultural History, 1794–1881* (Stanford, CA: Stanford University Press, 1985), pp.40–4.
9. See Alexander Orbach, *New Voices of Russian Jewry: A Study of the Russian-Jewish Press of Odessa in the Era of the Great Reforms, 1860–71* (Leiden, 1980).
10. For Goldfaden, see Nahma Sandrow, *Vagabond Stars: A World History of Yiddis Theater* (Syracuse, NY, 1996), pp.40–69.
11. *The Complete Works of Isaac Babel*, ed. by Natalie Babel (London, 2002), pp.129–195.
12. For a good examination of the role of Odessa in Babel's fiction, see Alice Stone Nakhimovsky, *Russian-Jewish Literature and Identity* (Baltimore and London, 1992), pp.97–106.
13. See John D. Klier, '1855–1894 Censorship of the Press in Russian and the Jewish Question', *Jewish Social Studies* 45.3-4 (1986), 257–68.
14. John D. Klier, *Imperial Russia's Jewish Question, 1855–1881* (Cambridge: Cambridge University Press, 1996), pp.40–50.
15. See Evreiskoe Statisticheskoe Obshchestvo, *Evreiskoe naselenie Rossii po dannym perepisi 1897 g. I po noveishim istochnikam* (Petrograd, 1917).
16. *Den': organ russkikh evreev*, 14:15/VIII/1869.

The Sorkin and Golab Theses and their Applicability to South, Southeast, and East Asian Port Jewry

JONATHAN GOLDSTEIN

Overarching Theoretical Considerations

In his seminal work on seventeenth to twentieth century Sephardi and Italian Jews living in Mediterranean, Atlantic, and West Indian seaports, historian David Sorkin isolated five characteristics which may also apply to contemporaneous Asian Jewish communities: India's Cochinim and Bene Israel Jews; Baghdadi Jews in India, Singapore, Hong Kong, and Shanghai; and Central and Eastern European Jews who fled Hitler and reached Shanghai in the late 1930s and early 1940s.[1] In an attempt to test the Sorkin thesis, this article examines these Asian port Jews as well as the Jewish community of Harbin [Haerbin/Kharbin], China, located some 1,500 miles inland. In a further attempt to clarify the histories of these Asian Jewish communities, this article applies U.S. immigration historian Caroline Golab's theory on the relationship between the duration of residence of an immigrant community and its institutional development.

As already noted, David Sorkin cited five characteristics of port Jews. They are:

- Migration and commerce: he observed a distinctive pattern of migration and commerce in which

    a Sephardi trade network ... connected the old Mediterranean routes with the Atlantic economy ... These merchants had the great advantage of being able to do business with, and draw bills of exchange on, relatives, friends, or business associates whom they could trust.[2]

- The valuation of commerce: Sorkin argued that the commercial utility of Jews to their host society ensured them 'admission to, or continuing residence in, a polity'.[3]

- Legal status: a third characteristic was that commercial utility gave port Jews other privileges and forms of legal equality which enabled them to move toward full emancipation. In some cases these were substantial privileges, over and beyond mere residential permission.

- Re-education and '*haskalah* [enlightenment] *avant la lettre*': Sorkin's fourth characteristic includes 're-education', the re-conversion of individuals who had involuntarily converted from Judaism to Christianity as a self-defence mechanism during the reign of the Inquisition. Although there most probably were some crypto-Jews or *conversos* in the European colonies of the Far East, there does not appear to be any evidence of this type of 're-education' of converts.[4] On the other hand, variations of what Sorkin terms '*haskalah avant la lettre*' may well have occurred in the Far East. This involved a community, not necessarily of converts, experiencing its Judaism in full compatibility with a larger culture, and without any formal awareness of Enlightenment tracts by Voltaire, Locke, Moses Mendelsohn, or others. In another publication Sorkin stresses the breadth of the term *haskalah*, which at various times has been defined as embracing acculturation, assimilation, emancipation, and modernisation.[5] In the Far East, over and beyond the totally assimilated 'Enlightened' Jews who rejected their Judaism for something more universal, it is clear that there were Jews who were 'Enlightened *avant la lettre*'. That is to say that, with or without benefit of Voltaire, Locke, or Moses Mendelsohn, they were comfortable retaining their Judaic beliefs while actively participating in a broad secular culture. Some considered Zionism as their 'Enlightened' Jewish awakening, an experience comparable to that of many of their nationalistic-minded non-Jewish Italian, Irish, Scottish and American contemporaries.[6]

- Identity and belief: Sorkin's fifth and final characteristic is intensification of Jewish identity. This characteristic, like '*haskalah avant la lettre*', has both Judaic and secular components. In defining Jewish 'identity' Sorkin refers not only to an individual's religious belief and practice but also to his or her work developing such communal institutions as primary and secondary schools, libraries, publications, hospitals, old age homes, and social services. In Mediterranean, Atlantic, and West Indian ports, many non-observant Jews 'continued to identify themselves as Jews and to support the community with their wealth and influence'. They supported a multi-institutional 'synagogue-based religion' even if they did not personally maintain Kashruth or observe holidays.[7] This essay cites examples of the aforementioned forms of philanthropy, as well as formal belief and practice, as evidence of affirmation of Jewish identity in the Far East.

Perhaps the most important concept that overarches all five criteria of the Sorkin thesis is that maritime trade created the conditions not only for Jewish institutional development and for affirmation of a broadly construed Jewish identity but also for a wide array of privileges that in some cases came close to full emancipation. As already noted, as a foil to this argument, I will apply Sorkin's thesis to Jews living some 1,500 miles inland, in the Chinese city of Harbin. Additionally, I will introduce another parameter for looking at port Jews, a concept derived from Caroline Golab's study of U. S. immigration history. In attempting to explain institutional and intellectual development among European immigrants in nineteenth and twentieth century America, Golab distinguishes between a 'migrant', or person who relocated from country A to country B with no clear intent of taking up permanent residence in country B; an 'immigrant', or individual who moved from country A to country B with the intention of establishing a new permanent residence; and a 'migrant' who became an 'immigrant'. Golab writes:

> By examining foreign migrants in greater detail we can see how intentions, desires, cultural belongings and pre-emigration experiences helped or hindered their attempts to adapt to established economic and demographic structures.[8]

Migrants became immigrants when 'conscious choice or force of circumstance' caused them to see their futures in new places rather than in their native lands. She concludes that 'their views of themselves as temporary or permanent influenced their goals and behavior'.[9] Her categories help explain institutional and intellectual development in the Baghdadi communities of India, Singapore, Hong Kong, and Shanghai, in other Indian Jewish communities, and in the Russian-Jewish community in Harbin. Her distinctions also help explain the absence of long-term institutional development in transient communities like that of the Holocaust survivors in Shanghai – individuals who in some cases spent years living next to their suitcases and with little or no interaction with their Asian hosts. These migrants could best be described as 'persons of Jewish origin temporarily living or working in ports' rather than as 'port Jews'.

What follows is not a comprehensive history of Jews in the Far East but rather thumbnail sketches of several communities. Each case will be discussed in terms of the degree it conforms with the Sorkin and Golab criteria.

India's Cochinim

Recent scholarship on Jews in the South Indian seaport of Cochin, in the province of Kerala, suggests that this community made the transition from migrant to immigrant status in Golab's sense and also conformed to all five criteria of the Sorkin thesis.[10] Copper plates dated 974–1020 AD and still preserved in the Cochin Synagogue contain inscriptions that Jews arrived on South India's Malabar Coast sometime after the destruction of the First Temple. Local legend maintains that the first Jewish merchants came to the coast with the ships of King Solomon's fleet, ca. 1000 BC. Dravidian loan words in the Hebrew scriptures attest to that possibility. Benjamin of Tudela's travelogue of 1173 speaks of 1,000 Jews living under the protection of the local Maharajah and participating in his international trade in ginger and other local spices. The Maharajah of Cochin recognised their economic utility and granted the head of the Jewish community special economic and ritual privileges, including exemption from paying taxes, the right to collect tolls, and the honour of using particular lamps, umbrellas, drums and trumpets associated with high ritual status. In the 1500s additional Jews arrived from Spain, Portugal, Aleppo, Constantinople, and the Land of Israel. They married into Cochin Jewish society and adopted the Malayalam language and Keralan customs. After a period of Portuguese oppression, Jews were more favoured under Dutch and English rule, and the head of the community assumed the traditional role of honorary Dutch Consul. According to anthropologist Barbara Johnson, because of the Jews' economic utility and the particular nature of the Indian caste system these migrants were able to transition into immigrants. As a 'caste apart', they enjoyed a separate but equal legal status alongside the majority Hindus.[11]

In terms of affirmation of identity and belief, Cochin Jews remained synagogue-centred in the Sorkian sense as they prospered. In 1968, in recognition of their equality in and value to Indian society, Prime Minister Indira Gandhi visited the main Cochin synagogue on its 400th anniversary. Simultaneously the Indian government issued a postage stamp commerorating what is arguably the oldest synagogue structure in the Far East.

In terms of Enlightenment/haskalah, the Cochin Jews, like their yet-to-be-discussed Bene Israel and Baghdadi co-religionists, enjoyed a prosperity which enabled a particular kind of intellectual emancipation. They availed themselves of English educational and cultural institutions in India and Britain and became both anglophile and Zionist in the course of the nineteenth and twentieth centuries. In this fashion Benjamin Isaac Sargon, son of Isaac Sargon of Cochin, received his law degree from the

Inns of Court in London and returned to practise law in Bombay in the 1930s. In 1933 he and his brothers Joseph and David established the *Jewish Tribune* in Bombay and counted world Zionist leader Chaim Weizmann among their columnists.[12] When the Jewish state was reborn in 1948, virtually the entire Cochin Jewish community, in spite of its prosperity and in the absence of anti-semitism, migrated en masse to Israel. In 2002 one is more likely to see the costumes and traditions of the Cochin Jews in the collective farms of Israel's Negev desert than on the main street of 'Jew Town', Cochin.

India's Bene Israel Community

Recent scholarship on the Bene Israel community of Maharashtra Province, North India, affirms that this community, like the Cochinim, were migrants who became immigrants. This community also conforms to Sorkin's five criteria for port Jews. According to legend, the Bene Israel's ancestors left the Land of Israel at the time of Antiochus (175–163 BC) and were shipwrecked at Navgaon in the Konkan region of Maharashtra, about thirty miles south of what is now Bombay. In one of the earliest documents about the community, the Scottish Presbyterian missionary John Wilson records visiting them in 1838 and finding them thoroughly Indianised, with only smatterings of Judaism. They abstained from work on the Sabbath, recited the *Shema*, or Hebrew-language catechism of the Jewish faith, circumcised infants on the eighth day, and ate only fish with fins and scales in conformity with Jewish dietary laws.[13] In the 1700s and 1800s, the Bene Israel were 'rejudaised' by members of the Cochin Jewish community. By the nineteenth century, many had sought their fortunes in Bombay as carpenters, construction labourers, stevedores, and 'sepoys', or native Indian employees of the British Navy. Although not merchants and middlemen like their Cochin co-religionists, the Bene Israel were very much port Jews, involved in vital maritime occupations in India's major seaport.

Like the Cochinim, the Bene Israel's 'Enlightenment' was their embrace of Zionism. About 12,000 members of the community left for the modern State of Israel after it was established in 1948. As of 1969 about 11,000 remained in India, with an emigration rate to Israel as late as 1989 of about 200 per year.[14]

Baghdadi Jews in India, Singapore, Hong Kong and Shanghai

The Baghdadi Jews of East, Southeast, and South Asia also conform to Golab's classic pattern of migrants who became immigrants. They created a mercantile infrastructure with ties to their kin in a far-flung diaspora much resembling that of Sorkin's Sephardi and Italian Jewish communities.[15]

The original settlement of Arabic-speaking Jews in the Far East occurred in Bombay. Here an industrious group of Baghdadis, in a fashion similar to that of the Cochinim and Bene Israel Jews, took advantage of favourable economic conditions created by the British colonial presence. Before long the Baghdadis surpassed their Indian co-religionists in terms of the scale of their enterprises. The pioneer Baghdadi immigrant to India was Suleiman Ibn Yakub, who anglicised his name as Solomon Jacob and was active in the Bombay opium export trade between 1795 and 1833. He and other Baghdadis shrewdly reinvested their opium profits in textile manufacturing and export, a strategy perfected by David Sassoon [1772–1864], who fled persecution in Iraq and arrived penniless in Bombay in 1833. Within a generation, Sassoon and his sons had built their own docks in Bombay harbour and were known as the 'Rothschilds of the Orient'. They built the first monumental Baghdadi synagogue, Magen David, in Bombay in 1861, and the first in the hill station of Pune in 1888. They sponsored a David Sassoon Hospital, an infirmary, a lepresarium, and, in 1855, the first Judeo-Arabic periodical in Bombay, *Doresh Tov Le-Ammo*. Sassoon's sons extended their empire eastward to Calcutta, Rangoon, Singapore, Hong Kong, and Shanghai, where the Baghdadis also built monumental synagogues.

In terms of Enlightenment, the Baghdadis of Calcutta and Singapore, like Bombay, sent their children west to be educated. Cases in point include Benjamin Meyer of Calcutta, who matriculated at London's Imperial College of Science and Technology; his wife Maisie J. Meyer, who received her doctorate from the University of London's School of Economics and Political Science; and his cousin Ezekiel Musleah, who received rabbinic ordination from New York's Jewish Theological Seminary. Singaporean David Saul Marshall (1908–95) studied law in London, was admitted to the English bar, and returned to his home island where, in 1955, he was elected Chief Minister. In that capacity Marshall gave Singapore its first measure of internal self-government and set the colony on its path to complete independence.[16]

Baghdadi prosperity occurred in all these British colonies after Jews forsook what they saw as worthless Ottoman citizenship for the greater privileges available from Great Britain. British citizenship guaranteed Jews full equality and protection of the Crown within each overseas possession. As in other free societies, some Jews assimilated completely and embraced Christianity while others used the opportunity to both prosper and intensify their cultural identity. Nowhere was the environment more nurturing for them than in Hong Kong, which, under the terms of the 1842 Sino-British Nanking Treaty, remained British for 150 years. Elias Sassoon, of Baghdad and Bombay, set up a branch of his family's business in Hong Kong in 1850 and quickly expanded into banking, transportation, and construction. The Sassoons supported the construction of the first Baghdadi synagogue, Ohel Leah, in Hong Kong in 1901. Sir Ellis Kadoorie (1865–1922), originally from Baghdad, settled in Hong Kong in the late 1800s. He established his own trading company with major interests in the Peninsula Hotel and Hong Kong and Shanghai Bank. His sons Lawrence (b. 1899) and Horace (b. 1902) held major interests in Hong Kong Light and Power Company. In 1909 Sir Ellis constructed the Jewish recreational club adjoining Ohel Leah. The Kadoories' charitable network included technical schools for Jews and non-Jews in Bombay, Baghdad, and in the Land of Israel, where, they helped endow the Hebrew University. Their agricultural school *Beth Sefer Kadoorie* was the alma mater of Israeli Defence and Foreign Minister Moshe Dayan and other important founders and leaders of the Jewish state.[17]

Shanghai was another Chinese city which the 1842 Nanking Treaty opened to British and, shortly thereafter, Jewish enterprise. This entrepot at the mouth of the Yangtze River never became an exclusively British colony like India, Burma, Singapore or Hong Kong. Instead, it was divided into a number of foreign concessions. This particular condition, and the inability of a weak China to do anything about it until the 1940s, made China's largest city an appealing environment for Baghdadi Jewish merchants.[18] In 1845 Elias David Sassoon established a branch of David Sassoon & Sons in Shanghai. He expanded the family business from opium trading to land speculation on the China coast and far-flung investment in the Yangtze valley. By 1850 three clerks of the firm are among 200 foreigners listed as residents of the city. In 1862 David Sassoon established Shanghai's first Jewish cemetery. In 1887 the Sassoons helped build Shanghai's first synagogue, Beth El, followed in the 1920s by Ohel Rachel and the monumental Beth Aharon, which benefitted from the largesse of fellow Baghdadi Silas Aaron Hardoon (1851–1931). Hardoon was reputedly the wealthiest person in Asia east of Suez, including the Indian Maharajahs. Like the Sassoons, he traded opium until 1918. Then he switched to real estate, ultimately owning 1,200 buildings in Shanghai alone. He was an Enlightened figure in many respects. One biographer records that 'quite apart from the exceptional nature of his rags-to-riches story, he was unique among Baghdadi Jews in that he established broad ties with the Chinese cultural milieu'.[19] He married a Eurasian woman and endowed both a Confucian and Buddhist university over and beyond his support of the Shanghai Jewish School and the aforementioned Beth Aharon synagogue.

At the opposite end of the Baghdadi intellectual spectrum from Hardoon, Nissim Elias Benjamin Ezra (1883–1936) co-founded the Shanghai Zionist Association in 1904. Its house organ *Israel's Messenger*, of which Ezra was Editor-in-Chief, was also the voice of the Jewish National Fund in China. In July 1914, on the eve of the First World War, Ezra wrote confidently to the Actions Committee of the International Zionist Association in Berlin that

> the future of Jewry is safe in the hands of our worldwide movement. Indeed, this is the only ray of sunshine illuminating us in our dark exile. We shall next week be celebrating our 'Black Fast', the day when the Jewish State had been overthrown [Tishah be-Av, memorialising the destruction of the Second Jewish Temple by the Romans in 70 AD.] The time is fast coming when we shall recover our own Jewish State and be proud of it once more.[20]

Ezra's efforts notwithstanding, Zionism was of minor concern to Shanghai's prosperous, early twentieth century anglophile Baghdadi community, which was formally organised as the Shanghai Jewish Community Association. Its long-term president, D.E.J. Abraham, elected in 1910, would still be in office when huge numbers of impoverished Jewish refugees would suddenly arrive on the Shanghai docks in the mid-1930s.

European Jews Fleeing to Shanghai to Escape Hitler, 1936–41: The Port City as a Port in a Storm

Closed to 20,000 Central and Eastern European Jews availed themselves of the openness of Shanghai and fled there in the late 1930s and early 1940s to escape Hitler. As already noted, these refugees were temporary residents who lived 'a life in the waiting room', as one of them entitled his memoir.[21] They did not establish roots or interact with the host culture and were 'migrants' rather than 'immigrants' in Golab's terms. Nor did they, as wards of Jewish charitable organisations, ever assume the commercially-linked characteristics of Sorkin's port Jews.

How did Shanghai become the haven for thousands of Austrian, Croatian, Czech, Dutch, German, Hungarian, Latvian, Lithuanian, Polish, Russian and stateless Jews at a time when no other place in the world, including the United States, would freely accept Jewish refugees? For reasons described above, until 1941, when the Japanese occupiers shut the gates of Shanghai, having earlier kept them open, Shanghai was the only place on earth just prior to the Holocaust where a foreigner could immigrate without any documentation whatsoever.

Transportation to Shanghai might be an obstacle, but the critical 'permission to enter' could not be denied. Ernest Heppner wrote that his family, and other Central and Eastern European Jews arriving in Shanghai in the late 1930s, could not believe that no one asked for their papers as they passed through the customs house. Hundreds of thousands of Jews in Europe, like the Baghdadis before them, were trying to find a country permitting them entry and 'here Jews could just walk ashore'.[22]

The refugees sat out the war years in Shanghai initially in five large refugee camps and ultimately in a ghetto. They survived on subsidies from the American Jewish Joint Distribution Committee and managed to recreate some aspects of their European lives, but no permanent institutions. These short-lived exercises included religious services ranging from Progressive/Liberal to ultra-Orthodox, a German-language press including three dailies, and sophisticated theatrical, radio, and musical productions. They founded two elementary schools and a dancing school and conducted adult-education seminars. A weekly paper in Russian and Yiddish covered current events and social activities. The Polish refugees included writers, actors, labour leaders, and the entire staff and student body of the Yeshiva of Mir, who managed to publish a Talmud in Shanghai for their use during the war years.[23]

The departure of virtually all Jews from China – Baghdadis, Central and Eastern Europeans – began almost immediately upon the formal surrender of Japan to the Republic of China and its allies on 2 September 1945 and the onset of civil war between Chinese nationalists and communists. Among the first to go were those ideologically committed individuals who had always viewed China only as a port in a storm. At one extreme, those emigrants included the students and faculty of the Yeshiva of Mir, who departed for Palestine and the United States. At an opposite ideological extreme, a contingent of the left-leaning Association of Democratic Germans in Shanghai [*Gemeinschaft der Demokratischen Deutschen in Shanghai*] repatriated to Germany aboard the U.S. troop carrier *Marine Lynx* in July 1947. The new Jerusalem for many of those anti-Fascists would be the German Democratic Republic.[24] Several dozen Jewish families who were long-term residents of China were among some 5,000 to 8,000 Soviet citizens who repatriated to the USSR between 1945 and 1948 for ideological and economic reasons.[25] By 1948, as the Republic of China's fortunes continued to worsen in its civil war with the Chinese communists, Shanghai Zionist leader Yaacov Liberman observed a 'hysteria of exodus' gripping 'the entire stateless community', those who were firmly ideologically committed as well as those who were not as ideological. He noted that 'embassies and consulates were flooded with desperate requests for entrance visas'. The most sought-after destination was the United States. Liberman's own parents departed for Cuba, and he soon after organised an exodus of several shiploads of Jews to the new State of Israel.[26] By the time the People's Republic of China was proclaimed on 1 October 1949, most of the Jews had left. Virtually all of the few thousand remaining left by the mid-1950s, signalling the end of a 'port in a storm' for some Jews and of long-term residence for others.[27]

Harbin Jews: Inlanders With Seaport Characteristics

An examination of the history of Jews in the Chinese city of Harbin, on the Sungari River 1,500 miles inland, provides yet another test of the Sorkin and Golab theses. The origins of the Harbin Jewish community date back to 1896, when Imperial China granted Imperial Russia territorial concessions across northern Manchuria.[28] Within that leasehold the Russians built and operated the Chinese Eastern Railway (hereinafter referred to as 'CER'), a straight course which connected their cities of Chita in Siberia with Vladivostok on the Sea of Japan. The CER was run by a private corporation which had a free hand to manage an extraterritorial zone [*Polasa Otchuzhdenia*] approximately 1,000 miles long and 20 miles wide and to exploit the natural resources of the area. In 1903 a 637-mile-long branch line was built to Port Arthur on the Yellow Sea.

The Russians enlarged the centrally-located Chinese hamlet of Harbin into their hub for all their Manchurian industrial and railway enterprises. The extraterritorial status of Harbin – it both was and was not part of Imperial Russia, like the Panama Canal Zone would be for the United States – made it an attractive destination for thousands of Imperial Russian subjects who sought greater prosperity and cultural and political freedoms than what they experienced in European Russia or Siberia. Thus the 'Russian' community of Harbin, while overwhelmingly Great Russian and Ukranian in its make up, also included Armenians, Estonians, Finns, Georgians, Latvians, Lithuanians, Poles, Tatars, and, of course, Jews. At the end of the Russo-Japanese War in 1905 many Russian army veterans chose to remain in Harbin, enlarging the Jewish population to about 7,000 by 1907. After the collapse of Imperial Russia in 1917 Harbin was ruled successively by an international coalition of allied powers, Chinese warlords, the Soviet Union, Japan, the Soviet Union again, and the Chinese Communists, all in a period of 35 years. The Soviets sold the railroad to the Japanese in the mid-1930s. Despite these changes in political organisation, the Jewish community as a whole prospered until at least 1940. Jews traded with one another in Sorkin's sense but also with a wider non-Jewish hinterland which was populated by Mongols and other native Siberian peoples, ethnic Russians, Chinese, Japanese, and Koreans. A secret report prepared by the Japanese-owned Southern Manchurian Railway Company in 1940 put the Jewish population of all Manchuria as 3,300, with 2,800 residing in Harbin. Although by then the Jewish population had dwindled from its height of about 13,000 in 1930, the Jewish firms still included banks, coal mines, lumber yards, hotels, restaurants, and establishments dealing in fur, grain, and soy bean processing, dry goods, transport, insurance, and real estate. These Jewish companies were capitalised at approximately 50 million yen (more than US $10 million in 1940 dollars), their annual transactions totalled more than 100 million yen, and annual profits reached almost 13 million yen.[29]

As Harbin Jews prospered, their community, 1,500 miles inland, enjoyed intensified belief and Enlightenment/*haskalah* in the broadest sense of those terms. Harbin's spiritual leader was Rabbi Aharon Mosheh Kisilev, born in 1866 in Ludvinovsk, Chernigov province [*guberniya*], Russia. He studied at the prestigious Volozhin Yeshivah under Rabbi Chaim Soloveitchik and was ordained by the distinguished Rabbi Chaim Ozer Grodzinski of Vilna. Kisilev's fellow students at Volozhin included future Hebrew poet Chaim Nacham Bialik and future Ashkenazi Chief Rabbi of Palestine Avraham Yitkhak Kook. All three were influenced by Rabbi Shmuel Mohilever, a Zionist predecessor of Theodore Herzl who founded the *Hoveivei Tsion* [Lovers of Zion] movement in Warsaw in 1881. Kisilev served the Harbin community continuously from 1913 until his death in 1949. During those years, according to his secretary, Harbin Jews became overwhelmingly Zionistic. A prolific writer, Kisilev published *The Waves of the Sea*, a commentary on the Jewish legal code *Shulkhan Arukh*, in Hebrew in Harbin 1925 or 1926. This book was republished in New York in 1991 and is still used as a seminal text. His volume *Nationalism and the Jews* was originally published in Russian in Harbin and subsequently in Hebrew. This book was a collection of sermons and lectures directed to the youth of Harbin about their Jewish heritage and religious Zionism. Kisilev's counterpart in the secular, Zionist world was Dr Avraham Iosifovitch Kaufman, born in 1885 in Mglin, also in Chernigov province. In 1903 he matriculated at the Russian Gymnasium in Perm but, because of Tsarist restrictions, had to go to Switzerland for his medical education. There he met his wife, also a doctor. Both moved to Harbin in 1912, where Kaufman became medical director of the new Jewish Hospital.[30]

Despite some ideological differences, Kisilev and Kaufman worked in tandem for nearly 35 years for the betterment of the Jewish community and for their common cause, Zionism. Indeed, Kaufman wrote the introduction to Kisilev's 1941 volume. They laboured indefatigably to build communal institutions to serve the needs of the immigrants pouring in from Russia. These establishments included a synagogue, religious school, library, old age home, cemetery, homeless shelter, kosher soup kitchen, and the aforementioned hospital. The institutions were governed by a democratically-elected, 40 member Jewish community council in which the plurality of delegates came from Dr. Kaufman's General (secular) Zionists but on which the non-Zionist Bund, Agudat Israel, Progressives, and others were also represented. Harbin became a centre for Jewish journalism in the 1920s and 1930s. Its periodicals included the Bund's Yiddish newspaper *Der Vayter Mizrekh* (the Far East) and the Russian-language periodicals *Evreiskaia Zhizn'* (Jewish life, of Kaufman's General Zionists) and *Gadegel*. The title of this publication was the Cyrillic rendition of the Hebrew words *ha-degel* [the flag]. *Gadegel* was the organ of Vladimir Jabotinsky's Zionist Revisionist Party, established in Harbin in 1929. Similarly, Harbin's two major Jewish sports organisations reflected the politics of the Russian Jews: Maccabi for the General Zionists, and Brit Trumpeldor [*Betar*] for the Zionist Revisionists. The latter organisation included para-military training in its regimen—a skill which was of value to the community during the periodic floods of the Sungari River, on occasions when the community had to defend itself against White Russian anti-Semitism, and in 1948–49, when nearly a thousand members of the community evacuated en masse to Israel.[31]

Conclusion: The Need for More Empirical Data on Port Jews

Golab's assertion of a linkage between migrant/immigrant status and institutional development is supported by evidence from all of the aforementioned Far Eastern Jewish communities. While it is also clear that the experiences of the Cochinim, Bene Israel and Baghdadis vindicate Sorkin's thesis, the experiences of Harbin Jews do not. Indeed, an examination of Harbin calls into question Sorkin's major argument that the economic opportunities provided by seaport cities helped Jews win an array of privileges and forms of legal equality. Although Harbin was not a seaport, it was a trading and distribution centre where long distance merchants made their headquarters and to and from which goods were shipped. Thus, the same dynamics which influenced seaports influenced Harbin. Perhaps it was the opportunities of a frontier environment, as suggested by historian Frederick Jackson Turner, or of an urban environment, maritime or inland, as suggested by sociologist Robert E. Park, that gave Jews the wherewithal to evolve ideologically and to win enhanced legal statuses and privileges.[32]

Additional research could cast more light on Sorkin's suggestions. What does the evidence show regarding Jews in such port cities as Tientsin [Tianjin], Dairen [Dalian/Dalny], Penang, Surabaja, Nagasaki, Kobe, Yokohama, and especially Rangoon, today Yangon in the Union of Myanmar? Although little remains of the latter community apart from its grandiose Musmeah Yeshua Synagogue and a cemetery, as late as 1940 Rangoon had a Baghdadi Jewish population of 2,200, two synagogues, a day school, a Zionist organisation, and had even provided the city with a Jewish mayor.[33] Raw data on these communities exists in local archives and can also be found in the Central Zionist Archives in Jerusalem, the American Jewish Joint Distribution Committee archives in New York City, and, perhaps most promisingly, in records of British Commonwealth Jewish communities in the Hartley Library of the University of Southampton, UK.[34] What we can say confidently at this point, according to Hebrew University historian Irene Eber, is that the history of Far Eastern Jewish communities 'underscores the importance of institutional life in the preservation and perpetuation of Jewish values and demonstrates the variety of Jewish secular culture in the assertion of Jewish identity'.[35] Whether or not those characteristics were products of seaport prosperity remains to be seen.

ACKNOWLEDGEMENTS

The author appreciates the editorial/research assistance of Peter Berton of the University of Southern California [emeritus], Michael Brown of Trinity College, Dublin, Parkes Centre Director David Cesarani, Jacques M. Downs of the University of New England [emeritus], Teddy Kaufman of the *Igud Yotsei Sin* (Association of Former Jewish Residents of China, Tel Aviv), Lois C. Dubin of Smith College, Ralph B. Hirsch of the Council on the Jewish Experience in Shanghai, Russel Lemmons of Jacksonville [Alabama] State University, and Jonathan Schorsch of Emory University. The author would also like to thank West Georgia's Learning Resources Committee for funding some of the basic research for this article, West Georgia's Dean of Arts and Sciences Richard G. Miller for providing the released time that made the writing of this article possible, and West Georgia librarian Myron House for bibliographical assistance.

NOTES

A Note on Romanisation: during centuries of East–West relations and of a Jewish presence in Asia, the Americas, Europe, and South Africa, several formal systems plus numerous arbitrary renditions have been used to convert Chinese, East Indian, Hebrew, Japanese and Judeo-Arabic words into the Roman alphabet. In this essay I have spelled foreign words according to their most common usage in American English, e.g. Chiang Kai-shek, Hong Kong, Jerusalem, and Nanking. Wherever feasible I have juxtaposed romanisations that are less commonly used in American English. Most Hebrew words are transliterated according to the standard rules given in *Encyclopedia Judaica*, Vol.1 (Jerusalem: Keter, 1973), p.90.

1. Arabic-speaking Jews from Baghdad, who are also referred to as Levantine Jews, should not, strictly speaking, be characterised as 'Sephardim', or Jews who were expelled from the Iberian Peninsula in 1492–93 and retained medieval Spanish or Portuguese as their mother tongue in varied places of exile. David Sorkin, 'The Port Jew: Notes Toward a Social Type', *Journal of Jewish Studies*, 50.1 (Spring 1999), pp.87–97.
2. Sorkin, 'The Port Jew' (see note 1), p.89. This Sephardi and Italian infrastructure was similar to the trade nexus which bound early American merchants from a particular city with each other and with their overseas financiers and agents. Economic historian Thomas C. Cochran observed that 'in spite of intercolonial trade in some items, each major (early American) port was a separate business community remote from its neighbors. The personal ties that bound the business world together were more often between American merchants and the houses of Liverpool or London than between men on this side of the Atlantic. Businessmen of Charleston were more at home in London than in Boston.' Thomas C. Cochran, *Basic History of American Business* (Princeton: Van Nostrand, 1968), p.28. On Philadelphia Quakers as a case in point, see Richard Waln, Jr., *Walnford Mill Accounts, 1772* (Historical Society of Pennsylvania, Philadelphia); Stephen Winslow, *Biographies of Successful Philadelphia Merchants* (Philadelphia: James K. Simon, 1864), pp.129–32; Jonathan Goldstein, *Philadelphia And The China Trade 1682–1846: Commercial, Cultural And Attitudinal Effects* (University Park and London: Penn State University Press, 1978), pp.11–12 and passim; and Jonathan Goldstein, 'America's First Sinologist: Philadelphia's Robert Waln, Jr. (1794–1825)', *Asian Culture Quarterly* (Taipei) 27.1 (Spring 1999), pp.1–13. A second case in point in colonial and early national America are the Huguenots.
3. Sorkin, 'The Port Jew' (see note 1), p.90.
4. ibid., p.92. With respect to South, Southeast, and East Asia, although the Inquisition existed in Portugal's colonies until the institution was abolished by King Joao VI in 1812, there is no record of converted Jews in the Far East returning to their original faith. Walter J. Fischel, 'Leading Jews in the Service of Portuguese India', *The Jewish Quarterly Review* (Philadelphia) 47 (July 1956), pp.37–57.
5. David Sorkin, *The Berlin Haskalah and German Religious Thought* (London and Portland, OR.: Valentine Mitchell, 2000), pp.1–3, pp.131–32, fns.1, 2; Lois C. Dubin, 'Trieste and Berlin: The Italian Role in the Cultural Politics of the Haskalah', in *Toward Modernization* ed. by Jacob Katz (New Brunswick, NJ and Oxford, UK: Transaction Books, 1987). In Trieste, for example, according to both Sorkin and Dubin, many Jews 'accepted the premise that secular and sacred studies were complementary'. Dubin, *The Port Jews of Habsburg Trieste: Absolutist Politics and Enlightenment Culture* (Stanford, CA.: Stanford University Press, 1999); Sorkin, 'The Port Jew' (see note 1), pp.92–4. There were many totally secularised free-thinkers among the Jews of South, Southeast and East Asia. Like their European counterparts, they espoused atheism, agnosticism, Second International Menshevism, Third International Socialism, and, in a few cases Maoism. Journalist Vincent Sheean wrote that the secular Jews he knew in China in the 1920s and 30s 'had risen so far above the prison walls of race, nation, and tradition that their Jewishness was altogether lost in their humanity; and their special passion, the purity and intensity in which the best of the Jewish heritage was expressed, burned itself out in a cause from which no human creature was excused. Only in such freedom could the Jewish genius give all it had to the developing conscious of mankind.' Vincent Sheean, *Personal History* (New York: Literary Guild, 1934), p.391.
6. As will be shown in this article, 'Enlightened' Jewish nationalists in the Far East included Anglophile Baghdadi Jews like Shanghai's Nissim Elias Benjamin Ezra who published and edited the Zionist monthy *Israel's Messenger* from 1904 to 1936, and Harbin General Zionist leader and hospital director Dr Avraham Iosifovitch Kaufmann. The ideologies of these Zionists were much akin to those of eighteenth-to-twentieth-century American, Irish, Italian and Scottish nationalists who took Enlightened world views but simultaneously and proudly affirmed their national identities. On Zionism and other

nineteenth century nationalisms, especially Italian, as expressions of Enlightenment thinking, see Hugh Trevor-Roper, 'Jewish and Other Nationalisms', *Commentary* 35.1 (January 1963), pp.19–20. He writes that Zionist leaders were 'Europeans of the Enlightenment (who) were not content with distant memories or merely religious traditions. If they revived the Hebrew language it was not merely to study the Scriptures or the Law. If they remembered their history it was not merely their ancient, sacred history. It was a Jew of the Emancipation, Heinrich Graetz, who wrote the first continuous history of the Jewish nation, carrying it through the destruction of the Second Temple, over the intervening centuries, to his own time. It was a Jew of the Emancipation, Moses Hess, who first urged escape from Europe to Jerusalem, and he urged it explicitly as a nationalist, secular movement, in imitation of the nationalist, secular Italian *risorgimento*. If Zionism was the age-old hankering of Jews for the Holy Land, it was that hankering secularised: a return to Israel without waiting for the Messiah, or led by a secular Messiah – one, moreover, who was half-assimilated into Europe... If [Zionism's] faithful masses came out of the Russian Pale, [their movement] was headed by half-assimilated men whom strict Jews might regard as little better than Gentiles and whose life was led in the Western Cosmopolitan cities of Paris and Vienna.' On the connection between Enlightenment thought and American, Irish, and Scottish nationalism, see David Dickson, 'Paine in Ireland', in Daire Keogh Dickson and Kevin Whelan (ed.) *The United Irishmen: Republicanism, Radicalism, And Rebellion* (Dublin: Lilliput Press, 1993), pp.134–50 and John Burns, 'Scottish Radicalism and the United Irishmen', in Dickson et al., *The United Irishmen*, pp.151–66. Biographer Eric Foner notes that, in spite of all his propagandising for an Enlightened internationalism, Tom Paine both 'called himself a "citizen of the world" and was an early advocate of a strong central government for America.' Foner, *Tom Paine and Revolutionary America* (London: Oxford University Press, 1976), p.xix.

7. Sorkin, 'The Port Jew' (see note 1), pp.95–6.
8. Caroline Golab, *Immigrant Destinations* (Philadelphia: Temple University Press, 1977), p.77. In her immigration history class at the University of Pennsylvania Golab gave, as a case-in-point of a rootless migrant, the nineteenth century Polish-American Leon F. Czolgosz. He spent one year in Pittsburgh, one year in Cleveland, and one year in Chicago where, at the age of 28, he heard Emma Goldman and latched onto anarcho-syndicalism. In 1901 he assassinated U.S. President William McKinley. McKinley's biographer concluded that Czolgosz was 'possessed of the idea that every king, emperor, president, or head of government was a tyrant and should be put out of the way'. Charles S. Olcott, *Life of William Mckinley, II* (Boston: Houghton Mifflin, 1916), p.385.
9. Golab (see note 8), p.49.
10. Seminal scholarship on the Cochinim includes Barbara C. Johnson, 'Cochin Jews and Kaifeng Jews: Reflections on Caste, Surname, 'Community', and Conversion' in Jonathan Goldstein, *The Jews Of China*, I (Armonk, NY and London: M. E. Sharpe, 1999), pp.104–19; Nathan Katz, 'The Judaisms of Kaifeng and Cochin: Parallels and Divergences' in Jonathan Goldstein, *The Jews of China*, I, pp.120–38; Barbara C. Johnson, ' "Our Community" in Two Worlds: The Cochin Paradesi Jews in India and Israel' (Ph.D. diss., anthropology, University of Massachusetts, 1985); Nathan Katz and Ellen S. Goldberg, *The Last Jews of Cochin: Jewish Identity in Hindu India* (Columbia, SC: University of South Carolina Press, 1993); Nathan Katz (ed.), *Studies of Indian Jewish Identity* (Ann Arbor: Association for Asian Studies Monograph Series; New Delhi: Manohar, 1994); and Thomas A. Timberg (ed.), *The Jews of India* (New Delhi: Vikas, 1986), pp.161–76.
11. Johnson, 'Cochin Jews and Kaifeng Jews' (see note 10), p.107.
12. Ezekiel Musleah, *On the Banks of the Ganga* (North Quincy, MA.: Christopher, 1975), p.426; Joan G. Roland, *Jews in British India: Identity in a Colonial Era* (Hanover, NH and London: Brandeis University Press/University Press of New England, 1989), pp.129, 167, 233, and passim; and *Encyclopedia Judaica*, Vol. 14, p.1294.

13. Shirley Berry Isenberg, *India's Bene Israel* (Berkeley, CA: Judah L. Magnes Museum; Bombay: Popular Prakashan, 1988); Isenberg, 'The Kaifeng Jews and India's Bene Israel: Different Paths' in Goldstein, *The Jews Of China*, I (see note 10), pp.87–103; Benjamin J. Israel, *The Bene Israel of India* (Bombay: Orient Longman, 1984); Walter J. Fischel et al., 'Bene Israel', *Encyclopedia Judaica*, Vol.1, pp.493–8.
14. Fischel et al. (see note 13) pp.493–8; Interview, Jonathan Goldstein with Israeli Consul General Giora Becher, Bombay, August 1989.
15. Major sources on Far Eastern Baghdadi Jews include Joan Roland, 'Baghdadi Jews in India and China in the Nineteenth Century: A Comparison of Economic Roles' in Goldstein, *The Jews Of China*, I (see note 10), pp.141–56; 'Silas Aaron Hardoon and Cross-Cultural Adaptation in Shanghai' in Goldstein, *The Jews Of China*, I (see note 10), pp.216–29; Maruyama Naoki, 'The Shanghai Zionist Association and the International Politics of East Asia Until 1936' in Goldstein, *The Jews Of China*, I (see note 10), pp.251–66; Cecil Roth, *The Sassoon Dynasty* (London: Robert Hale, 1941); Maisie J. Meyer, 'The Sephardi Jewish Community of Shanghai 1845–1939 and the Question of Identity' (Ph.D. dissertation, University of London, London School of Economics, 1994); Moshe Yegar, '*Le-Toldot Ha-Kehillah Ha-Yehudit Be-Singapoor*', (Hebrew: On the History of the Jewish Community in Singapore), *Gesher* 1.78 (1974), pp.50–65; Musleah (see note 12), passim; and Roland, *Jews in British India* (see note 12), passim.
16. On the career of David Saul Marshall, see his obituary in the *Washington Post*, 13 December 1995, p.5; Denis D. Gray, 'Jewish Lawyer is Singapore's Crusading Conscience', *Jerusalem Post*, 1 May 1994, p.3; and *Encyclopedia Judaica* Vol. 7, p.1059.
17. On the Baghdadi Jews of Hong Kong see Dennis A. Leventhal, 'Environmental Interactions of the Jews of Hong Kong', in Goldstein, *The Jews Of China*, I (see note 10), pp.171–86; Dennis Leventhal, *The Jewish Community of Hong Kong: An Introduction* (Hong Kong: Jewish Historical Society of Hong Kong, 1985, rev. ed. 1988); and Dennis Leventhal and Mary W. Leventhal (eds.), *Faces of the Jewish Experience in China* (Hong Kong: Hong Kong Jewish Chronicle, 1990).
18. On the Baghdadi Jews in Shanghai, see Chiara Betta, 'Silas Aaron Hardoon and Cross-Cultural Adaptation' in Goldstein, *The Jews Of China*, I (note 10), pp.216–29; Maisie J. Meyer, 'The Sephardi Jewish Community' (note 15); Roland, 'Baghdadi Jews in India and China' (note 15), and Roth, *The Sassoon Dynasty* (note 15).
19. Betta (see note 18), p.216; *Passage Through China: The Jewish Communities Of Harbin, Tientsin and Shanghai (Derekh Erets Sin: Ha-Kehillot Ha-Yehudiot Be-Harbin, Tiyeng'tsin Ve-Shanghai)* (Tel Aviv: Beth Hatefutsoth, Nahum Goldman Museum of the Jewish Diaspora, 1986) (exhibition catgalogue), pp.v–vi. Chiara Betta, 'Marginal Westerners in Shanghai: The Bagdadi Jewish Community, 1845–1931' in Robert Bickers et al., *New Frontiers* (Manchester: Manchester University Press, 2000), pp.38–54.
20. Letter: N. E. B. Ezra, Shanghai, to the Actions Committee of the International Zionist Organization, Berlin, 16 July 1914. Yad Vashem Archives, Jerusalem, file 078/54.
21. Georg Armbruester, '15,000 Appellieren an die Welt', (German: 15,000 appeal to the world) in *Leben Im Wartesaal: Exil In Shanghai 1938–47 [Life In The Waiting Room: Exile In Shanghai, 1938–47]* (Berlin: Jüdisches Museum im Stadtmuseum Berlin, 1997), pp.74–77. For a general history of the exodus of Central and Eastern European Jews to Shanghai, see David Kranzler, *Japanese Nazis & Jews* (Hoboken, NJ: Ktav, 1988); Ernest G. Heppner, *Shanghai Refuge* (Lincoln, NE and London: University of Nebraska Press, 1994), translated into German by Roberto de Hollanda as *Fluchtort Shanghai: Erinnerungen 1938–1948* (Bonn: Weidle Verlag, 1998); Yaakov Liberman, *My China* (Jerusalem and New York: Gefen, 1997); Isaac Lewin, *Remembering the Days of Old* (New York: Research Institute of Religious Jewry, 1994); Zorach Warhaftig, *Refugee and Survivor* (Jerusalem: Yad Vashem, 1988); Avraham Altman and Irene Eber, 'Flight to Shanghai, 1938–1940: The Larger Setting', *Yad Vashem Studies* (Jerusalem) 28 (2000), pp.51–86 and Jonathan Goldstein, 'Answered and Unanswered Questions About Motivation in Holocaust Rescue: The Case of Jan Zwartendijk in Lithuania, 1940' in

Lessons And Legacies VI: The Presence of the Holocaust ed. by Jeffery M. Diefendorf (Evanston, IL: Northwestern University Press, forthcoming 2002).
22. Heppner (see note 21), p.40. The absence of passport controls in Shanghai has often mistakenly been described as the 'non-requirement of visas'. The absence of controls was due to the absence of authority in Shanghai of both the Chungking [Chongqing]-based Chinese Nationalist government of Chiang Kai-shek and the Nanjing-based Japanese puppet government of Wang Jingwei. Altman and Eber (see note 21) pp.51–86.
23. David Kranzler, 'Shanghai', in *Encyclopedia of The Holocaust* ed. by Israel Gutman (New York: Macmillan, 1990), pp.1346; *Yeshivat Mir* ed. by A. Bronshteyn et al., 2 vols (Bene Berak, Israel: Sifrei Kodesh Mishor, 1990); Lewin, *Remembering the Days of Old* (note 21), passim; Warhaftig (note 21), passim; Kranzler, *Japanese Nazis & Jews* (note 21), passim; Goldstein, *The Jews of China*, I (note 10), passim.
24. Telegram: Jointco, Shanghai, to Jointdisco, New York, 24 July 1947, American Jewish Joint Distribution Committee Archives, New York; 'Association of Refugees from Germany' in *Almanac Shanghai 1946/47* ed. by Ossie Lewin (Shanghai: Shanghai Echo, 1947), p.81; Sonja Muehlberger, 'From Shanghai to Berlin', *Points East* (Menlo Park, CA), 13.2 (July 1998), pp.1, 10–11; Georg Armbrezuster, 'Exil in Shanghai' in *1945: Jetzt Wohin? Exil und Rückkehr* [German: 'Exile in Shanghai' in '*1945: Now whereto? Exile and return'*] (Berlin: Verein Aktives Museum, 1995); Armbruester, '15,000 Appellieren an die Welt' (note 21); Genia and Guenther Nobel, 'Als politische Emigranten in Schanghai', *Beitraege Zur Geschichte der Deutschen Arbeiterbewegung* 21. [German: 'As Political Immigrants in Shanghai' in *Contributions to the History of the German Workers' Movement* 21] (Berlin/DDR: n.p. 1979); Walter Laqueur, *Generation Exodus* (Hanover, NH and London: Brandeis University Press, 2001), pp.183–4.
25. Isador A. Magid, ' "I Was There": The Viewpoint of an Honorary Israeli Consul in Shanghai, 1949–1951', in *China And Israel, 1948–1998: A Fifty Year Retrospective*, ed. by Jonathan Goldstein (Westport, CT and London: Praeger, 1999), pp.41–5; Liberman (see note 21), pp.57, 95–7, 151, 158–65.
26. Liberman (see note 21), pp.159–60; Heppner (see note 21) pp.172–74.
27. Kranzler, 'Shanghai' (see note 23), p.1347. The major part of the exodus ended in 1950 with the departure of a hospital ship from Tientsin that carried over 700 sick and disabled people to Israel. Irene Eber, 'Introduction', in *Passage Through China* (see note 19), p.xii.
28. On the origin and development of the Harbin Jewish community, see Alexander Menquez (pseud.), 'Growing Up Jewish in Manchuria in the 1930s: Personal Vignettes', in Jonathan Goldstein, *The Jews of China*, II, pp.70–84; Israel Epstein, 'On Being a Jew in China: A Personal Memoir', in Goldstein, *The Jews of China Jews*, II, pp.85–97; Yosef Tekoah, 'My Developmental Years in China', in Goldstein, *The Jews of China*, II, pp.98–109; Boris Bresler, 'Harbin's Jewish Community, 1898–1958: Politics, Prosperity, and Adversity' in Goldstein, *The Jews of China*, I, pp.200–15; Zvia Shickman–Bowman, 'The Construction of the Chinese Eastern Railway and the Origins of the Harbin Jewish Community, 1898–1931' in Goldstein, *The Jews of China* (note 10), pp.187–99; Joshua A. Fogel 'The Japanese and the Jews in Harbin, 1898–1930', in Robert Bickers et al., *New Frontiers* (note 19), pp.88–108; Herman Dicker, *Wanderers and Settlers in the Far East* (New York: Twayne, 1962); Soren Clausen and Stig Thogerson, *The Making of a Chinese City: History and Historiography in Harbin* (Armonk, NY and London: M. E. Sharpe, 1995); David Wolff, *To The Harbin Station* (Stanford, CA: Stanford University Press, 1999); Liberman, *My China* (see note 21), passim; Magid (see note 25), passim.
29. Mantetsu Chosa Bu [Japanese: South Manchuria Railway Company, Research Department], *Zai-Man Yudaya Jin No Keizai-Teki Kako Oyobi Genzai* [*The Economic Past and Present of Jews in Manchuria*] (November 1940), *Yudaya Mondai Chosa Shiryo Dai 27 Shu* (No. 27 in The Jewish Problem Investigation Materials Series), marked 'Gokuhi' [Top Secret], pp.20–1, 44–6, in Menquez (see note 28) p.70.
30. Aharon Mosheh Kisilev, *Mishbere Yam: Sheelot U-Teshuvot Be-Arbaah Helke Shulkan

Arukh [Hebrew: The Waves of the Sea: Responsa on the Four Parts of 'The Set Table']
(Harbin: Defus M. Levitin, 5686 [1925 or 1926], reprinted Brooklyn, NY: Katz
Bookbinding, 1991); Kisilev, *Natsionalizm I Evreistvo: Stat'i, Lektsii, I Doklady*
[Russian: Nationalism and the Jews: Articles, Lectures and Reports] (Harbin:
Evreiskaia Zhizn', 1941); Kisilev, *Imre Shefer* [Hebrew: 'Good Words' or 'Beautiful
Sayings'] (Tel Aviv: Betsalel-Levitsky, 1951); *Evreiskaya Zhizn'* [Jewish Life] (Harbin)
47 (2 November 1938), pp.14–16, 23–25; no. 48 (25 November 1938), pp.7–10, 24–25;
Interview, Jonathan Goldstein with Teddy Kaufman, Tel Aviv, 2 January 2002; Violet
Gilboa, comp., *China and the Jews* (Cambridge, MA.: Harvard University Library,
1992), pp.40, 43; Dicker (see note 28), pp.21–60.

31. *Passage Through China* (see note 19), pp.vii–xii; Dicker (see note 28), pp.21–60;
Liberman (see note 21), passim.
32. According to sociologist Robert E. Park, the emancipated Jew's 'pre-eminence as a
trader, his keen intellectual interest, his sophistication, his idealism and his lack of
historical sense, are the characteristics of a city man, the man who ranges widely,
...who, emerging from the ghetto in which he lived ... is seeking to find a place in the
freer, more complex and cosmopolitan life of [the] city.' Robert E. Park, 'Human
Migration and the Marginal Man', *American Journal of Sociology*, 33.6 (May 1928),
p.892. See George Mosse's comments on the Turner frontier thesis in *Confronting
History: A Memoir* (Madison, WI.: University of Wisconsin Press, 2000), pp.152–63.
33. On the Baghdadi Jews of Rangoon, Burma, see Lindsey Shanson, 'Twilight in Burma',
Jewish Chronicle (London), 23 May 1986; Sue Fishkoff, 'Burmese Jews Hang on Despite
Dire Predictions', *Jerusalem Post*, 18 August, 1993, p.7; obituary for David Meyer
Sofaer in *Washington Jewish Week*, 10 March 1994, p.40; and Robert Horn, 'Burma's
Jewish Remnant', *Jerusalem Post*, 28 December 1995, p.7.
34. Collections in the Hartley Library include massive clipping files, in English, French,
and German, on the Jews of Burma, China, Hong Kong, Indonesia, Japan, Malaya, the
Philippines, and Thailand. The collection also holds unpublished World Jewish
Congress reports, including Isi J. Liebler's on his 1981 meeting with Indian Prime
Minister Indira Gandhi.
35. Irene Eber, 'Introduction', in *Passage Through China* (see note 19), p.12.

Conclusion: Future Research on Port Jews

DAVID CESARANI

This book joins several others that have attempted, in some cases literally, to map Jewish history according to maritime trade routes, overseas expansion and port cities. They are part of a continuing endeavour to understand Jewish history and culture in the light of other disciplines including geography, economics, ethnography and cultural studies. The future research agenda is rich, to say the least, since only a fraction of the port cities that are possible candidates for exploration have been examined in these terms.

First of all, however, it will be necessary to work through the tensions identified in this volume and to clarify the applicability of the concepts of 'port Jew', 'port Jewry' and 'Jews in port cities'. The results of this process will determine, to some extent, whether and how research is extended to other port cities in different regions and over different time periods. There is potential for research that applies the 'social type' of the port Jew to case studies in the Mediterranean and Atlantic regions from antiquity to the modern era to determine if there are common features including migration, commercial activity, local commercial ethos, positive legal status, programmes of improvement and changing identity. Or the concept may need to be diversified, leaving the original definition intact while adding a variant that incorporates such issues as transmigration, diasporic connections, and the image and perception of Jews in ports. David Sorkin and Lois Dubin linked the 'port Jew' to the process of modernisation, but can it be deployed to similar locations independent of the transition to modernity?

Is there a distinct 'social type' that can be called a port Jew or port Jewry in the nineteenth and twentieth centuries, too? Previous work has concentrated on the Jews, but what of the changing perceptions of the port city and its Jewish inhabitants: is there scope for examining the imagery and perception of the port and 'the Jew'? Should comparative studies embrace non-Jews in port cities, too?

Finally, there is the question of what constitutes a 'port' and whether some characteristics of a maritime trading centre may occur inland. There are also lake ports (such as Chicago), river or canal ports (such as the Danubian cities and Manchester), and transport hubs or cities on trade routes that are thousands of miles from the sea or nearest major waterway (such as Aleppo, Bukhara and Harbin). Not unconnected with this question is the scope of the port city. The study of Jews in a city port cannot really be divorced from the relationship of Jews in these locations to Jews and non-Jews in their hinterlands and other significant urban centres, such as imperial capitals.

In other words, the study of Jews and the sea, ports, and port cities is only just beginning. Potential case studies include: Aden, Alexandria, Barcelona, Bombay, Buenos Aires, Cape Town, Charleston, Gothenberg, Haifa, Marseilles, Montreal, New York, Riga, Smyrna, Sydney, Venice. It is hoped that some of these places will be the subject of research connected with the Arts and Humanities Research Board Parkes Centre project on port Jews and will feature in the international conference which it is intended to convene in Cape Town, in collaboration with the Kaplan Centre for Jewish Studies in January 2003. The organisers of this conference are eager to hear from other researchers in this field and to combine in what must be a truly international and interdisciplinary programme that will reveal the Jewish historical experience in a new light. Further information about the project may be found at www.soton.ac.uk/~parkes or obtained from The AHRB Parkes Centre, Department of History, University of Southampton, Highfield, Southampton, SO17 1BJ, UK.

Notes on Contributors

David Cesarani is Professor in Modern Jewish History at the University of Southampton. He is Director of the AHRB Parkes Centre and also leads two of the individual projects, including Port Jews. He is author of *The 'Jewish Chronicle' and Anglo-Jewry, 1841–1991* (1994) and *Arthur Koestler: The Homeless Mind* (1998).

Brian Hoyle has recently retired as reader in Geography at the University of Southampton. He is author of *Cityports, Coastal Zones and Regional Change: International Perspectives on Planning and Management* (1996) and *Ports, Port Cities and Coastal Zones: Development, Interdependence and Competition in East Africa* (1997).

David Sorkin is Frances and Laurence Weinstein Professor of Jewish Studies and Senior Fellow at the Institute for Research in the Humanities at the University of Wisconsin-Madison. He is the author of *The Transformation of German Jewry, 1780–1840* (1987), *The Berlin Haskalah and German Religious Thought* (2000) and co-editor of *Profiles in Diversity: Jews in a Changing Europe, 1750–1870* (1998) and *New Perspectives on the Haskalah* (2001).

Lois Dubin is Associate Professor of Religion and Director of the Jewish Studies Program at Smith College. She is author of *The Port Jews of Habsburg Trieste: Absolutist Politics and Enlightenment Culture* (1999). She works on the culture and politics of port Jews, the history of civil marriage and divorce, and Jewish feminist theology and ritual.

Jonathan Schorsch holds a two-year post-doctoral fellowship in the history of the Portuguese Atlantic at Emory University, having spent last year at the Institute of Jewish Studies, Hebrew University of Jerusalem as a post-doctoral fellow. In 2000 he completed his PhD on Jews and Blacks in the Early Modern Mediterranean and Atlantic Worlds, 1450–1800 at the University of California-Berkeley.

Rainer Liedtke teaches at the University of Giessen, having held positions at the University of Michigan and the Technische Universität Berlin. He is author of *Jewish Welfare in Hamburg and Manchester, c.1850–1914* (1998) and with Michael Brenner and David Rechter was co-editor of *Two Nations: British and German Jews in Comparative Perspective* (1999).

Professor **Tony Kushner** is Head of the Parkes Institute for the Study of Jewish/non-Jewish relations at the University of Southampton. He is author with Katharine Knox of *Refugees in an Age of Genocide* and editor with Todd M. Endelman of *Disraeli's Jewishness* (2002).

Mark Levene is Reader in Comparative History at the University of Southampton. His recent publications include *The Massacre in History* (with Penny Roberts, 1999) and he is currently completing *The Coming of Genocide* (2003).

Maria Vassilikou is Post-Doctorate Scholar of the German Academic Community (DFG) at Potsdam University. She is the author of articles published in Greek and English periodicals on Greek anti-semitism in inter-war Salonika, Jewish education in Salonika, and the Jewish Cemetery of Salonika.

John D. Klier is Corob Professor of Modern Jewish History at University College London and is Head of the Department of Hebrew and Jewish Studies. He is author of *Russia Gathers Her Jews: The Origins of the Jewish Question in Russia* (1986), *Imperial Russia's Jewish Question, 1855–1881* (1995), and *Westjuden: Germany and German Jews through East European Eyes* (1998). He is also the co-editor of the scholarly journal *East European Jewish Affairs*.

Jonathan Goldstein is Professor of History at State University of West Georgia, where he teaches courses on China, Japan, India and the Holocaust. He is author of *Philadelphia and the China Trade* (1978), *Fresh Perspectives in Qing Dynasty Maritime Relations* (1988), *The Jews of China* (1999) and *China and Israel: A Fifty-year Retrospective* (2000).

Abstracts

Fields of Tension: Development Dynamics at the Port-City Interface
BRIAN HOYLE

Although there is no single, simple model of the port city, the idea of the cityport is derived from the frequently close but often tense relationships between port functions and coastal urban development, both spatially and over time. This essay explores the cityport concept from a geographical perspective, outlines factors involved in cityport origins, growth and development, introduces models of port-city linkages and the cityport interface, and debates dimensions, perceptions and interpretations of change, using a range of case-studies. Conclusions emphasise factors involved in the continuing transformation of the cityport interface over time but question the continuing interdependence between port activities and urban phenomena.

Port Jews and the Three Regions of Emancipation
DAVID SORKIN

Current conceptions of emancipation are inadequate since they tend to be geographically exclusive and chronologically truncated as well as to presume a bipartite east–west divide. A more inclusive understanding of emancipation requires defining a range of statuses (toleration, civil inclusion, partial emancipation, full emancipation) as well as fashioning a tripartite model (west, central and eastern Europe). The notion of the Port Jew is integral to the status of civil inclusion and the 'west' European experience of emancipation.

Researching Port Jews and Port Jewries: Trieste and Beyond
LOIS DUBIN

This article traces the development of the concept of port Jews, stressing its value for the comparative study of communities (port Jewries) as well as social types (port Jews). Focusing on the eighteenth-century Habsburg Free Port of Trieste and its Jewish community engaged in international maritime commerce, it emphasizes utility as a key factor in the perception of a port Jewry and analyses constructions of utility in Enlightenment, reforming absolutist and Haskalah discourses. Further, it argues that comparative study of port Jews and Jewries facilitates analysis of the respective roles of economics, society, and culture in Jewish history.

Portmanteau Jews: Sephardim and Race in the Early Modern Atlantic World
JONATHAN SCHORSCH

Using both texts and examples of social practice from various Atlantic communities, especially Amsterdam, this essay traces some of the ways in which individual Sephardim and the Sephardic collective wielded the social status of whiteness in the seventeenth century in order to navigate their ambiguous insider/outsider position as Jews or suspected Jews in a Christian milieu. Sephardic identity was shaped in part by Iberian racism and many (ex-)conversos found anti-blackness useful in enabling them to see themselves (and be seen) as part of the dominant culture and class, as whites, regardless of their religious otherness.

Germany's Door to the World: A Haven for the Jews? Hamburg, 1590–1933
RAINER LIEDTKE

Hamburg, Germany's dominant port city for centuries, also contained one of the largest, richest and culturally most productive Jewish communities of the German-speaking lands. The supposedly cosmopolitan and open environment of this major German entrepot provided a stable legal framework which protected the economic interests for all minorities but failed to deconstruct social and political barriers that prevented Jews from participating fully in the city's formation. At the centre of the investigation is the question of how Jewish–non-Jewish interactions developed between the settlement of the first members of the minority in the late sixteenth century and the onset of the Nazi period.

A Tale of Two Port Jewish Communities: Southampton and Portsmouth Compared
TONY KUSHNER

This article explores the neglected histories of Portsmouth and Southampton Jewry, arguing that the concept of Port Jews needs to be extended chronologically, geographically and with a less elitist focus. While context with regard to location and era is crucial, it argues that Port Jews across the ages have something in common – the importance of place. Ports have experienced a greater cosmopolitanism than other urban settlements, producing particular forms of the expression of Jewishness, blurring categories of local, national and global. In Portsmouth and Southampton it produced positive and negative results for their Jewish minorities, encouraging freedom and restraint. They attempted to achieve balance between local loyalty and diaspora connections, producing fascinating and multi-layered identities, further complicated in the case of Southampton through the presence of transmigrants, a marginalised but highly significant feature of modern and especially European Jewish history.

The Forgotten Port Jews of London: Court Jews Who Were Also Port Jews
DAVID CESARANI

The Jews of London are neglected in histories of the city and the port, yet the development of the Jewish community since the readmission was shaped by its connections with both the court and the port. During the seventeenth and eighteenth centuries the crown protected Jews from rival mercantile interests during conflicts which challenge the assumption that ports were automatically cosmopolitan, benign places for Jewish settlement. Jews occupied a precarious, marginal position in the city's maritime economy. Later, economic and social change interacted with Jewish mass migration to foster a negative image of the Jew as port dweller.

Port Jewry of Salonika: Between Neo-colonialism and Nation-state
MARK LEVENE

Can the Port Jew model be applied to communities temporally and geographically distinct from that of an Atlantic-orientated mercantilism? This essay argues that it can with regard to late nineteenth century Salonika. But it also seeks to show the model's problematic down-side. Salonika's new status emerged under the aegis of a neo-colonialism, the culmination of which was the bid for international free-port status in 1912. Salonika Jewry thereby found itself at odds with the town's other ethnic communities and with competing external national interests. In microcosm, a diasporic embrace of an emerging world economy came face to face with its other reality, the nation-state.

Greeks and Jews in Salonika and Odessa: Inter-ethnic Relations in Cosmopolitan Port Cities
MARIA VASSILIKOU

Greek-Jewish relations in Salonika and Odessa are a classic case study of inter-ethnic relations within the cosmopolitan environment of a port city. Both communities were part of a far-flung trading diaspora and shared characteristics of internal cohesion. However, historians have tended to concentrate on the differences and conflicts between the two groups. This article suggests that both communities were internally fissured and that strong ties existed between different strata across the ethnic-religious divide. In business, welfare, and political activities Jews and Greeks commingled and offered a model of integration informed by a self-conscious cosmopolitanism.

A Port, Not a Shtetl: Reflections on the Distinctiveness of Odessa
JOHN D. KLIER

This article emphasises the unique aspects of Odessa and their influence on the history of East European Jewry. These included the city's newness (founded in 1798) and openness to settlers of any ethnic or religious background. The numerous economic opportunities – so different from the shtetl economy of the Jewish heartland in the Pale of Settlement – attracted Jewish settlers from both the Russian and Austrian Empires. Given its unique characteristics, the city played a major role in the development of Jewish culture, but primarily those contributions marked by novelty and innovation. These included the ideologies of Zionism and Jewish varieties of socialism, as well as a modern Jewish press in Russian, Hebrew and Yiddish, and the modern Yiddish stage. The economic dynamism of Odessa gave rise to socio-economic differentiation in the Jewish community which was far different from that of the towns of the Pale of Settlement.

The Sorkin and Golab Theses and their Applicability to South, Southeast, and East Asian Port Jewry
JONATHAN GOLDSTEIN

The experiences of the larger Far Eastern Jewish seaport communities tend to validate David Sorkin's thesis that Jews in seaport cities enjoyed distinct opportunities for economic advancement and political and intellectual emancipation. Conversely, the Jews of Harbin, China, 1500 miles inland, also enjoyed these types of progress, calling into question the applicability of Sorkin thesis in a Far Eastern context. All of the above-mentioned communities conform to immigration historian Caroline Golab's thesis that institutional and political development depends on length of residence, with long-term immigrants developing institutions more extensively than transitory migrants. Additional research on Jews in smaller Far Eastern seaports is needed to further test the Sorkin/Golab hypotheses.

Index